AMAZING
TRAIN
Journeys

60 unforgettable rail trips and how to experience them

NEW ZEALAND'S TRANZALPINE: p282

COLOMBO TO BADULLA: p150

Contents

© ALEX_ALADDIN | GETTY IMAGES

THE EASTERN & ORIENTAL: p121

WEST COAST WILDERNESS RAILWAY: p287

THE NORTHERN EXPLORER: p291

Foreword

MARK SMITH THE MAN IN SEAT 61

There's something magical about a journey by train. Sometimes the magic is inside – on a train you have room to move and meet people, dine in a restaurant car with white tablecloths, sleep in a private compartment between crisp, clean sheets with the sound of steel wheel swishing on steel rail beneath you. Sometimes the magic is outside, in the landscape the train traverses – an adventure, an experience, an insight into the heart of a nation.

I've been hooked on the magic of train travel since the tender age of 13. I saved my pocket money for years – well, several weeks at least – until I had amassed £2.73, enough for my first solo overseas trip, a child-rate cheap day-return from London to the Isle of Wight. My parents had no idea where I'd gone, but when I eventually returned home were too relieved to scold me. The fascination with train travel didn't end there and railways became my career, first with British Rail, and now running the train travel website The Man in Seat 61, through which I try to share my passion with others.

I don't think even I realised quite how magical a train journey could be until I took a trip from London to Verona in the luxurious 1920s-vintage cars of the Venice Simplon-Orient-Express. Frankly, even though I needed to research the trip for my website, I had doubted that any 24-hour train ride could possibly be worth £2000. But one year the stars aligned: a 25% discount was offered at the end of the season, and on discovering with horror that my girlfriend had never

visited Italy, I booked tickets. We'd only been going out for six months. But that special train weaved its very special magic: the name of our first-born son was decided in our wagons-lits that night, and the next day something happened as the train swept south in a blizzard through the Brenner Pass. We still talk about who said what to whom (although I remember the important details, such as in which 1927-built S-type sleeping-car we were staying), suffice it to say when that train arrived in Verona we were engaged. And here I am 13 years later with a wife, two small kids, two small cats and one large mortgage. Powerful magic indeed.

In this book you'll find many of my own favourite journeys – some well known, some less so, some luxurious and expensive, others true bargains. The California Zephyr from Chicago to San Francisco is perhaps the best of all the Amtrak routes across the USA, and the fabulous Bernina Express is, in my opinion, the best Swiss Alpine ride of all. The spectacular railway from Belgrade to Bar through the mountains of Montenegro, and the wonderful journey from Mandalay to Lashio in Myanmar are two of the most scenic train rides you've probably never heard of, with a fare of just €20 for the former and US$6 for the latter. And naturally my favourite British train route makes an appearance, the West Highland Line to Mallaig. I hope this book inspires you to make some of the journeys it features, and that you too can discover – if you don't already know – just how magical a train ride can be.

MANDALAY TO LASHIO, MYANMAR: p134

INLANDSBANAN: p256

THE GHAN: p272

THE RUPERT ROCKET: p82

About this Book

● **TOM HALL** EDITORIAL DIRECTOR, LONELY PLANET

Here at Lonely Planet we've always had a soft spot for trains. It may have something to do with our history, firmly rooted in overland travel, in following lines on maps and seeing where they lead, and delighting in the people and places encountered along the way. Or it might be that, whatever the reason for departure, we know the moment a train pulls out of a station bound for somewhere fantastic is when the adventure truly starts. Generations of travellers have experienced that feeling with a Lonely Planet travel guide by their side, whether that's in Chicago's Union Station, the Gare de Lyon in Paris, Mumbai's Chhatrapati Shivaji Terminus or another great train station of the world. The book you are currently holding aims to distil that feeling and point the way to other fabulous trips.

When we first devised *Amazing Train Journeys*, we started, as we often do at Lonely Planet, by asking 200 or so travel writers to tell us their favourites. We got many more suggestions than we could include here, with many different reasons for championing their cause. Some were international journeys epic in length and adventure, others short suburban routes along a stretch of coast or leading to somewhere special. Some offer incredible feats of engineering, others seem to work only due to sheer force of will of local railway workers. And while some are so celebrated they've achieved Unesco World Heritage status, my favourites are the little-known routes you might otherwise not give a second glance to as they flash by on a clacking Solari board.

This tribute to our love affair with the world's railways is published at a time when steel rails and wheels have been enjoying a 21st-century renaissance. After decades of decline, new high-speed rail, urban lines and ultra-long-distance freight services are underscoring the importance of railways in the world's economy. This book showcases some of these relative newcomers, from riding the (extended) Ghan from Australia's north to south coast, to taking the world's highest train to Lhasa, Tibet. A more rail-friendly world view has also led to a greater appreciation of small yet perfectly formed lines such as the Darjeeling Toy Train and Slovenia's well-kept secret from Nova Gorica to Jesenice, both featured here.

There's more to come too – by the time you read this you should be able to once again take a train from Addis Ababa to Djibouti, on brand-new track and rolling stock, and, looking further ahead, railway expansion is planned in places around the world as varied as Mexico, Iran, Scandinavia and East Africa. And just to show you we're as sentimental about past golden ages as anyone else, it feels right to offer a nod of appreciation to the remarkable number and quality of heritage railway lines around the world, often volunteer-run and adding to the richness of rail travel anywhere they're found.

We're excited to bring our passion for 'the permanent way' to the pages of *Amazing Train Journeys*. Whether you prefer high-speed or deliberately go-slow, hopefully you'll be inspired to get out on the rails again.

● **KEY TO ICONS**

Tourist train · Passenger train · Recommended stop · Detour · Budget: ticket <US$50
Steam train · High-speed train · View · Train life · Mid-range: ticket US$50–$100
Railway architecture · Food and drink · Top end: ticket >US$100

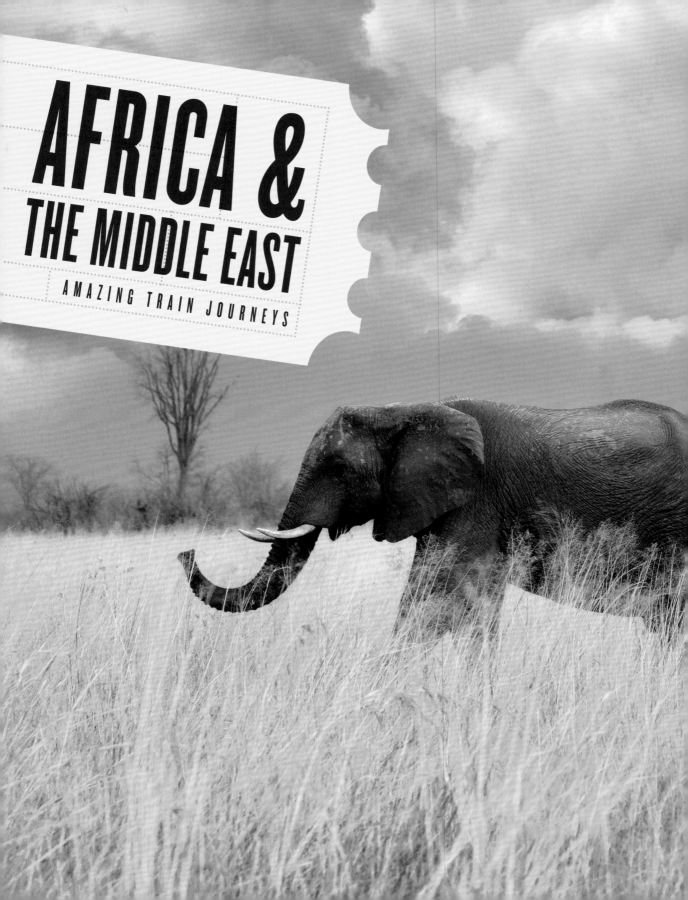

AFRICA &
THE MIDDLE EAST
AMAZING TRAIN JOURNEYS

Johannesburg to Cape Town

SOUTH AFRICA

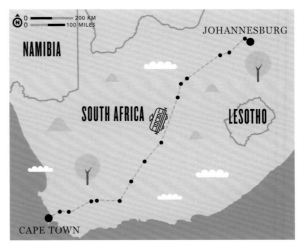

START **JOHANNESBURG**

END **CAPE TOWN**

DEPARTS **4 PER WEEK**

DISTANCE **930 MILES (1500KM)**

DURATION **27 HRS**

The overnight service between Johannesburg and Cape Town crosses the Great Karoo, a mythical desert at the heart of South Africa and its imagination, where tumbleweeds roll down dusty roads and mountains ripple along the horizon. Formerly known as the Trans-Karoo Express, the train leaves Johannesburg's razor-wire-wrapped suburbs and crosses the northern bush, hurtling across the Karoo as its passengers sleep and the desert stars twinkle, before emerging among the Cape's breathtaking tapestry of mountains and vineyards. Finally, an air of camaraderie fills the train as it follows the Atlantic coast towards the welcome outline of Table Mountain.

❶ RIDING THE RAILS

Most visitors to South Africa cross the country's vast interior on a two-hour flight from Johannesburg to Cape Town. However, there is another way: a local secret, shared by khaki-clad old timers in bush lodges from Kruger to the Kalahari. You may hear it referred to by its old, more-romantic name of the Trans-Karoo Express. It follows the same route as the world-famous Blue Train but for the price of a budget flight. It's the Shosholoza Meyl tourist-class sleeper, a train that traverses the arid, little-visited core of this epic nation, a rite of passage through scrubland, before arriving at the postcard views and fine wines around Cape Town.

Pay heed to those old timers, and buy them a cold beer, because passengers soon discover that this trip is hotter than the Karoo in summer. Fleeing the edginess of downtown Johannesburg, the train chugs into the surrounding bushveld, stopping in working-class Afrikaner towns. Instead of mountain ranges glimpsed from a plane window, this railway journey offers a close-up of South Africa in all its blotchy glory, from sweeping Karoo vistas to railway-siding scenes worthy of an African Edward Hopper painting. On small-town platforms beneath the harsh afternoon sun, train staff catch up with station porters in the slang of this many-tongued country: 'Howzit...' 'Is it...' 'Agh, shame man'.

Then there are the characters you meet stretching their legs in the corridor. Maybe it will be a Cape Coloured auntie, a grizzly old Afrikaner, a young black

Cape Town – seen from the rocky
shoreline on Robben Island.

© GARY LATHAM | LONELY PLANET

professional or a gathering of all three, passing the long desert hours in their diverse accents. Corridor-window conversations lurch and lapse as the train rattles onwards, until passengers find themselves gazing at an industrial skyline in the darkness. 'It's the biggest hole in the world,' someone says. Stop sniggering back there in economy class: this is Kimberley, site of the 705ft (215m) deep Big Hole – one of the world's largest hand-dug craters, dating to the city's 19th-century diamond-mining heyday. You can relive those prospecting days by visiting the hole and its reconstructed mining village, the historic pubs and museums, or by taking a ghost tour.

The train clatters onwards through the diamond fields and into the mighty Karoo, which takes its name from a Khoe-San word meaning 'land of thirst' and covers about one third of South Africa. Toast the velvety darkness from the dining car, and then awake after a good night's sleep in your bunk to find the semi-desert still out there – and going nowhere for the rest of the morning.

Descending from the great inland plateau of the Karoo to the Breede River Valley and the Cape Winelands, a rollercoaster ride of mountain passes awaits, before the train crosses the coastal flats towards the beckoning mass of Table Mountain. Excitement mounts about arriving at the Cape, with the well-rested passengers crowding the windows to chat like old friends and enjoy the city views. Alighting in the mid-afternoon, there's plenty of time to check into your hotel before taking another journey: on the cable car up Table Mountain for sunset.

❷ LIFE ON BOARD

True to operator Shosholoza Meyl's motto – 'A pleasant experience' – tourist class offers no-frills sleeper compartments with artificial-leather bench seats.

TAKE THE CAR

It's possible to combine a railway journey with a road trip by transporting your car on the train. This service is available on the tourist class and Premier Classe sleepers linking Johannesburg with Cape Town, Port Elizabeth and Durban.

Two- and four-berth options are available, respectively known as coupés and compartments, each with a washbasin and a shared toilet and hot shower. Solo travellers are usually placed in a shared compartment; buy two tickets to have a coupé to yourself. Bedding is available and, although there is no air-conditioning, you can open the windows for fresh air and Karoo views. Economy class is in reclining seats.

You're likely to spend at least a few hours enjoying the views from the dining car, which serves snacks and meals, beer and wine throughout the day – perfect for sampling the local vino as the train swishes on through the Cape Winelands. The chicken curry would also pass muster in a stationary restaurant. The one drawback is that the sleepers are only lockable from the inside, so you may wish to keep valuables on you as a precaution, although the train feels totally safe overall.

Pass the 988-acre (400-hectare) Kamfers Dam and its thousands of lesser flamingoes, north of Kimberley.

Experience the Karoo in Prince Albert, where 19th-century cottages nestle below the Swartberg Pass.

Wander the perfectly preserved street of Matjiesfontein, with its grand hotel and two museums.

Johannesburg

Kimberley

Prince Albert

Matjiesfontein

LEFT & BELOW: The Shosholoza Meyl train pulls into downtown Johannesburg; riding through the Great Karoo.
OPENING PAGE: The Karoo desert.

❸ UPGRADES

South Africa's classic luxury railway journey is the Blue Train (www.bluetrain.co.za) between Pretoria and Cape Town, which provides tours of diamond-mining Kimberley and the colonial Karoo resort of Matjiesfontein on the southbound and northbound trips respectively. Luxury operator Rovos Rail (www.rovos.com) also plies the trans-Karoo route in style, while Shosholoza Meyl's Premier Classe service (www.premierclasse.co.za) offers deluxe but affordable travel on the same route.

❹ MAKE IT HAPPEN

Trains depart four days a week. You can book tickets direct (www.shosholozameyl.co.za) and collect them at major train stations. For convenience and peace of mind, though, book instead through agency African Sun Travel (www.africansuntravel.com). Bookings open 90 days before departure and places fill up, so reserve your place as far ahead as possible.

Most people cover the journey in one go, but the historic diamond town of Kimberley, the charming Karoo *dorpies* (towns) of Prince Albert and Matjiesfontein, and wine-farming Wellington and Paarl are possible stop-offs. Southbound to Cape Town is the more romantic direction. Travel in autumn (February–April) to see beautiful colours in the vineyards, or spring (August–October) for wildflowers.

Most Western travellers are given a 90-day visa upon arrival in South Africa; for more information visit www.home-affairs.gov.za. **JB**

© GREG BALFOUR EVANS | ALAMY STOCK PHOTO

© PETE TITMUSS | ALAMY STOCK PHOTO

Enjoy the dramatic Hex River Pass, descending from the Karoo into the Breede River Valley.

Get your camera ready for the mountains and vineyards between Worcester and Paarl.

Salute the distant beacon of Table Mountain as you approach your final stop, Cape Town.

| Worcester | Wellington | Huguenot (Paarl) | Cape Town |

Andimeshk to Dorud

IRAN

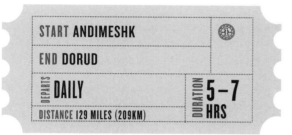

START **ANDIMESHK**	
END **DORUD**	
DEPARTS **DAILY**	DURATION **5–7 HRS**
DISTANCE 129 MILES (209KM)	

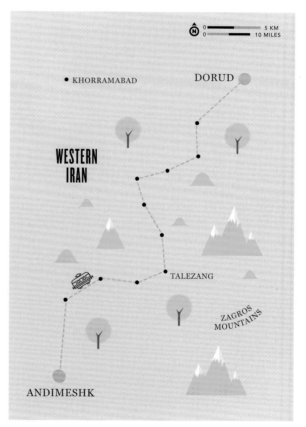

 One of the world's least known, but most spectacular railway journeys winds like a Silk Road caravan through the mountainous heart of ancient Persia. This dazzling engineering marvel, blasted through Iran's unforgettable Zagros Mountains, clings to the side of remote river valleys, tunnels under immense, crumbling peaks, bridges gaping chasms and passes gently cascading waterfalls, and comes framed against a stark and unforgiving landscape. As it climbs over 3280ft (1000m) from the flat Khuzestan plain to the high plateau of fabled Lorestan, the awe-inspiring scenery is only matched by the legendary hospitality of your fellow travellers.

❶ RIDING THE RAILS

The raw, jagged mountains of the Zagros loom nearer as you stare mesmerised out the window. The sun's rising and you're drinking sweet tea with your new friends, an Iranian family sharing your compartment. The mother presses another cookie on you. Smiling, you accept while her kids take selfies with the *turiste*. Flat, featureless Andimeshk already seems miles away, though you've been travelling less than an hour.

The Trans-Iranian Railway links the Persian Gulf with the Caspian Sea, and the 129-mile (208km)

convoluted section through the wild and barren Zagros Mountains is especially scenic. The line from Andimeshk strikes out north, then skirts across eroded badlands to avoid the massive reservoir of Dez Dam. The first of many, many tunnels is entered. By Balaroud the tracks are shadowing a river bed and several viaducts are crossed en route to Mazou.

Commissioned by Reza Shah Pahlavi in the 1930s, the mountain phase of the Trans-Iranian was

"The train pops into a precipitous gorge above the sediment-filled River Dez. You gasp in surprise."

completed by European engineers who battled salt mountains, shifting bedrock, insane gradients and yawning abysses. Shortly afterwards, the US, UK and Soviets commandeered the line during World War II to protect their oil and to provide an arms supply conduit to Stalin.

'What country you?' as another cookie slides your way. 'Iran good? Children? Married?' Hand-signals and smiles compensate for a lack of Farsi and by journey's end you'll have gained some weight, a phone full of new contacts and possibly a dinner invitation.

Viaducts and tunnels proliferate after Mazou as the route twists east through bizarrely striped barren ridges until tunnelling into the Zagros proper after the tiny village of Shahbazan.

Prelude over, the scenery ramps up as the train pops out into a precipitous gorge above the sediment-filled River Dez. Even the Iranians pause mid-mouthful, but no sooner do you gasp in surprise than blackness again engulfs, and tunnel cat-and-mouse is played all the way to atmospheric Talezang on a bend in the river.

In 2017, the Trans-Iranian's system of tunnels, viaducts and overlapping spirals, originally engineered in the 1930s, were submitted for World Heritage inclusion. A thought to ponder as upstream on the Dez the line soon burrows directly under the massive Kuh-e Kornas mountain (6149ft/1980m), returning to daylight just as the river splits into two tributaries. Cross the Bakhtiari and follow the western Sezar to nearby Tang-e Panj via a particularly fetching viaduct traversing a Mordorish landscape.

Welcome to Lorestan.

Suddenly, the whole train disembarks. Is it terminating in the middle of nowhere? 'Don't worry, we go talk to God' informs the conductor. Prayer stops are common on Iranian trains – take advantage of the 20 minutes to stretch your legs. Back on board, the line crosses the Sezar several times before disappearing back into the earth under Kuh-e Hamid (4547ft/1386m). Someone in your compartment starts singing, others join in. Emerging near Tang-e Haft, they look at you expectantly. Feigning sleep may work.

Continuing north with the river, the tracks tunnel into the huge, crumbling lump of Zarrin Kuh (2969ft/905m), which dwarfs the village of Keshvar, before heading east again along the widening valley. Tick off Chamasangar before reaching Sepid Dasht, beautifully ringed by 5250ft (1600m) rocky spires, where the line loops over itself in a figure-eight climb onto the greener Lorestan plateau.

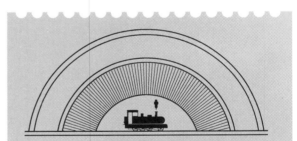

SHEVI WATERFALLS

From Talezang, a popular 6-mile (10km) trek leads to a pair of photogenic waterfalls in a gorge of a tributary of the River Dez. The approach takes several hours and requires some scrambling. Most parties take a tent and stay overnight, as the surrounding mountains offer excellent hiking. Spring (March–May) is the best time to visit.

Make new Iranian friends as you settle into your compartment after boarding in Andimeshk.

Cross the bizarrely striped barren ridges between Mazou and Shahbazan.

Enjoy the first glimpse of the precipitous River Dez gorge after exiting the Shabazan tunnel.

Trek from Talezang to the remote Shevi Waterfalls.

Andimeshk   Balaroud   Mazou   Shabhazan   Talezang

LEFT & BELOW: Relaxing on the journey; sunlit Zagros landscape. **PREVIOUS PAGE:** One of many viaducts en route.

Enjoy the cooler air and verdant landscape on arrival at pretty Bisheh, where a waterfall spills down behind the station. Seek out fortress-like Kuh-e Pariz (9652ft/2942m) as the line enters yet another narrow gorge for the final push to Dorud. Arriving is an anticlimax, so consider staying on the train, perhaps all the way to Tehran? Got another cookie, mama?

❷ LIFE ON BOARD

In summer, slow regional trains can be crowded beyond belief, and the reservation numbers on your ticket mean little, but as a foreigner you'll be offered a seat. Expresses have six- or eight-berth compartments complete with refreshment packages of cake, juice and bottled water. Some trains have a buffet car. You'll be the height of interest so expect to share food and be ready for an onslaught of questions and selfies.

❸ MAKE IT HAPPEN

Several trains ply the route daily in both directions, though usually only one will travel during daylight hours. Schedules change frequently. Book seats (up to one month) in advance from a travel agency within Iran or any station, or queue early on the day.

The route can be travelled in either direction. Leaving from Andimeshk gives you the option of continuing onto Tehran. Thursdays and Fridays (the Iranian weekend) are busy. Avoid No Ruz, the Iranian New Year (around March equinox), when the whole country is on the move.

Bring your own refreshments and share. Avoid photographing anything structural (stations, bridges, tracks, etc). Citizens of the US, UK and Canada have stricter visa conditions than other Western countries. For more information visit www.rai.ir. **SW**

Cross the Bakhtiari and ford the Sezar on numerous viaducts around Tang-e Panj.

Be amazed by the rock spires surrounding Sepid Dasht as the train ascends the figure-eight loop.

Stay overnight in Bisheh to view its waterfall without the crowds.

Tang-e Panj   **Keshvar**   **Chamasangar**   **Sepid Dasht**   **Bisheh**   **Dorud**

Bulawayo to Victoria Falls

ZIMBABWE ●

START **BULAWAYO**	⊚
END **VICTORIA FALLS**	
DEPARTS **DAILY**	DURATION **12HRS 30 MINS**
DISTANCE 295 MILES (472KM)	

A night spent rattling through the savannah of southern Africa by train – waking to gaze at Zimbabwe's Zambezi-fed bushveld from the window of a British-built carriage straight from the 1950s, sleepy eyes suddenly alert to the possibility of spying antelopes and elephants by the trackside – is an experience that stays seared to the synapses of your brain for life. And that's before you get a glimpse of the planet's most impressive cascade. Even if the finer details are a little dusty after decades of runaway economic decline in Zimbabwe, this remains a classic journey to one of the world's great wonders.

❶ RIDING THE RAILS

Despite the final destination's designation as one of Africa's biggest attractions, the train trip from Bulawayo to the thundering vapour of Victoria Falls is far from a touristy experience. Travellers who choose to shoot this route by rail – instead of flying or squeezing into a cramped bus – will find most of their fellow passengers are locals, with the train becoming a veritable village on wheels.

During holiday season, boarding in bustling Bulawayo can be lively, as families and passengers peruse the carriages. The train is a long, serpentine beast, though, which easily swallows its colourful human cargo, and the service sets off close to the advertised departure time of 7.30pm most evenings.

From Zimbabwe's second city, which sits at 4455ft (1358m) above sea level, the lackadaisical loco meanders across the Matabeleland plateau, chugging first through the agricultural areas where maize and peanuts are grown by the Bantu-bantering Ndebele.

However, even at the height of the southern summer, the sun sets shortly before 7pm and the last vestige of twilight evaporates within the hour, so much is left to the imagination as the train rolls into the deepening night. The air is fresh at this altitude, and with windows down to feel the evening breeze, extra layers are often required before bedtime.

Unless you opted for the really cheap seats (an uncomfortable and unnecessary option, given the modest price of 1st-class travel), you'll be slumbering in a sleeping car built in Britain in the 1950s, complete with wood panelling if you're really lucky, but most likely featuring more contemporary (but less charismatic) Formica frills.

Note the 'RR' logos on windows and mirrors, historic reflections of Rhodesia Railways, which once operated some of the largest and most powerful locomotives in the southern hemisphere – including a rampaging gang of 200-tonne Garratt steam engines.

The paintwork on carriages retains the old colonial company's colour palette too, but the hue of the experience has changed considerably since 1980, when the country secured independence and changed its name, and the insignia of the National Railways of Zimbabwe (NRZ) was emblazoned on the newly nationalised industry's equipment.

Tourism thrived in the 1980s and early '90s, but Zimbabwe's financial fortunes plummeted faster than a thrill-seeking bungee jumper leaping from Victoria Falls Bridge during the turbulence and controversy that buffeted the country in recent decades. An attempt to recapitalise the railway was made in 2017, but the bounce is yet to come and, unsurprisingly, upkeep of rolling stock has not been the nation's number-one priority in the meantime.

So, the buffet car will likely be shut or missing, some lights might not work, bedding will be in short supply, the sink won't feature running water, and door latches and window blinds might not function as intended. But despite these chips, chinks and cracks in the veneer, the charm of the experience itself survives – and who wants to pull a blind across a moving vista of Africa's epic plains anyway?

Admittedly, at the numerous stops – some of which seem simultaneously unscheduled but expected, judging by people waiting to board at unofficial bush 'stations' – inquisitive eyes will automatically alight on the sight of international travellers. If you're concerned about privacy or security, especially while sleeping, compartments come with lockable doors,

© MIKE ABRAHAMS I ALAMY STOCK PHOTO

Observe the daily life of locals in villages, on stations and aboard the train itself.

Get snug in your sleeping bag as the train rat-a-tats across Matabeleland's cool plateau.

Bulawayo **Mpopoma** **Nyamandlovu** **Sawmills**

LEFT & BELOW: Elephants can cause delays; a passenger is transfixed.
PREVIOUS PAGE: Victoria Falls.

RAILWAY MUSEUM

Before boarding, check out Bulawayo's NRZ Railway Museum near the station, which features Cecil Rhodes' sumptuous 1890s private carriage. A controversial colonial figure, Rhodes ordered the Victoria Falls Bridge be built so close to the great cascade that passengers could feel spray through the windows.

and you can always improvise a more comprehensive window blind/door stop. The atmosphere is generally friendly and the staff does its best with what they have – you just have to come prepared.

Overnight the train puffs from plateau to savannah, skirting the eastern edge of huge Hwange National Park and rat-a-tatting across one of Africa's longest stretches of straight railway. As dawn approaches, the first fingers of light start colouring in the Lowveld bush, and ephemeral curtains of morning mist part to reveal evocative valleys. By daybreak proper, the train is trespassing through the wilderness of Zambezi National Park, with real-time safari scenes playing out on the widescreen portal that is your window.

While the train maintains its somnambulant pace, passengers rub the sleep from their eyes and scour the msasa, mopane, baobab and sausage trees, hunting and hoping for a flashing glimpse of wildlife, including giraffes, impalas, springboks and baboons.

Mischievous monkeys occasionally climb on the carriages, and sometimes elephants will stray onto the line, causing delays.

Pachyderm problems aside, by breakfast the journey's finale fast approaches, with the train following the flow of the mighty Zambezi, rolling along just a few hundred metres from the banks of the beautiful river, where the water is seconds away from plunging over the edge of the abyss between Zimbabwe and Zambia.

At Victoria Falls Station, Mosi-oa-Tunya ('The Smoke That Thunders', as the Tonga call the falls) dominates the senses. The roar – created by over 35,000 cubic feet (1000 cubic metres) of water rolling over a 324ft (108m) chasm every second – resonates right around the town, which is veiled by a delicate mist rising from the impact zone in the gorge below.

'Scenes so lovely must have been gazed upon by angels in their flight,' is how Livingstone famously

Wake at dawn to see the rising sun setting the Zimbabwean savannah ablaze.

Spot wildlife – including elephants, giraffes, antelopes, springboks and baboons – from your train window.

Gwaai   Dete   Hwange   Matetsi

described the Zambezi during his approach to the falls on 16 November 1855, shortly before he became the first known European to clock the cascade.

It had taken the explorer, already maimed by a lion attack, two years to bash through bush and negotiate crocodile-infested rivers to reach this point – which makes 13 hours on an overnight sleeper train seem somewhat luxurious, even if the lights in the 1st-class coupé don't all work.

❷ LIFE ON BOARD

First-class sleepers have two-berth rooms (coupés) and four-berth rooms (compartments) with leatherette bench seats converting to bunks, plus a fold-out washbasin. Compartments are single sex. For your own coupé, book two tickets. Second-class sleepers have three-berth coupés and six-berth compartments.

❸ UPGRADES

Charter steam-train trips are an option for rail enthusiasts travelling in Zimbabwe, Zambia and South Africa, with options incorporating the Bulawayo–Victoria Falls route. Short sunset steam trips can also be taken across Victoria Falls Bridge. See www.rovos.com or www.victoriafalls-guide.net.

❹ MAKE IT HAPPEN

Trains run every evening from Bulawayo to Victoria Falls. It's no longer possible to buy tickets 30 days in advance – purchase tickets at Bulawayo Station's reservation office on the day of travel only. There are three classes: 1st and 2nd are both in sleepers, while economy is seat only. Zimbabwe dollars are no longer accepted; US dollars are now general currency.

Bedding isn't always available; bring your own sleeping bag. Also take a torch, and in the absence of a buffet car, buy supplies from Bulawayo's Pick 'N' Pay supermarket. More info is found at www.nrz.co.zw. **PK**

Arrive at Victoria Falls, with the mist and cacophony of the incredible cascade filling the air.

Victoria Falls

Canoeing on the 'gazed upon by angels' Zambezi River at sunset.

Tazara Railway

TANZANIA & ZAMBIA

START **DAR ES SALAAM**	
END **KAPIRI MPOSHI**	
DEPARTS **TWICE A WEEK**	DURATION **46 HRS**
DISTANCE **1160 MILES (1860KM)**	

On a continent where taking things slowly is compulsory, it won't come as much of a surprise that the 46-hour journey along the 1160-mile (1860km) route from Tanzania's port city to New Kapiri Mposhi in Zambia often ends up taking far longer. Then again, few trains in the world offer the chance – and we should point out that it's a chance rather than a guarantee – of spotting big game from your seat, but the Tazara (Tanzania and Zambia Railway Authority) does exactly that. For many, the highlight is neither the scenery nor the wildlife, though; it is the chance to spend two days watching everyday life out of the window, and enjoying the clamour and chaos when the train pulls to a halt, scheduled or unscheduled.

❶ RIDING THE RAILS

Even the most jaded of trans-continental travellers must surely feel excited boarding the Mukuba Express at Dar es Salaam's Tazara Station. From here, the next two days will slowly unfold: an unforgettable cross-Africa journey taking in city, plains, hills and rivers. The handsome station building at Dar was constructed, like the rest of the line, by Chinese engineers in the 1970s to facilitate the transportation of copper from Zambia to the sea.

A Friday afternoon departure from the bustle and noise of Dar es Salaam may mean that you're still digesting a street-food lunch of barbecue grilled chicken, or looking forward to a slow train after spending time on the buses that cover much of the rest of the country. The happy lurch of the Mukuba Express begins the slow procession west and south, and the line runs first across the coastal plain and then traverses hundreds of miles of dream-like savannah scenery. An open window allows all the sounds, smells and warmth of southern Tanzania to drift into your compartment.

Most travellers will not have undertaken this trip on the promise of a cheap safari, but as the line passes through Selous Game Reserve on the first evening of the journey there is a decent chance of seeing giraffe, elephant and other big names of African wildlife. If you're unlucky there should at least be a glorious sunset to gawp at from the moving train, and the promise of more beautiful scenery to

© CATHERINA UNGER | AWL

GREAT UHURU

Originally built to free Zambia from having to export minerals through neighbouring white-ruled territories, the Tazara was dubbed the Great Uhuru ('freedom' in Swahili) Railway. Today the line carries both freight and passengers on one of Africa's great rail adventures.

come. Of course, away from the big city lights the night sky is also stunning to behold.

The next day brings the rolling hills of the southern uplands of Tanzania, heralded by the towns of Makambako and Mbeya. Intrepid travellers can head into the highlands from Makambako, exploring the plateau and then heading on to Lake Nyasa. Staying on board, close to Mbeya is Mbeya Peak, the highest in the area and a wonderful hike through lush terrain if you have time to linger.

The train rolls on to the border, which is an event in itself: visas are acquired, customs cleared and money changed. Once in Zambia the population soon becomes denser, and everyday life in all its glory can be witnessed through the train window. Nowhere more so than upon arrival at New Kapiri Mposhi station. If you've drifted into a reverie after a couple of days on board, you'll find this abruptly snapped in

the cacophony of a classic southern African transit terminal. Expect plenty of noise, bartering and general commotion until you find your ride on to Lusaka or elsewhere in Zambia.

❷ LIFE ON BOARD

Settle in for a long, rolling ride. There are clean and comfortable 1st-class (four-berth) and 2nd-class (six-berth) sleepers, which are single sex unless you have reserved the entire compartment. Seated tickets are also available. There is a bar and a dining car, and meals can be served at your seat in sleeper compartments, though you should bring your own snacks and water. Some provisions are available at stations. Although there are money-changers at the border, you'll get a predictably worse rate than in a bank or at big-city exchanges.

☆ The non-stop waves and shouts of people passing by your train window ensure there's never a dull moment on board.

👓 Have your binoculars at the ready as you pass through Selous Game Reserve.

👓 Gasp at the Rift Valley scenery spotted en route through Tanzania's southern highlands.

Dar es Salaam   Kisaki   Ifakara   Mlimba   Makambako   Mbeya   Vwawa

CLOCKWISE FROM LEFT: Trackside traders along the Tazara Railway; young lions at play; giraffes can sometimes be seen from the train. **PREVIOUS PAGE:** Cape buffalo in Selous Game Reserve.

❸ ALTERNATIVE ROUTES

Another Tanzanian railway adventure heads out from Dar es Salaam to Kigoma on Lake Tangyanika, from where the MV Liemba ferry makes its timeless journey to Mpulungu in Zambia. The train leaves from Dar es Salaam central station, not the Tazara station.

❹ UPGRADES

Rovos Rail's 15-day, five-star luxury journey from Cape Town to Dar es Salaam on the Pride of Africa includes the Tazara route. It comes in at US$12,450 (£9300) based on two sharing (www.rovos.com). Should you be wavering over the price, there is an observation car.

❺ MAKE IT HAPPEN

Two trains per week run in each direction. One train (leaving Dar on Fridays and heading the other way on Tuesdays) is the Mukuba Express service, while the other is a slower train with many stops, rather marvellously named Kilimanjaro Ordinary.

Given the absence of online booking and the need to do some old-fashioned things, such as visiting a station or picking up the phone to reserve a seat, which may or may not be a reliable process, we recommend you make use of the traveller's grapevine. The booking information at www.seat61.com is regularly updated, and includes phone numbers, travel agencies and details of which trains will run on which service. You'll also find information at tazarasite.com. **TH**

Experience the fun and games and passport stamps on the border crossing between Tanzania and Zambia.

Enjoy (at least) two African sunsets on board.

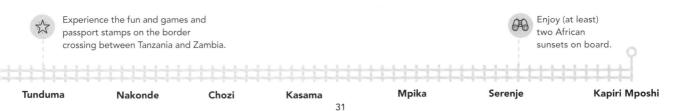

Tunduma   Nakonde   Chozi   Kasama   Mpika   Serenje   Kapiri Mposhi

© FEARGUS COONEY | ALAMY STOCK PHOTO

© JT PLATT | GETTY IMAGES

Iron Ore Train

MAURITANIA

START **ZOUÉRAT OR CHOÛM**	
END **NOUÂDHIBOU**	
DEPARTS **DAILY**	DURATION **17 HRS**
DISTANCE **435 MILES (700KM)**	

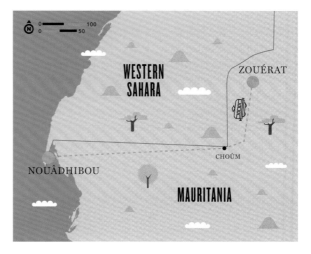

As much a sand-blasted Saharan legend as a means of getting from desert A to B, and considerably more geared towards freight than passengers, Mauritania's Iron Ore Train connects remote inland mines with the Atlantic coast. Hardy local Moors and Sahrawi perch atop the sooty mounds of iron ore, holding their turbans across their faces as their robes billow in the night. This is one of the world's longest trains at more than 1.25 miles (2km) in length, and of its approximately 200 carriages, just one serves as passenger transport. Before recent security issues, the train was a classic Saharan route leading deep into the desert.

❶ RIDING THE RAILS

Mauritania is as enormous as it is obscure, covering about 380,000 sq miles (1 million sq km) of the Sahara's western stretches or an area four times the size of the UK. A population of less than 4 million brave its rocky hamada. To the north lies the disputed territory of Western Sahara, much of it carpeted with minefields, while the Senegal River, defining Mauritania's southern border, unofficially marks the beginning of sub-Saharan Africa. In between, the inhabitants of the forbidding desert covering three quarters of Mauritania eke out a traditional nomadic existence.

The Iron Ore Train serves the mining hub of Zouérat, but most travellers board or disembark in Choûm, where the track turns west and follows the Western Sahara border to Nouâdhibou on the Atlantic coast. Choûm is accessed from Atâr, which, apart from having harboured Saddam Hussein's family during the Gulf War, is the launchpad for visiting the 13th-century caravan town of Chinguetti. The adventure thus begins long before you board the train: getting to Choûm entails squeezing into a bush taxi in Atâr, normally a battered Land Rover that follows piste trails into the Adrar region and navigates the plains by the driver's knowledge of local rock formations. It's a relief to arrive in Choûm, although there's little there except a flophouse for escaping the searing heat and drinking tea until the train arrives.

As with everything in Saharan life, the general attitude in the waiting room is that the train will arrive *inshallah* (God willing), and the assembled company seems resigned to any eventuality. But their sleepy fatalism quickly vanishes when the locomotive appears. There's a stampede towards the sole passenger carriage at the rear of the train, with men and women alike lifting their colourful robes to sprint across the sand, hauling a motley collection of faded holdalls, sacks and goats. Hitting the ladder into the carriage, everyone tries to scramble up and squeeze through the door at once, not giving a millimetre of ground in the competition for the best position inside.

The single carriage is bare inside, apart from a narrow wooden bench along one wall, and a layer of dust covering everything. By the time it reaches Choûm, almost every patch of bench and floor space is occupied. Packed like sardines, everyone spends the night shifting and turning, bending their legs and angling their backs according to the contours of the neighbouring bodies. One or two unfortunates crawl into the recess under the bench, their voices emerging from their stuffy lair like those of desperate desert Gollums. In this manner, passengers on the Iron Ore Train cross one of the world's least populated countries, surrounded by empty plains and dunes.

Night soon descends on the Sahara. The passengers sprawl in the darkness, all keeping their heads near the bench to accommodate the tea service. This consists of a man stumbling up the carriage with a tray heaving with glasses of piping-hot tea, picking his way over the carpet of legs. There is some camaraderie for travellers to enjoy with their tea, as curious young men with intense eyes framed by their turbans ask in Arabic-accented French (Mauritania's colonial language) exactly how you came to be riding through the Sahara in the middle of the night. The hot tea and the broken conversation help to pass the time, and

© GARY COOK | ALAMY STOCK PHOTO

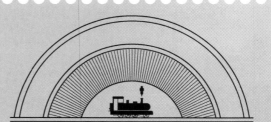

GETTING TO NOUÂDHIBOU

Bush taxis cross the border between Nouâdhibou and Dakhla in the Western Sahara, which is well connected to Morocco by daily flights and buses. Taxis also connect both Nouâdhibou and Choûm to the Mauritanian capital, Nouakchott, making it possible to ride the Iron Ore Train as part of a circuit.

⭐ Drink tea with turban-wrapped Moors and Sahrawi as you wait to board your train.

Catch a bush taxi south from Choûm to explore the Adrar Plateau.

Zouérat

Choûm

CLOCKWISE FROM LEFT: The (very long) Iron Ore Train; young women passengers; traversing the desert. **PREVIOUS PAGE:** Economy class.

there's plenty of that to kill as the night presses at the dirty windows and the passengers murmur and groan.

And so the cramped passengers arrive at dawn in Nouâdhibou. Here the train unceremoniously disgorges its human cargo on the outskirts of town, leaving you to find a taxi and tiredly haggle with the driver. Still, the Iron Ore Train is the only way to cross northwest Mauritania and is typical of the hardships endured by the inhabitants of this desert nation.

❷ LIFE ON BOARD

Thrifty travellers can ride the Iron Ore Train for free by clambering into an ore wagon. Dress warmly in preparation for a night in the open desert, and wrap your luggage in plastic to keep off the dust and grime. In addition to the seats inside, there is an extremely worn sleeper section with bunk beds.

❸ MAKE IT HAPPEN

Trains depart daily. You can buy a ticket on the train, though they sometimes sell out, so you may wish to make inquiries and buy one a few days in advance, especially for the sleeper compartment. Most people travel one-way between Choûm and Nouâdhibou (12 hours). Avoid the gruelling peaks of Saharan heat by visiting during the cooler winter season between November and March. Nights are colder at this time of year, so wrap up warm on the train, which travels overnight in both directions.

Always check your government's travel and safety advice before visiting Mauritania. Tourist visas should be available on arrival, but it's probably safer to obtain one at the Mauritania embassy in your own country. Food and water aren't available on the train, so make sure you bring plenty of both. **JB**

 Look out for Ben Amira, a 2077ft (633m) granite monolith.

 Arrive in Nouâdhibou as Mauritania's second city is waking up, then go birdwatching in the Parc National du Banc d'Arguin.

Nouâdhibou

AMERICAS

AMAZING TRAIN JOURNEYS

The Sunset Limited

USA

START **NEW ORLEANS**

END **LOS ANGELES**

DEPARTS **3 PER WEEK**

DISTANCE **1995 MILES (3211KM)**

DURATION **2 DAYS**

The ultimate American railroad ride: east to west, coast to coast, clean through from the bars of New Orleans to the breakers of the Pacific Ocean. If you've always dreamed of crossing the States, but don't much relish the prospect of two weeks spent cooped up in an automobile, then a ride on the Sunset Limited is the answer. Sit back and let America's landscapes buzz by: from Louisiana's

bayous, past the high-rises of Houston, across the deserts of Texas and Arizona, over the Californian hills all the way to LA's golden beaches. Saddle up, pardner: it's gonna be quite a ride.

❶ RIDING THE RAILS

Inaugurated in 1894, the Sunset Express, as it was originally known, was the second coast-to-coast train line to be completed in the United States (the Pacific Railroad, finished in 1869, was the first). It opened up trade between America's coasts and the rich plantations of the southern states, and also revolutionised transcontinental passenger travel: a journey that had previously been measured in weeks could now be completed in days.

Amazingly, it's still in service more than a century and a half later. Rebranded the Sunset Limited, it's the oldest named train service in the United States, and

a fabled route for America's boxcar buffs and railway fanatics. These days, the train runs three times a week, completing its cross-country journey in just under two days. Sleeper cabins mean you can stay on the train for the whole journey, should you so wish – but one of the best things about the Sunset Limited is that you can hop out at any stop along the route, and rejoin the service the next time it steams through town. So if you feel like taking time out to explore Houston, El Paso or Palm Springs, no problem – another Sunset Limited will roll by in a couple of days. It's like boxcar-jumping across the continent, except in considerably greater luxury. Seen from another angle, it's a spin on the classic pan-American adventure: the railroad version of Route 66.

Just as it has for the last 123 years, bar a brief hiatus thanks to the ravages of Hurricane Katrina, which wiped out several sections of track, the Sunset Limited's route begins in downtown New Orleans, a short walk from the jazz joints of the French Quarter. From here, it rolls west past the curves of the Superdome and crosses the 4.5-mile (7.25km)

THE LOST FLORIDA CONNECTION

A branch line connecting with the Sunset Limited originally enabled travel all the way to Orlando in Florida, but the line was largely washed away by Hurricane Katrina in 2005. Various plans have been put forward to rebuild the route, but so far none have made it off the drawing board.

Cruise through the tangled bayous and gator-filled creeks of Louisiana.

Have dinner in the dining car as Houston's cityscape rattles past.

New Orleans   **Houston**   **San Antonio**

CLOCKWISE FROM FAR LEFT: Big easy does it in N'Orleans; stately in San Antonio; crossing the desert of New Mexico; a train conductor at Alpine Station. **PREVIOUS PAGE:** Passengers in the viewing car of the Amtrak train.

Huey P Long bridge before trundling into Louisiana's backwaters, where willows droop along the creeks and gators lurk in the shallows. By mid-afternoon, the train crosses the state border, switching the lush, green bayous for the rocky deserts of southern Texas. Oil wells and cattle ranches appear through the train windows, followed a few hours later by the skyscrapers of Houston, America's oil central. Many passengers break their journey here; those who don't will bunk down in their sleeper cabins as the Sunset Limited rattles on into the desert night.

By mid-morning on day two, the train reaches the little town of Alpine – a frontier settlement which, 150 years ago, marked the beginnings of the Wild West, deep in the heart of Apache and Comanche country. These days it's better known for the important observatory at nearby Fort Davis, which hosts regular night-time star-gazing parties, and for its proximity to Big Bend National Park – a desert wonderland of canyons, cliffs and rock formations running along the banks of the Rio Grande. Gloriously wild, it's also among America's least-visited national parks: superb for hiking in solitude.

West of Alpine, the train rattles past El Paso, skirting the Mexican border before rolling on into New Mexico and Arizona. By evening on day two, it'll have arrived in Tucson, a town celebrated for its cinematic connections: many of the classic Hollywood westerns were shot around town, and you can still visit some original movie sets at kitschy Old Tucson. This part of Arizona is also the home of the saguaro cactus – the bulbous, barbed backdrop to countless westerns, but which actually can only be found here. It's so rare, it even has its own national park.

The last route on the Sunset Limited travels west through Maricopa and Yuma, passing Palm Springs and Pomona in the middle of the night before

© KRIS DAVIDSON | LONELY PLANET

See right over the Rio Grande into Mexico as you go through El Paso.

Bag a prime seat in the Sightseer Lounge as you cross the vast, parched deserts of Texas and Arizona.

El Paso   **Tucson**   **Maricopa**

arriving at LA's grand Union Station at 5.35am. While the city battles with rush hour, the best way to end the journey is to hop, bleary-eyed, on board the metro line to Santa Monica. Stepping out of the station, you'll spy gulls wheeling overhead and smell the salt-tang of the sea; the Pacific Ocean lies just a few blocks west. As you stroll down towards the pier, you'll pass surfers carrying their boards down to the waves and fishers casting their lines into the surf along the boardwalk. Somewhere near the pier's end, a sign marks the official end of Route 66 – and, fittingly, the last stop for America's most epic train ride.

❷ LIFE ON BOARD

There's a choice of accommodation on the Sunset Limited. The cheapest way to travel is to book a standard coach seat, but if you're doing the whole route, trust us – you'll be glad you booked a sleeper cabin. There are two options: a Superliner Roomette, which has two seats that fold down into a lower berth, plus a second fold-down berth above, and shares corridor bathroom facilities with other sleeper cabins. A more luxurious option is to book a Superliner Bedroom, which has a bit more space and its own bathroom cubicle. Family-sized bedrooms are also available. There's a dining car on every train: if you have a sleeper ticket, meals are included in the price, and room service is also available. The best views are from the Sightseer Lounge, which has swivel seats and panoramic floor-to-ceiling windows.

❸ MAKE IT HAPPEN

Trains depart weekly in each direction. Bookings for the Sunset Limited are made through Amtrak (www. amtrak.com/sunset-limited-train). Prices fluctuate according to demand and departure dates, so it pays to be flexible and book as early as possible. You can get off at any station and catch the next train, but it will work out more expensive, as you'll be incurring single fares between each point. **OB**

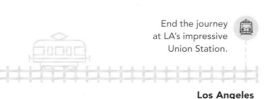

End the journey at LA's impressive Union Station.

Los Angeles

© KIT LEONG | GETTY IMAGES

The grand Union Station in
Los Angeles

La Trochita

ARGENTINA ●

START **ESQUEL**

END **ESQUEL**

DEPARTS **ONCE A WEEK** (IN SEASON)

DISTANCE 22 MILES (36KM)

DURATION **3 HRS**

In the foothills of the Argentinian Andes, far away from almost everything, an antique steam train chugs through a desolate landscape. La Trochita ('Little Gauge'), as the local name suggests, is a narrow railway, the cars so compact that you can barely stand up inside. Heated by old-fashioned wood-burning stoves and dwarfed by the mountainous terrain, the train has to stop at regular intervals when gusty winds blow hard across the sweeping scenery. Welcome to one of the southernmost railways in the world, a train that's best known to most of the world by its official name, El Viejo Expreso Patagónico (the Old Patagonian Express).

PATAGONIA

ESQUEL

NAHUEL PAN

0 — 5 KM
0 — 2.5 MILES

❶ RIDING THE RAILS

In the mid-1970s, the great American novelist and travel writer Paul Theroux set out on a grand locomotive adventure. Starting at his home in Massachussetts, Theroux travelled across the Americas, aiming to go as far south as possible by train. The end of the line, deep in the wilds of Argentina, was La Trochita – a narrow-gauge train that ran through the foothills of the Andes, connecting the city of Esquel with the far-flung ranches and

settlements of Patagonia. Enchanted by the dramatic landscape and the quaint train cars lined with wood and leather, Theroux immortalised the experience in his 1979 classic *The Old Patagonian Express*.

The railway, of course, was around for decades before Theroux brought it to the attention of an international audience. La Trochita was originally part of the Argentinian government's grand plans to build a national railway system to connect the Andes, on the country's western edge, to the Atlantic seaports on the eastern side. Construction stalled, then halted altogether, in the economic recession after World War I.

With a few key exceptions, that is. After the war, narrow-gauge equipment was cheap and widely available; the government decided to build a railway across the valley of the central province of Chubut, importing coaches and wagons from Belgium, Germany and the USA. The train line opened in 1935, but was only used for freight until 1950, when passengers boarded the train to travel between Esquel and the capital city of Buenos Aires.

By the 1960s and '70s, La Trochita was already on the decline. The destinations served – not just Esquel, but other lines that connected to it – were remote, and buses had become a more popular form of transportation. It was Theroux's account of his train trip to Argentina, and the avid readers and travellers that followed in his footsteps, that helped keep La Trochita alive and running.

Today, visitors can only access a short segment of the original journey. On Saturdays, the Old Patagonian

Express departs from the train station in Esquel, chugging along the 11-mile (18km) railway to the indigenous settlement of Nahuel Pan. After a short break at the rural station, during which passengers are free to disembark and wander around the village, browsing artisan goods and sampling *tortas fritas* (fried pastries) and maté (a tea-like beverage made with herbal yerba maté leaves), the train makes the return journey to Esquel.

In total, the trip takes just three hours. It's a fraction of the 250-mile (402km) expanse that the old train lines used to cover. But the experience of riding the train is much the same as it was in its early days. Instead of plush seats, La Trochita is furnished with wooden benches; instead of central heating, the train is warmed with its original wood-burning stoves. The train still pauses on the tracks when the winds outside are too strong. And the view from the train window – marked by empty, wide-open spaces and quickly shifting weather – hasn't changed, either. A ride on La Trochita is a journey into the past.

© EDUARDO RIVERO | GETTY IMAGES

SHOPPING FOR TRAINS

In 1922, when the Argentinian government decided to develop the narrow-gauge line, it opted for top-of-the-line train cars made by some of the world's finest manufacturers. They ordered 75 locomotives: 50 from Henschel & Son in Kassel, Germany, and 25 from Baldwin Locomotive Works in Philadelphia, USA.

Board the antique La Trochita at the old train station in Esquel.

Squeeze into a window seat and view the Andean foothills as the train pulls out of town.

From a distance, observe the tiny village of Nahuel Pan, framed by mountains.

© INTERTOURIST | GETTY IMAGES

❷ LIFE ON BOARD

Tall travellers, be forewarned: La Trochita's petite cars are out of another era, and passengers ride in closer quarters than usual. Take a seat on a wooden bench and watch the scenery go by, or squeeze into the tiny cafe car for a steaming hot bowl of tea or *café con leche*. On the return journey from Nahuel Pan, you'll often enjoy the scenery with a soundtrack of live music: a guitarist or singer, eager to entertain passengers with traditional Andean music, often climbs aboard for the ride back to town.

❸ MAKE IT HAPPEN

La Trochita usually runs once a week on Saturdays. The journey is always a round trip. Be aware that there's limited service in winter months (May to August), and there are extra departures during the peak months of January and February. Check the website (www.latrochita.org.ar) for up-to-date details.

Travel agencies in Esquel sell tickets for the journey, and it's recommended to buy at least a day in advance in high season. Otherwise, you can buy tickets on the day of departure at the train station. Dress warmly. **BG**

 Wander around Nahuel Pan, peeking down rustic alleyways and stopping for traditional snacks.

Soak up the empty, quiet landscape of the valley on the return journey to Esquel.

Nahuel Pan

Esquel

The Rocky Mountaineer

CANADA

START VANCOUVER	
END BANFF	
DEPARTS TWICE A WEEK	**DURATION** 37 HRS
DISTANCE 594 MILES (957KM)	

Clattering across the wild Rocky Mountains along a pioneering 19th-century railroad, this train journey is all at once a geological field trip, a sightseeing adventure and a wildlife safari. It promises cinematic views of Canada's quintessential mountain landscapes, plus a bevy of engineering marvels, from dizzying bridges to logic-defying tunnels. And with luck you might even spy a bald eagle, a moose or a grizzly bear – and there aren't many train trips that can promise that, now, are there?

❶ RIDING THE RAILS

The origins of the Rocky Mountaineer date back to the 1870s, when ambitious plans were laid for a trans-Canadian line connecting the Pacific and Atlantic seaboards. Unfortunately, there was one rather large obstacle in the way – or rather, lots of large, spiky obstacles: namely, the Rocky Mountains. After years of planning, the newly formed Canadian Pacific Railway laid its first track in 1881; five years later, on 28 June 1886, the first train ran from Montréal all the way to Port Moody, near Vancouver – a gargantuan feat of engineering that, in many ways, marked Canada's emergence as a modern nation.

Sadly, the Rocky Mountaineer is now the only passenger train that travels along this historic stretch of railway. Along its route, it traverses thunderous rivers, sparkling lakes, dense forests, plunging canyons and craggy mountains, but just because the scenery is wild and raw doesn't mean the comfort levels are

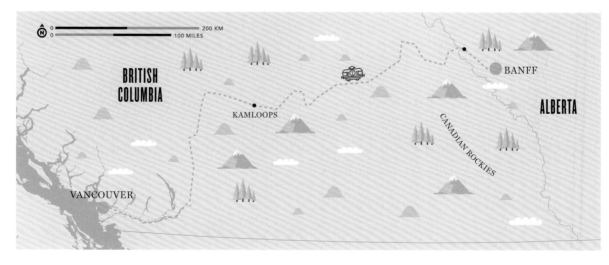

© PETE SEAWARD | LONELY PLANET

SPIRAL TUNNELS

The first train to attempt the 'Big Hill' at Kicking Horse River derailed in 1884, killing three people, and emergency spurs had to be built in case trains ran out of control. The problem was solved in 1909 by a young engineer called JE Schwitzer, who designed corkscrew shafts modelled on those used by Swiss railway builders.

compromised; with its bubble-windowed viewing carriages, smart dinner lounge and snappily-dressed staff, this is a train that makes a point of spoiling its passengers at every opportunity.

The classic Rocky Mountaineer route, known as the 'First Passage to the West', starts in Vancouver and follows the original Canadian Pacific track to the mountain town of Banff. The departure is at 8am sharp, often accompanied by the drone of a bagpiper – a heraldic send-off befitting such a landmark train. Beyond the city suburbs, it rattles along the banks of the Fraser and Thompson Rivers, then begins its long climb towards the mountains. Waterfalls, log-jams and canyons zip past, and as the trees thin out, the distant silhouettes of the Rockies loom along the skyline. The train's huge, curved windows bring the landscape right into the carriage, a bit like a 3D film – only here, the landscapes rushing past are very real.

Get your camera ready for the thunderous cascade of Hell's Gate, where 750 million litres of water are forced through a narrow gorge.

Snap a selfie as you traverse the Cisco Crossing, two rust-red iron bridges spanning the Fraser River.

Vancouver

Kamloops

CLOCKWISE FROM LEFT: An attendant on the upper deck; Banff National Park rolls by; in the dining car; **PREVIOUS PAGE & OVERLEAF:** Banff National Park.

Riding the Rocky Mountaineer is a communal experience. In the viewing cars, passengers swap tales of their sightings, passing round binoculars and oohing and ahhing as each curve in the track unveils a stunning new view: a moose mooching along the riverbanks, say, or an osprey's nest perched high in the treetops. The holy grail is a grizzly or a black bear sighting, but only travellers with the keenest eyes – and the longest lenses – are likely to spot them.

The first day covers the land west of the Continental Divide, followed by an overnight stop in Kamloops. Day two is when the mountain scenery really kicks into high gear. Past the shores of Shuswap Lake and the historic waypoint at Craigellachie, where the west and east tracks met in 1885, the train trucks up into the Rockies proper, rolling through Mt Revelstoke and Glacier parks, and clattering over the steel arches of Stoney Creek Bridge along the way. Next comes the mighty Columbia River and the ski town of Golden, followed by the peaks and vast pine forests of Yoho.

The canyon of Kicking Horse River presented one of the major challenges for the railway's builders: reaching a 4.4% gradient, it was infamously dangerous to descend. The Spiral Tunnels, which circle right through the mountainside, are a marvel of modern railway-building – and a hallowed sight for train buffs.

And then, almost too soon, the Rocky Mountaineer is nearing journey's end. The train rattles past the turquoise bowl of Lake Louise, overlooked by glaciers studded in the mountainside, then veers southeast along the Bow River into Banff National Park.

Finally, passengers step out into the crisp mountain air at Banff town, breathing in the scent of pine sap as they stretch their legs and gather luggage. Yesterday the journey began on the shores of the Pacific Ocean, today it ends in the middle of North America's greatest mountain range. It might be short, but the Rocky Mountaineer packs a mighty sweet scenic punch.

© PETE SEAWARD | LONELY PLANET

© PETE SEAWARD | LONELY PLANET

 Between Revelstoke and Golden, look out for Stoney Creek Bridge, one of the highest on the Canadian Pacific route.

Take a window seat as you pass through the stunning mountain scenery of Yoho National Park.

 Admire the ingenuity of the engineers who constructed the Spiral Tunnels as you climb over Kicking Horse Pass.

Lake Louise

❷ LIFE ON BOARD

There are two classes on the Rocky Mountaineer. Silver Leaf passengers travel in the single-decker coach, with complimentary breakfast, lunch and snacks served at your seat by train attendants. Gold Leaf buys access to the premium double-decker carriage, with viewing deck on the top level and dining room on the lower level. The standard of service is extremely high, comparable to business class on an international flight, only with much better views.

❸ ALTERNATIVE ROUTES

In addition to the First Passage to the West, the Rocky Mountaineer offers three other routes. The Journey through the Clouds follows the track as far as Kamloops, then heads north to Jasper. The Rainforest to Gold Rush route travels north via Whistler into the ranch lands of the Cariboo Plateau and the gold-panning lands around Quesnel, then loops east to Jasper. The Coastal Passage Route adds on an extra stretch of track along the Pacific seaboard from Seattle.

❹ BUDGET ALTERNATIVE

Main-line trains run by Canada's national railway, VIA Rail, follow the same route as the Rocky Mountaineer's Journey through the Clouds (see p104).

❺ MAKE IT HAPPEN

The First Passage to the West service runs twice a week, leaving Vancouver on Mondays and Fridays, although some services leave on Tuesdays. The two-day package includes meals and drinks on both days, plus one night's hotel accommodation in Kamloops. May to September are the priciest months to travel; discounts are available in April and October. The train doesn't run from November to March. Book direct through Rocky Mountaineer (www.rockymountaineer.com). **OB**

Banff

© PETE SEAWARD | LONELY PLANET

Perurail's Lake Titicaca Railway

PERU

START	**PUNO**		
END	**CUZCO**		
DEPARTS	**3 PER WEEK**	DURATION	**10 HRS**
DISTANCE 241 MILES (388KM)			

Traversing the Altiplano, from the shores of Lake Titicaca to the beating heart of the Inca capital, the railway from Puno to Cuzco cuts a ponderous but picturesque path through the snow-dusted peaks and voluptuous valleys of the Andes. Between drinks in the bar and enjoying entertainment and fine food in the restaurant, passengers aboard Perurail's Lake Titicaca train can ogle the vista from an open-air observatory car, as they rumble across the epic Peruvian plains, passing hardy bowler-hatted llama farmers and travelling through remote towns and villages.

❶ RIDING THE RAILS

Famous for floating islands and fantastic reed boats, Lake Titicaca – an immense inland sea between Peru and Bolivia – was believed by the Incas to be the birthplace of the sun god and great creator, Viracocaha. On the Peruvian side, Puno is the primary port, and the terminus for arguably South America's most scenic train trip.

Thrice a week, a determined diesel locomotive pulls out of Puno's Titicaca Station and traces the shoreline of the lake for several miles, before trundling northwest across the Collao Plateau.

About 28 miles (45km) later, the train toots and tiptoes its way through the busy town of Juliaca, where women in bowler hats and men pedalling impossibly overladen three-wheeled bikes cross the rails, barely glancing at the advancing metal serpent.

A kaleidoscopic tapestry of market stalls unzips as the loco approaches, then knits back together in the carriages' wake. Goods are laid on blankets right across the tracks; some vendors don't bother moving their wares at all, the train simply rolls right over the top of them.

Vegetables, shawls, brimming sacks of coca leaves, llama foetuses... Peru's frenetic markets offer a brain-boggling mix of local produce and peculiarities. But the train trundles nonchalantly onwards, bound for higher ground among the apparently impenetrable peaks that erupt from the edge of the Altiplano.

In the comfortable bar car, passengers pucker up to pisco sours and glasses of Inca Kola, while outside a

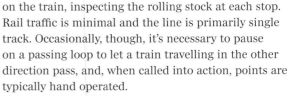

smattering of settlements occasionally punctuate the scratchy scrubland, and llamas, alpacas and vicuñas (camelids with fabulously fine wool worn only by royalty under Inca law) compete with sheep for the dry stubble that passes for grass.

The service dawdles through such villages and towns as Ayaviri and Marangani, where local children with ruddy round cheeks and hungry eyes often appear near the tracks. Inhabitants of contrasting worlds make eye contact through the thin window here – where on one side of the glass a gourmet three-course feast is about to be served, and on the other such basic commodities as pens and paper are treated like treasure.

The standard-gauge line between Puno and Cuzco carries the world's third-highest train service, and the conditions are as breathtaking as the views, with some symptoms of *soroche* (altitude sickness) possible for those insufficiently acclimatised.

The locomotive labours hard through the valleys, travelling at walking pace, carefully crossing rivers and passing through ravines where loose-looking rocky outcrops tower overhead. Derailments, landslides and rockfalls are familiar features of rail travel here, causing little more delay than leaves on the line can in some Western countries. But here they're dealt with immediately; a fitter often travels

on the train, inspecting the rolling stock at each stop. Rail traffic is minimal and the line is primarily single track. Occasionally, though, it's necessary to pause on a passing loop to let a train travelling in the other direction pass, and, when called into action, points are typically hand operated.

At the 14,170ft (4319m) La Raya pass, the train reaches the roof of the route and passengers hop out to purchase pan pipes and woolly hats, surrounded by a crown of ice-capped peaks. It's downhill from here, and the snowmelt from these mountains will run into rivers that race the train towards Cuzco.

Neck-and-neck the railway and Urubamba River flow through Urcos – alleged location of a legendary lost golden chain, hidden by Incas from the grasp of Spanish conquistadors – and from here the Huatanay River streaks ahead towards the outskirts of Cuzco.

The descent into the city is delightfully dramatic – despite taking place at a snail's pace, with the train negotiating numerous switchback bends during the drop – and travellers arrive in the capital of the old Inca Empire in time for a traditional teatime feast of roasted *cuy* (guinea pig).

❷ LIFE ON BOARD

Ticket price includes snacks, a three-course gourmet lunch (with wine) and afternoon tea. Bottled water is free; bar beverages are extra. Take one carry-on bag on board; additional bags are stored in the luggage car. Entertainment is provided, in the form of live local music and dancing.

❸ ALTERNATIVE ROUTES

Perurail also operates trains from Cuzco to Aguas Calientes, beneath Machu Picchu. There are various options, from the cheap (Expedition) to the super luxury (Hiram Bingham). All now leave from Cuzco's Poroy Station, descend into the Sacred Valley and follow the Urubamba River.

© PHILIP LEE HARVEY | LONELY PLANET

 Trundle along the banks of Lake Titicaca, watching reed boats bob on the water.

Take in the colours and chaos of the trackside markets in Juliaca.

 Spot llamas, vicuñas, guanacos and alpacas grazing on the immense Altiplano plains.

Puno (Lake Titicaca)

Juliaca

LEFT & BELOW: Bowler hat–wearing Aymara woman in Juliaca; a reed boat on Lake Titicaca. **PREVIOUS PAGE:** The Andean Puno–Cuzco train negotiates peaks and valleys between Puno at Lake Titicaca and Cuzco.

LOCAL KNOWLEDGE

Over the past two decades train travel in Peru has become big business, and rail trips between popular destinations have been tailored specifically for tourists. Locals do still ride the rails, on unadvertised trains with wooden seats that are available only to Peruvian nationals and for a fraction of the price foreigners fork out.

❹ UPGRADES

In May 2017, Perurail launched a new luxury overnight service travelling both ways between Puno and Cuzco (and beyond, to Unesco-listed Arequipa). The service is called the Belmond Andean Explorer (not to be confused with the daytime service formerly of the same name, now rebranded as the Perurail Lake Titicaca train, described above).

With various itineraries available, these services offer fine dining, a berth in a private sleeper car with en suite, a lounge bar with evening entertainment, and use of a spa car.

❺ MAKE IT HAPPEN

Trains run three times a week in each direction, leaving Puno early on Monday, Thursday and Saturday to arrive at Cuzco late on the same afternoon. Travelling in the other direction, trains leave Cuzco's Wanchaq Station early on Wednesday, Friday and Sunday. Book and buy tickets online from the website: www.perurail.com. Fares include your seat, meals and entertainment but not additional drinks at the bar.

Note the 'Andean Explorer' was the former name given to the day service described here, which is now called the Perurail Lake Titicaca train. **PK**

Reach the apex of the journey at the 14,170ft (4319m) La Raya pass.

Sip a pisco sour in the observation car while gazing up at Andean peaks.

Watch the Huatanay River rushing over rapids during the final descent into Cuzco.

La Raya   **Urcos**   **Cuzco**

Metro-North Hudson Line

USA

START **NEW YORK CITY**	
END **POUGHKEEPSIE**	
DEPARTS **DAILY**	DURATION **2 HRS**
DISTANCE 73.5 MILES (118KM)	

Depart from New York City's iconic beaux arts Grand Central Terminal, stopping to admire the ornate astronomical ceiling painting in the vaulted Grand Concourse and to slurp up oysters and a martini at the famous Oyster Bar. Then roll through Manhattan and the Bronx and into the glorious green Hudson River Valley, getting off at any number of charming historic towns along the way.

❶ RIDING THE RAILS

Some iconic New York activities are desperately overrated. But sucking down a platter of fresh, ocean-cold Blue Point oysters at the Grand Central Oyster Bar is definitely not. The century-old restaurant is just one of the things that make Grand Central so magical. There's the viridian-green vaulted ceiling of the main concourse, painted with gold constellations. There's the four-faced brass clock atop the information booth, perhaps the most famous meeting place in the world. There are mosaics and classical sculptures galore, there are cathedral arched windows and grand staircases, there are more platforms than any other railway station in the world.

It's from this extraordinary station that we begin our journey. Hugging the eastern banks of the

Hudson River, New York's Metro-North Hudson Line travels deep into American history. The names of the stops along the way speak to the area's origins: Native American (Ossining, Poughkeepsie); Dutch (Spuyten Duyvil, Yonkers, Cortlandt, Peekskill); English (Hastings-on-Hudson, Scarborough). It's a land so famously beautiful an entire art movement – the Hudson River School – was once dedicated to

"industrial buildings give way to small marinas with sailing boats, and bucolic river towns"

capturing its glory. For the cost of a burger and a beer, this view can be yours for two hours.

Travelling underground through much of Manhattan, the train then clacks through the Bronx, past brick high-rise apartment blocks, baseball diamonds, and warehouse buildings with banners offering cheap storage. But the real magic begins 11 miles (18km) into the journey, when the tracks join the Hudson. Suddenly the dramatic basalt cliffs known as the Palisades come into view on the far side of the river. Stretching 20 miles (32km) from Jersey City northwards, these crenelated grey cliffs reach heights of more than 500ft (150m).

As you leave New York City behind, the industrial buildings give way to small marinas with motorboats and sailing boats, and the bucolic river towns of Hastings-on-Hudson, Dobbs Ferry and Irvington. Past Hastings-on-Hudson, the river gradually widens into Haverstraw Bay, which is about 3.4 miles (5.5km) at its widest. On sunny days it's often dotted with sailing boats. Less charming, but undeniably fascinating, is the moment when the train cuts directly through the infamous Sing Sing prison at Ossining, where criminals have been sent 'up the river' to complete their sentences for nearly 200 years. You get a clear view of the prison's stone walls and guard towers.

By Peekskill you're in the furthest reaches of Westchester County, leaving behind the commuter suburbs of New York and heading deeper into what's simply known as 'upstate'. Many of these Hudson River towns once thrived on manufacturing – mills, ironworks, chemical companies. Beacon was the 'Hat-Making Capital of the United States'. Wappingers Falls had one of the biggest printworks in the country. By the mid-20th century, however, most of them had

fallen into deep decline, leaving warehouses and grand industrialists' mansions to crumble. Many of these towns have since undergone revivals, with artists turning factories into studios, and former city dwellers rehabbing the gracious old homes.

One of the river's most photo-worthy sights reveals itself at the S-shaped curve in the river just after Garrison Station. Here, the commanding Norman-style granite buildings of the US Military Academy at West Point dominate the lower slopes of the Hudson Highlands. The site has been used by the military since the Revolutionary War; the academy itself was established by Thomas Jefferson in 1801.

Don't miss the steep crag of Storm King Mountain, a favourite subject of Hudson River School painters, rising from the riverbank past Cold Spring Station. Then, just past the Breakneck Ridge flag stop you'll see a small island from which rises an eerie vision: the ruins of a turreted castle, five storeys high and dripping with vines. This is Bannerman's Castle, built in the early 20th century by a Scottish industrialist,

STATION TO STATION
Architecture lovers should explore the line's historic stations. There's the grand beaux arts Yonkers Station, built in 1911 of red brick and tile. The fin-de-siècle Ardsley-on-Hudson Station was once part of a country club that counted Vanderbilts and other New York luminaries as members. And don't miss the half-timbered Tudor Revival of Philipse Manor.

Start with oysters at Grand Central Terminal.

When the tracks finally join the Hudson River, the breathtaking Palisades come into view.

The train line cuts right through the razor wire-topped stone buildings of notorious Sing Sing prison.

Grand Central Terminal (NYC)   **Yonkers**   **Dobbs Ferry**   **Tarrytown**

CLOCKWISE FROM LEFT: The Metro-North train runs past the Hudson River; a conductor and a railroad rep share a story in Grand Central. **PREVIOUS PAGE:** Main concourse of Grand Central Terminal.

© ROB CRANDALL | GETTY IMAGES

© MARIO TAMA | GETTY IMAGES

who used it as a storage facility.

From here you'll stop in the arty river town of Beacon, then pass two interesting bridges – the industrial Newburgh-Beacon cantilevered bridge and the graceful Mid-Hudson suspension bridge – before pulling into Poughkeepsie Station. Completed in 1918, its high arched windows and dramatic, cathedral-like ceiling are meant to reflect the architecture of Grand Central Terminal, where your journey began 73.5 miles (118km) ago.

❷ LIFE ON BOARD

This is a commuter railway, so expect no frills. The upright vinyl seats are reasonably comfortable, but you probably won't be lulled into a nap. The days of the bar car are long gone, leaving passengers to sip flasks surreptitiously.

❸ MAKE IT HAPPEN

Trains depart from Grand Central Terminal multiple times an hour from before 6am until nearly 2am daily. Buy tickets on the Metropolitan Transportation Authority (MTA) eTix app or website (www.mta.info), or at station ticket machines or windows. You can buy them on board too, but they're more expensive.

You can choose to travel nonstop to enjoy the view, or get off at any of the river towns along the way for antique-hunting, art gallery-hopping and food. The best times of day to travel are before or after the peak commuting hours of 6:15am to 9:30am and 4:30pm to 7pm when Grand Central becomes a swarm of fast-walking New Yorkers. Autumn (September–November) offers leaf-peeping from your seat and is the prettiest season. Sit on the left side of the train heading north for the best river views. **EM**

The fortress-like granite buildings of the US Military Academy at West Point make a great photo opp.

The dramatic slopes of Storm King Mountain hulk on the west banks of the river.

Bannerman's Castle, decaying alone on its overgrown little island, is a creepy sight.

Ossining　　　　　Cold Spring　　　　　Beacon　　　　　Poughkeepsie

The Copper Canyon Railway

MEXICO ●

START CHIHUAHUA	
END LOS MOCHIS	
DEPARTS DAILY	**DURATION 16 HRS**
DISTANCE 418 MILES (673KM)	

From the arid altitudes of Chihuahua city in the Sonoran Desert down to the balmy Pacific Ocean via the world's biggest and most breathtaking string of canyons… this is a rail ride that will have you exclaiming at its engineering alone, then start you oohing all over again at the startling scenery. Cresting 7875ft (2400m) at the topmost point and needing over 120 tunnels and bridges to deal with the route's rocky topography, these tracks teeter along canyon edges and transport you deep into the heartlands of two of Mexico's most interesting cultural groups, the Tarahumara and the Mennonites.

❶ RIDING THE RAILS

Chihuahua is a sprawling, dusty, desert city with a proud history coloured by its pivotal place as a capital of the Mexican Revolution. But standing at its train station in the pre-dawn gloom, queuing to buy your ticket from the bleary-eyed attendant, there is little sense of spectacle for those waiting to embark on this epic excursion – even though this is the nation's last remaining long-distance passenger train trip, and an odyssey encompassing the best of Northern Mexico.

Departures for the train, affectionately dubbed El Chepe (using the Spanish initials of 'Chihuahua' and

'Pacífico'), are early (6am starts, whichever way you do it, for the full route) so it is a blessing that there are a couple of hours for dozing through unremarkable desert before the scenery picks up.

The going gets green and undulating around Cuauhtémoc, a city that has become a haven for one of the world's most significant groups of Mennonites. Tracing origins to Menno Simmons, the Dutchman who founded the sect in the 16th century, these often blonde-haired, blue-eyed people are prized for their agricultural prowess, but often at odds with governments for their refusal to swear loyalty to anyone other than God. Their singular, spiritual community is intriguing to visitors, and tours to see how the Mennonites make up northern Mexico's cultural mix can be arranged here.

After Cuauhtémoc, a corkscrewing climb into the Sierra Madre Occidental begins and it is here, too, that true appreciation of the railway's construction kicks

© NINA RAINGOLD | GETTY IMAGES

THE TARAHUMARA

The distinctive Tarahumara community often use two dwelling places: caves up in the higher, cooler reaches of the canyons and a hut down near the far-warmer canyon base. They are perhaps most renowned for their long-distance running, sometimes covering 200 miles (321km) barefoot: a phenomenal feat given the ruggedness of the Barrancas del Cobre.

CLOCKWISE FROM ABOVE: Creel, home to indigenous Tarahumara communities; rolling through canyonland; the verdant Copper Canyon. **PREVIOUS PAGE:** The Chihuahua al Pacífico train crossing the lofty Copper Canyon.

in, as gradients get markedly steeper. With 86 tunnels, 37 bridges, innumerable twists and turns and even points where the route runs back over itself to gain elevation, the line ascends 3280ft (1000m) between Chihuahua and Creel before descending nearly 8200ft (2500m) to sea level. But it was not the altitude that caused builders headaches so much as the canyons gouging out these mountains. Today, an engineer's nightmare – there were 81 years between the line's conception and its completion – is a passenger's dream.

After trundling through Creel, an outdoor-adventure hub boasting the best facilities of any of the canyon

Explore Chihuahua's revolutionary roots at Museo Francisco Villa, which celebrates the fabled freedom fighter.

Check out Creel's host of canyon-themed adventures, such as the Cascada de Basaseachi waterfall.

Pause for heart-in-mouth yet majestic vistas at Divisadero.

Chihuahua　　　　　　**Cuauhtémoc**　　　　　　**Creel**　　　　　　**Divisadero**

settlements, El Chepe hits its high point and, arguably, highlight. The tracks run virtually to the rim of one of the world's deepest and longest canyons at Divisadero, where dizzying views plunge to the faint line of the Río Urique squiggling along the canyon floor far below. You are now atop the colossal network of canyons collectively referred to as the Barrancas del Cobre, which can be further appreciated from the nearby adventure park where zip lines whoosh you right over those vertiginous canyon drops. All trains pause for roughly 15 minutes at Divisadero, allowing time for a snack and a photo opportunity.

This sector of the Sierra Madre Occidental is known as the Sierra Tarahumara on account of the indigenous people, the Tarahumara, who call these canyons home. At Divisadero and, to a greater extent, at the less-touristy stops thereafter, Posada Barrancas and Bahuichivo, you can alight to discover more about this resilient people, purchasing Tarahumara traditional street food or handicrafts. Bahuichivo is the best place to disembark for forays down the canyon to charming villages, such as Cerocauhi or Urique, and these remoter lower echelons are naturally where the most meaningful insights into canyon livelihoods and traditions are likely to be gained.

Great side trips away from the rails include a visit to Mexico's second-highest waterfall, the mesmeric Cascada de Basaseachi (from Creel, active in the wet season only) or a boat ride through the bird-rich Bosque Secreto, a rare remnant of subtropical dry forest (from the penultimate stop, El Fuerte).

And then, some 16 hours after it sallied forth, El Chepe comes to a standstill at Los Mochis. Here you can board a bus for the short jaunt to Topolobampo, its tawny-gold band of beach abutting the Pacific, and marvel at how you travelled all the way from the mid-Mexican desert on little more than a set of sleepers.

Swoop over the world's most amazing canyon on zip lines at Parque de Aventuras Barrancas del Cobre.

Take a detour to the pretty canyon-bottom village of Urique, home to a famous ultra-marathon.

Posada Barrancas   **Bahuichivo**   **El Fuerte**

RIGHT: Copper Canyon, one of the colossal network of canyons that makes up the dizzying Barrancas del Cobre.

❷ LIFE ON BOARD

The main difference between the 1st-class Primera Express and the cheaper Clase Económica (economy class) services that El Chepe offers is not the on-board comforts but the degree of procrastination on the line. The Primera Express sticks closer to its schedule and makes a handful of defined stops in stations of interest to tourists; the Clase Económica, used more by locals, potters along with umpteen request stops en route, arriving at the end destination an hour or upwards later. Both services sport reclining seats and air-con. First class has an elegant dining car, 2nd class just a snack bar – but it's still best to bring bottled water and snacks with you to fall back on. Taking toilet roll is a wise move too.

❸ MAKE IT HAPPEN

The Primera Express runs each way every day, while the Clase Económica makes three weekly journeys in either direction.

Information is available on the train website, www.chepe.com.mx, but for online bookings you must email requests to chepe@ferromex.mx. It is almost always possible to purchase tickets for the following day at the stations in Chihuahua or Los Mochis; at stops in between you can board then buy tickets on the train (have the fee in Mexican pesos). Most people tackle the journey one-way and break this across at least two days. The most popular overnight stop-off is Creel.

Topographical (and therefore climatic) contrasts en route are so varied that all times of year have their bonuses. Even rainy season (June to August) is beguiling, with mountainside flora blooming. **LW**

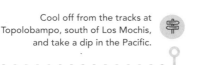

Cool off from the tracks at Topolobampo, south of Los Mochis, and take a dip in the Pacific.

Los Mochis

© CAROLYN BROWN | GETTY IMAGES

The California Zephyr

USA ●

START **CHICAGO**

END **SAN FRANCISCO**

DEPARTS **DAILY**

DISTANCE **2438 MILES (3924KM)**

DURATION **52HRS 40 MINS**

For soaking up the scenic grandeur of the North American continent, nothing compares with Amtrak's California Zephyr train. This classic three-day journey travels nearly 2500 miles (4000km) across prairies, deserts, the Rocky Mountains and the Sierra Nevada on its way from Chicago to San Francisco. Scenery is magnificent throughout – especially when seen through the floor-to-ceiling windows of the lounge car – but if you can only do one section, opt for the riveting 185-mile (298km) stretch between Denver

and Glenwood Springs, where the train travels through an often roadless wilderness of deep, narrow gorges near the Colorado River's headwaters.

❶ RIDING THE RAILS

'Now boarding: Amtrak's California Zephyr!' – five words, and Chicago's beaux arts Union Station buzzes with anticipation. In a nation with only four transcontinental passenger rail routes, crossing the country by train is a once-in-a-lifetime experience, and virtually every ticket-holder under the Great Hall's barrel-vaulted skylight has come for the Zephyr's scenic and nostalgic appeal. Speed and convenience be damned; here it's still about the journey, kindred spirits coming together for a slow, epic voyage on the rails.

A whistle and a lurch and the double-decker train chugs onto the great American prairie. East of the Mississippi in Illinois, the farmland still has the verdant lushness of the eastern United States – but we're bound

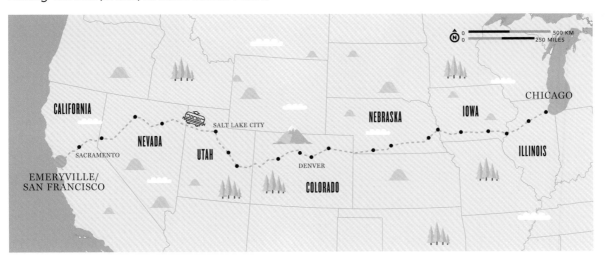

DONNER PARTY

As you cross the Sierra Nevada in lounge-car comfort, consider the Donner Party, America's most ill-fated mid-19th-century pioneer expedition. Plagued by a disastrous detour off the Oregon Trail and an early November blizzard, the San Francisco–bound group was forced to overwinter beside frozen Truckee Lake, and eventually resorted to cannibalism.

for drier, vaster landscapes: the sparsely populated expanses of the American West. In late afternoon, at the Illinois-Iowa border, the Zephyr crosses America's iconic dividing line – the Mississippi River – and forges into the corn, soybean and wheat fields that stretch clear across Iowa and Nebraska. Grain elevators rise silhouetted against the dusk, and somewhere between Ottumwa and Osceola, night falls.

Day two dawns over the bleak high plains of eastern Colorado, with the Rocky Mountains looming on

the horizon, as yawning passengers filter into the panoramic lounge car at the centre of the train. With its seats turned sideways to face floor-to-ceiling picture windows, this is unquestionably the place to be for the journey's stunningly scenic second day. Performance artist Spalding Gray once called the lounge car 'one big rolling confessional', and indeed, sitting side-by-side with perfect strangers while the American landscape rolls inexorably past seems to inspire people to share stories and secrets they might never voice elsewhere.

After a 50-minute stop in Denver, the Zephyr climbs dramatically into the heart of the Rockies, crossing through Moffat Tunnel (9239ft/2816m) and bursting into high meadows fringed with Colorado blue spruce. Here the train enters a series of rugged canyons and, near Granby, begins following the Colorado River. The journey's highlight is Gore Canyon, whose 1000ft (300m) cliffs and Class V white water make it accessible only by train or kayak – one of those rare and wonderful

Contemplate the mighty Mississippi River as you cross from Illinois to Burlington, Iowa.

Emerge from the 6.2-mile (10km) Moffat Tunnel into Rocky Mountain wonderland near Fraser-Winter Park.

Snake along 1000ft (300m) cliff faces above the Colorado River in remote Gore Canyon.

Chicago   **Omaha**   **Denver**

© BLAINE HARRINGTON III | ALAMY STOCK PHOTO

CLOCKWISE FROM LEFT: Denver's Union Station; Alamo Square in San Francisco; views from the observation car. **PREVIOUS PAGE:** the route crosses most of the US.

❷ LIFE ON BOARD

The Zephyr has two classes of service: coach and sleeper. Amtrak's large, padded coach seats recline more fully than economy-class aeroplane seats, permitting a relatively comfortable sleep. True sleeping accommodation – which ranges from claustrophobic 'roomettes' to slightly more spacious family rooms – costs hundreds of dollars extra. Showers are available in both coach and sleeper cars. Full meals and snacks are served in the dining and lounge cars respectively, but bringing your own provisions is also highly advisable.

❸ ALTERNATIVE ROUTES

Amtrak operates two other cross-country routes from Chicago to the Pacific. The Empire Builder's northerly run to Seattle crosses through Wisconsin, Minnesota, North Dakota, Montana, Idaho and Washington, skirting the edge of Glacier National Park en route. The Southwest Chief traverses the prairies of Missouri and Kansas, traces the southeastern edge of Colorado's Rockies and finishes its run to Los Angeles through the deserts of New Mexico, Arizona and California.

❹ MAKE IT HAPPEN

One train departs daily in each direction. Book tickets at www.amtrak.com. For the best fares, reserve well in advance. Most people travel one-way. It's a long trip, so breaking the journey en route is highly recommended. Good stop-offs include Denver, Glenwood Springs, Reno and Truckee. This route is beautiful any time of year, but best between June and October, when the Rockies' full natural splendour is on display. **GC**

American places you simply can't reach by car. A second Colorado River canyon, Glenwood, opens out onto the mesa country of western Colorado, followed by sunset over the glowing red-rock desert of eastern Utah.

Sunrise on day three reveals an entirely different desert: the blinding-white alkali flats and ghostly grey mountains near Winnemucca, Nevada. Just beyond the gambling-happy little city of Reno, the Zephyr climbs into the foothills of the Sierra Nevada, then enters California's imposing granite high country beyond the photogenic frontier town of Truckee.

Guides board the train here, narrating the 19th-century story of Donner Lake, where 39 California-bound settlers succumbed to bitter temperatures and were eaten by their companions, and Emigrant Gap, where pioneers once lowered stagecoaches by rope to navigate the steep cliff faces. Leaving the mountains behind, the Zephyr's final descent leads through gold-rush country to the promised land of San Francisco Bay.

Pause to swim in Glenwood Springs' gargantuan hot springs or raft through Glenwood Canyon.

Test your slot machine fortunes beneath the neon arches of Reno, Nevada's 'Biggest Little City'.

Check out the historic Sacramento Locomotive Works, next to the city's State Railroad Museum.

Glenwood Spring   Salt Lake City   Reno   Sacramento   Emeryville/San Francisco

The Hershey Train

CUBA ●

START **CASABLANCA (HAVANA)**

END **MATANZAS**

DEPARTS **DAILY**

DISTANCE 53 MILES (85KM)

DURATION **3 HRS 25 MINS**

Cuba's chocolate train clicks and clatters through farmland and clumps of royal palms as it shudders along the island's north coast, just over a mile shy of the sea, from the capital Havana to the port city of Matanzas. American confectioner Milton S Hershey needed more sugar to boost his Pennsylvania chocolate empire; he found fertile soils and a ramped-up sugar industry in newly independent Cuba and moved in, exporting the sweet stuff for

his Hershey Kisses, and to Coca-Cola for its fizzy pop. Pondering how to get his sugar to port, the chocolate baron built the electric Hershey Train in 1922 along 53 miles (85km) of single-track rails.

❶ RIDING THE RAILS

Casablanca, a fraying-at-the-edges fishing village, is a world away from the manicured fringes of Spanish colonial Old Havana, but the Hershey train departs from here – because the Brits, who owned all the railway tracks in Havana at the time, resisted US competition on the doorstop of their rail hub in the Cuban capital. An ancient rusty ferry chugs across the bay of Havana right to the Hershey Terminal.

The bare-bones sage-green and grey carriages, hooked to their electric lines above, sway and judder at no more than 25 miles (40km) per hour, tooting to scare stray dogs and cows off the tracks, as they arc

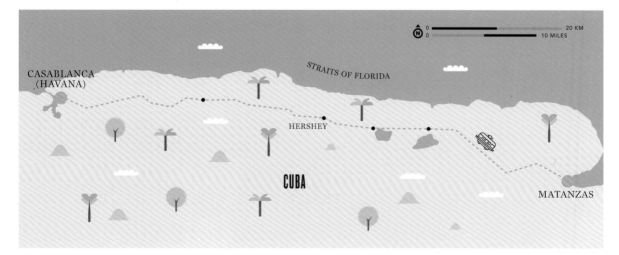

© OLGA KOLOS | ALAMY STOCK PHOTO

CUBA SUGAR FACTS

Matanzas province profited immensely in the sugar industry stakes. In 1852, the Cárdenas region had 221 mills, the largest number in the country at the time. In 1841 the mills employed 53,331 slaves. In 1890, a mill in central Cuba produced 135,000 sacks of sugar, the largest harvest in the world at the time.

CLOCKWISE FROM ABOVE:
Guanabo beach; beautiful Boca de Canasí; a driver's view departing Casablanca; leaving Hershey. **PREVIOUS PAGE:** A Cuban flag waves over Havana.

© THE WASHINGTON POST | GETTY IMAGES

out of the bay of Havana on the rails, and straight into rural pastures with pink pigs and white horses spied on by circling vultures. Cuban locals board the Hershey train to travel from tiny hamlets, wrapped in cactus fences, embedded in farmland, citrus trees and palm groves, either to Havana, Matanzas, or a couple of stations down the line. The train brakes, all rust screeching and jolting, at all 46 stations – some are no more than unmarked concrete platforms in the thicket.

Cubans board with livestock – birds in delicate wooden cages, an unhappy pig stuffed in a bucket, and bleating goats trussed up in white sacks – as well as pastel-bright cakes in boxes, bales of root vegetables,

Alight at Guanabo, a white-sand beach popular with Cubans, with plenty of B&Bs for rent.

Explore Hershey town, including a pharmacy with wooden interiors and a grocery with Moorish tiles.

Casablanca (Havana)   **Guanabo**   **Hershey**

and ballooning pumpkins bursting out of jute carriers. The handful of tourists who ride are mostly train fans, the curious adventurous, or history-minded (or chocoholic) Americans. In between the chirruping and loud protests of the wildlife, passengers mull over the latest news, hot gossip, the exorbitant prices of trainers in the shops, or read the communist party newspaper, *Granma*.

Hershey town – now renamed Camilo Cienfuegos after one of Cuba's 1959 revolution leaders – is the star turn on the railway journey, and it's worth taking some time to explore here. In 1920 Cuba was filthy rich from sugar exports; the island enjoyed an era of prosperity known as the 'Dance of the Millions'. Its total crop more than doubled in value from US$455 million in 1919 to a staggering US$1 billion the following year. The beet fields of Europe had been devastated during World War I, leaving a global shortage of sugar. Sniffing an opportunity for his candy business, Milton S Hershey came to Cuba in 1916 and invested US$40 million. By 1917 the sugar mill had opened, and later a distillery. He built a small American-model town – Central Hershey – of 180 homes, 25 miles (40km) east of Havana, flanked by a hotel, a golf course, workers' houses and a school for orphans. By 1922 the Hershey electric train sparked into life, considered the first of its type in the world to transport sugar to ports, along 84 miles (135km) of total track. By 1924 the Hershey Railway had a fleet of 17 electric passenger cars and seven electric locomotives; today it runs with a batch of cars bought from Catalonia 20 years ago. The colourful clapboard homes of sleepy Hershey, in neat lines along tree-lined roads, are dwarfed by the sugar-mill carnage – the towering chimneys and iron wreckage of the mill that was decommissioned in 2002, and is currently being dismantled for recycling. The Hershey Gardens, just north of the town, are a good stop for

© CLAIRE BOOBBYER

© ALUN JOHN | ALAMY STOCK PHOTO

The beaches of Jibacoa, backed by limestone cliffs, with snorkelling offshore, are the best sands close to Havana.

The Boca de Canasí offers snorkelling, hiking, and swimming.

Jibacoa

Canasí

RIGHT: Another sleepy town on the Hershey line...welcome to a very different type of Casablanca.

Cuban cocktails and meals at its scattered restaurants.

The train rocks and sways onwards. If you've remembered to pack your trunks, Canasí is a great jumping-off spot for snorkelling, hiking and swimming at the gorgeous Boca de Canasí.

At the end of the line is Matanzas, an overlooked, untouristy, emerging urban star. Go for the rumba, Afro-Cuban tunes, history, art galleries, handcrafted books store, and the world's only preserved 19th-century French pharmacy – a cornucopia of ancient pills, bottles, prescriptions and ravishingly beautiful stained-glass windows.

❷ LIFE ON BOARD

The train usually runs with two interconnecting spartan carriages fitted with wooden and black plastic seats aligned in groups of four – two seats face another two seats. When buying a ticket at Havana or Matanzas you're given a seat number. Sweet snacks are sold at Hershey Station and the Hershey Gardens hosts a couple of restaurants. There are no bathrooms on board; there's a (decrepit) toilet at Hershey Station.

❸ MAKE IT HAPPEN

Trains depart three times a day from both Havana and Matanzas, year-round. The timetable has been known to vary so it's advisable to be there at least one hour before the scheduled departure. Book tickets in person at the terminals in Casablanca or Matanzas, or on board if you get on at smaller stops. Booking in advance is not recommended as the train can be cancelled if the electricity goes down. It's best to travel to Casablanca on the ferry from the terminal in Old Havana. Don't bring pen knives or similar, as there is airport-style security at the ferry terminals. **CB**

Matanzas boasts music, art, history, handmade books, and a preserved 19th-century French pharmacy.

Matanzas

76

New England's Amtrak Downeaster

USA ●

START **BOSTON**

END **BRUNSWICK**

DEPARTS **DAILY**

DISTANCE 145 MILES (233KM)

DURATION **3 HRS 25 MINS**

As car-free city breaks go, this train escape is hard to beat, chugging from the downtown main streets of urban Boston to Maine's rural greens in under four hours. That's from the seventh most densely populated city in the US to the state with the highest percentage of forest coverage, all in less time than it takes to cook an old-style Yankee plum pudding. Even better, every stop along the way features historic New England cities and towns, parks and seascapes, cottage arts and crafts, world-class shopping and stellar foods fashioned from farm- and sea-fresh ingredients.

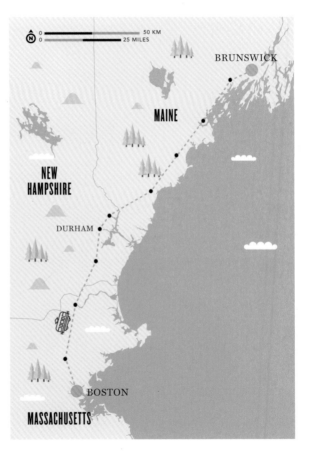

❶ RIDING THE RAILS

The Downeaster is a standalone part of Amtrak's nation-spanning system. It's the only Amtrak service to depart from Boston's North Station, beneath the TD Garden arena. Shortly after clickety-clacking out of the greater Boston area, a pervasive sense of contentment settles over the train. In spring and summer, the far-reaching field, forest and sea views put riders at their ease. In autumn, it's the fabulous fall foliage. Even in winter, the unmasked sight lines through denuded trees take in soothing snow-blanketed pastures. Was that flash of russet a fox? Yes, perhaps it was!

Most people on the Downeaster embrace and amplify the insouciance. They're an easy-going slice of New England life that includes commuting professionals, students at universities in and around Boston (the Phillips Exeter Academy at Exeter, the University of New Hampshire at Durham and Bowdoin University in Brunswick, all stops on the train), and, on game days, families and friends sporting bright team colours on the way to or from seeing the Red Sox, Celtics or Bruins in Boston.

Of course, there are also out-of-staters keen for a taste of 'It's All Here' Massachusetts, 'Live Free or Die' New Hampshire and 'Vacationland' Maine. Some of them fall into conversation with volunteer goodwill ambassadors, who, coordinated by TrainRiders Northeast, share information about the Downeaster service and the destinations through which it passes.

And what a varied assortment of destinations; only Boston boasts a population of more than 70,000 people (most places have fewer than 20,000). There are many-layered, richly storied glimpses into small-town life in the northeast of America – college municipalities alive with youthful energy, formerly industrial riverside communities (Haverhill and Saco), and coastal resorts (Old Orchard Beach) or outlet-shopping meccas (Freeport) rolling out a regular welcome to a steady flow of visitors.

Of course, in between townships are long stretches of fertile land, some of it tamed by agriculture and

rural settlement, while other parts, such as southern Maine's Wells National Estuarine Research Reserve and Rachel Carson US Wildlife Preserve, conserve coastal wetlands for birds, animals and the people who love them. For many travellers choosing not to pause along the way, these glimpses pass in colourful flashes, brushed aside by the determined rhythm of wheels against tracks and frequent full-throated bellows from the locomotive.

But many people do stop short of the current (but perhaps not future) Brunswick terminus. Old Orchard Beach has a wide, seven-mile (11km), crescent-shaped strand that is commonly considered Maine's best. The seasonal train station is mere feet from the Coney Island-like Palace Playland, the only seaside amusement park in New England, as well as a historic century-old pier jutting 500ft (150m) into the water. The next stop is in harbour-front Portland, where many people alight and head for the revitalised Old Port District or the Arts District, packed with museums, music venues big and small, historic parks

IMAGE COURTESY OF AMTRAK

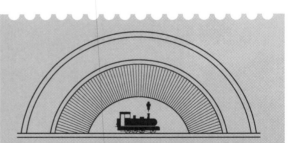

THE LAST SHALL BE FIRST

The present-day Amtrak Downeaster first ran between Boston and Portland on 15 December 2001. It is the most recent Amtrak service. Ten years later, in 2011, it was the first service to pilot on-board wi-fi and e-ticketing. It is also registered as a potential high-speed rail corridor.

The train's departure point is in the North End, a historic part of Boston with a distinctly European character.

The route passes through the venerable University of New Hampshire at Durham.

| Boston | Haverhill | Exeter | Durham | Dover |

CLOCKWISE FROM LEFT: Portland Head Lighthouse in Maine; Boston's skyline; leaf peeping at its best. **PREVIOUS PAGE:** A farmhouse in rural Maine.

and delectable restaurants. The next and penultimate station is Freeport, where the brick sidewalks lead past the LL Bean flagship store and dozens of other brand outlets and local speciality shops.

For travellers wishing to leave trip organisation to professionals, all of these destinations and many others feature in family-friendly, culinary and romantic travel packages at https://downeasterpackages.com.

❷ LIFE ON BOARD

The Downeaster has wide, reclining seats with generous legroom. In business class, it's even more spacious, seats are fully reclining and leather upholstered. There's also a complimentary newspaper and a non-alcoholic drink. Free wi-fi and electrical outlets round out the in-seat amenities.

Food and drink, including alcoholic beverages, are available in the Downeaster Cafe, which is open to all passengers.

❸ MAKE IT HAPPEN

The Amtrak Downeaster makes its round-trip journey every day of the week, five times a day, although two services begin and stop short in Portland, Maine.

Tickets for both classes of service – reserved coach and business – can be booked through the Amtrak website at www.amtrak.com. Reservations are required to board and may be available until the last minute, although it is best to secure tickets in advance, when they may also be cheaper.

The Downeaster is a special treat all year round, but in autumn's peak leaf-peeping season, the forest views are particularly wonderful. **EG**

Maine's premier stretch of sand, beachfront amusement park and pier, is at Old Orchard Beach.

Portland is a picturesque, harbourside city with fantastic museums and restaurants.

The postcard-perfect village of Freeport is home to the famous LL Bean store.

Old Orchard Beach   **Portland**   **Freeport**   **Brunswick**

The Rupert Rocket

CANADA

START JASPER	
END PRINCE RUPERT	
DEPARTS **3 PER WEEK**	DURATION **2 DAYS**
DISTANCE **286 MILES (1160KM)**	

Canada's famously scenic railway lines lure travellers from around the world. But while you'll always meet international visitors on some routes, VIA Rail's charming two-day Jasper-to-Prince-Rupert service combines stunning backcountry scenery with plenty of chances to meet the northern British Columbia locals, who use the three-times-a-week trundle as a regular link between the area's remote communities. Add the excitement of wildlife-spotting opportunities plus vintage

steel-sided carriages that echo the golden age of streamlined travel, and this train – fondly nicknamed the Rupert Rocket – becomes one of Canada's greatest rail journeys.

❶ RIDING THE RAILS

The train lurches unannounced from Jasper's steeply gabled old station, startling several nearby deer that are feasting on stray grain dropped by passing freight cars. As it gathers speed towards the surrounding sawtooth mountains, suspense ripples through the carriages and expectant passengers glue themselves to the windows.

But while cameras snap at the receding Canadian Rockies town and the dense woodlands closing in alongside, not everyone is ogling the scenery. The rhythmically juddering Rupert Rocket might be a once-in-a-lifetime trip for some but it's simply a way of life for others – including its veteran train attendants.

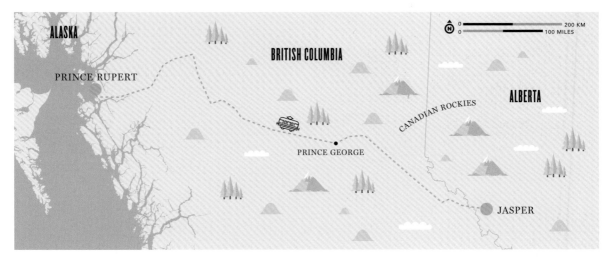

Passing silvery lakes and snow-frosted crags, these friendly folk point out the landmarks to newbies. There's the surging Fraser River flashing between the trees, lofty trestle bridges that seem to curve through the sky, and neck-cricking Mt Robson, its mist-fingered crown appearing to levitate over the area. Chatting to attendants and locals as you stroll through the carriages is a good way to gather insider tips about the region – as well as suggestions for what to look for en route. Wildlife rules this region, and keeping at least one eye on the ever-changing nature diorama unfurling alongside is essential.

Huge ruminating elk, statue-still longhorn sheep and dainty deer that spring from the tracks like jack-in-the-boxes are popular sights among passengers. But bears of both the black and grizzly variety are everyone's favourite lens magnet – especially if they happen to be ever-watchful mothers with a gaggle of ungainly cubs in tow. After exhausting your camera battery, it's usually time to examine the train. It's like touring in a mobile museum: the Rocket's steel cars

were built in the mid-1950s, recalling a bygone age of romantic rail travel – especially in the train's double-decker Park Car, with its domed upper-level seats and cosy little downstairs lounge.

After the service stops for the night in Prince George – northern BC's biggest city – day two of the journey feels even more laid-back. Many passengers know each other now and the 12-hour trundle is relaxed and even a little snoozy...until the surrounding views take a dramatic turn.

The Rockies were yesterday's news and the grand Coast Mountain range now rushes to meet the train. Sheer cliff faces fill the windows as veiny waterfalls tumble behind flagpole-straight trees. Trestles and tunnels take centre stage, testament to the death-defying challenges of building this line more than a century ago.

There are long stretches of reverential vista-watching now as the train threads past forest-framed little settlements Doreen and Telkwa. By mid-afternoon, the locomotive is inching alongside some

IMAGE COURTESY OF VIA RAIL CANADA

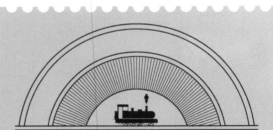

HISTORIC STATIONS

Originally built by the Grand Trunk Pacific Railway, there were once dozens of small, flare-roofed wooden train stations dotting this route. Among the remaining few, the largest is in McBride, where the train often stops, allowing passengers to hop off for photos and to pick up coffee from the station's chatty cafe.

Crane your neck for the best views of Mt Robson, the Canadian Rockies' highest peak.

Snap panoramic scenes while crossing the giant Raush River Bridge, one of the route's longest.

Jasper

IMAGE COURTESY OF VIA RAIL CANADA

© MLORENZPHOTOGRAPHY | GETTY IMAGES

CLOCKWISE FROM LEFT: Classic BC scenery; a black bear cub; the Rupert Rocket is unhindered by snowfall.
PREVIOUS PAGE: The steamlined Rupert Rocket takes in some of Canada's finest scenery.

gargantuan peaks and there are so many bald eagles whirling overhead that passengers soon become blasé. By mid-evening, with the train's metronomic rat-a-tat fostering a Sunday afternoon drowsiness, the Rocket reaches the wide, sunset-glittered Skeena River. It's time to skirt the long shoreline towards end-of-the-line Prince Rupert. Sliding past ghostly remnants of forgotten fish-canning operations, the train eventually squeals across its final bridge to a slow, juddering halt.

❷ LIFE ON BOARD

From mid-June to September, passengers can opt for touring class: spacious Panorama Car seats, airline-style meals and exclusive Park Car access. Additionally, economy class operates all summer and throughout the rest of the year, offering older but perfectly comfortable seats.

❸ MAKE IT HAPPEN

Trains leave Jasper on Sunday, Wednesday and Friday year-round. Services stop overnight in Prince George – reserve your hotel in advance. Book tickets from VIA Rail's website at www.viarail.ca. Touring class should be booked far in advance, with economy class more readily available.

Visitors often travel one-way from Jasper. After Prince Rupert take the spectacular BC Ferries service to Vancouver Island's Port Hardy or the service to the islands of Haida Gwaii for an immersive introduction to First Nations culture. Fly on to Vancouver from Prince Rupert, Haida Gwaii or Port Hardy. Summer is popular but autumn delivers breathtaking fall foliage views. Economy class passengers often bring food and drink, though they may also be bought on board or at stops. **JL**

Peer over steep-sided trestle Seeley Gulch Bridge as the train slows to a scenic crawl.

Pass the North Pacific Cannery, then return the next day to this evocative museum.

Trundle into evening-time Prince Rupert, joining the locals for dinner and a few craft beers.

Prince George

Prince Rupert

Lima to Huancavelica via Huancayo

START **LIMA**

END **HUANCAVELICA**

DEPARTS **TWICE A MONTH**

DISTANCE **286 MILES (460KM)**

DURATION **17–19 HRS**

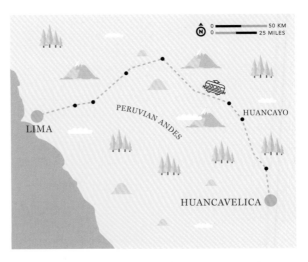

This monolithic two-part Peruvian adventure ushers you through the greatest elevation change of any railway journey in the world: from sea level to nearly 16,000ft (5000m). Prepare yourself to traverse the Andean cordillera, to visit the planet's second-highest set of tracks and highest passenger railway station, then for the finale of the odyssey, to board Peru's only remaining non-tourist train to the bewitching city of Huancavelica. In the process, you will pass through one of the most tradition-rich and rural parts of the country, a time-trapped tract of Peru very different from the modern metropolis of Lima from which you depart.

❶ RIDING THE RAILS

Lima's Desamparados Station is one of South America's most architecturally astonishing: a beaux arts beauty from 1912 with a gorgeous stained-glass skylight. Get here early to savour the sense of theatre which themes this trip throughout. It's a fitting beginning to the more luxurious first leg of the journey.

Rattling away from the capital and the coast, the first dramatic stop is at San Bartolomé where, as the Andes close around, the engine has to be turned manually on a turnstile so as to deal with the steep,

tightly twisting ascent ahead. The mountains, by turns arid and luscious, are a poor part of Peru as a rule, with mining one of the few sources of wealth; eerie mining settlements such as Casapalca and La Oroya dot this route.

Between the two, the Ferrocarril Centro Andino reaches its highlight: the highest point of any passenger railway anywhere on the globe. From Ticlio, on the Pacific side of the Andes, the train dives into the La Galera tunnel, which goes through to the mountains' Atlantic side: in the process passing the topmost sleeper at approximately 15,692ft (4783m). This is not even the loftiest part of the line: a spur used just for mining purposes reaches 15,843ft (4829m). Post-tunnel, there is just time at lonely La Galera Station to set foot on the platform, which at 15673ft (4777m) is the planet's highest for passengers. The train then descends into the lush Río Mantaro valley, renowned throughout the country for handicrafts, such as its decorated gourds, and bathed by this time in radiant late-evening sunlight, and hits Huancayo an hour after sundown.

Huancayo is the big city of the Central Andes, with one of Peru's best dining scenes. It's a cosmopolitan, culturally dynamic journey-breaker before stage two of this rail romp: a six-hour chug over mountainous massif to Huancavelica. The train on the Ferrocarril Huancayo–Huancavelica service is a locals' train, which bears the moniker 'El Tren Macho', because, according to a local joke, 'he left when he wanted and arrived when he could'. Besides the ride through another delightful swath of altiplano (high-altitude Andean plateau), this part of the journey is magical for a different reason: its insight into life hereabouts. Watch villagers jump on and off at tiny photogenic communities scattered along the way: giggling children attending school, farmers transporting livestock (chickens and guinea pigs are common fellow passengers), and vendors baying about their foodie treats for sale. And then, amid the squawking,

hawking and breathtaking views, Huancavelica appears, spreadeagled along the valley floor, its myriad colonial church spires gleaming like a dream.

❷ LIFE ON BOARD

Ferrocarril Centro Andino's run to Huancayo is done with tourists in mind. Two classes, *clásico* and *turístico* (roughly equating to standard and 1st class), are both fairly comfortable, with padded leather seats. *Turístico* benefits from more leg-room and reclining seats. It also has access to an open car where you can best view the scenery, and proximity to the bar coach, where drinks and snacks are served. Because of the prices and the route's infrequency, passengers are mostly tourists. This is in stark contrast to the Ferrocarril Huancayo–Huancavelica, very much a locals' ride. Again there are two classes (buffet class is about a dollar dearer, more comfortable, but still no-frills). This journey is full of colour and clamour compared to the rather less frenzied Lima–Huancayo tourist service.

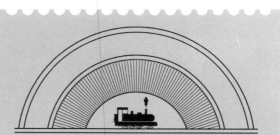

HIGHEST IN THE WORLD?

The Qinghai–Tibet railway has the world's highest station (Tanggula; 16,627ft/5068m), but you can't disembark. Bolivia's Río Mulatos–Potosí route boasts the second-highest station, Cóndor (15,702ft/ 4786m), but is solely for mining access. Thus Ferrocarril Centro Andino has the world's highest passenger rail station (La Galera; 15,673ft/4777m).

Marvel at the beaux arts Desamparados Station in Lima, a vestige of the railway's glory days.

Watch the engine being swivelled on a turnstile at San Bartolomé, ready for the ascent into the Andes.

Alight at La Galera, the highest passenger railway station in the world.

| Lima (Desamparados) | Choisica | San Bartolomé | Casapalca | Ticlio | La Galera |

IMAGE COURTESY OF RAIL SOUTH AMERICA

CLOCKWISE FROM LEFT: The Huancayo train crossing a viaduct; party time in the bar coach; llamas; a family shops at Peru's Lircay market. **PREVIOUS PAGE:** Plying the lofty high-line between Lima and Huancayo.

© PETER LAUFFER

❸ MAKE IT HAPPEN

Cutbacks, cutbacks: the Lima–Huancayo leg now makes merely a couple of runs per month at most. Discover the month's schedules and book tickets at the Ferrocarril Centro Andino website (www.ferrocarrilcentral.com.pe). The train leaves Lima's Desamparados Station early in the morning, enabling passengers to see the best of the route during daylight. Bring snacks, water and warm clothes, plus something to counteract possible altitude sickness. The train lays over in Huancayo for a couple of days, giving you plenty of time to see the city.

Departures for the Huancayo–Huancavelica leg are far more frequent (three days a week in each direction). Again, water and warm clothes are wise things to bring. Just turn up at Huancayo Chilca Station beforehand to buy tickets. **LW**

© ECATERINA LEONTE | ECATERINALEONTE | 500PX

Wander through the resplendent Santa Rosa de Ocapa convent near Concepción.

Browse Peru's best handicrafts centres in the Río Mantaro valley near Huancayo.

| La Oroya | Jauja | Concepción | Huancayo (Chilca) | Izcuchaca | Huancavelica |

The New Mexico Rail Runner

USA ●

START	ALBUQUERQUE	
END	SANTA FE	
DEPARTS	DAILY	DURATION 1 HR 30 MINS
DISTANCE 75 MILES (120KM)		

One of America's great unsung commuter railways, the New Mexico Rail Runner is a regional train that runs down the Rio Grande Valley, connecting the state's largest city, Albuquerque, with its cultural and political capital, Santa Fe. On the way it crosses wide, high desert, giving views of arid mountains in all directions, and even passes through several of the state's Native American tribal lands. A no-nonsense, clean and quick journey, its highlights are the sweeping views from the upper seats of the double-decker carriages. Taken as a day trip or a scenic-but-practical form of intra-state transport, the Rail Runner is a wonderful introduction to New Mexico's epic landscapes.

❶ RIDING THE RAILS

Meep meep! The doors whoosh closed. The train's door-closing chime leaves you in little doubt where you are: it's impossible to forget you're in New Mexico and on a train punningly named for the state bird, the road runner. And as the train zips northward from the state's largest city, Albuquerque, to its capital, Santa Fe, you might feel a little bit like you're passing through the landscape of that famous cartoon.

But you won't find the Road Runner out-birding

the Coyote here, though the land nods to your imagination. Red-brown mesas flatten off into purple-grey cones of ancient volcanoes, but this is real life and there is something about this landscape that gets instantly into your blood. It's not the animated vistas of Old-West movies, but it's poetically close.

The Rail Runner has no snack car, and although it's a short enough ride (just an hour and a half), you'll want to have a giant breakfast of huevos rancheros at old-school New Mexican favourite, Barelas Coffee House, before you embark. And because this is New Mexico and food is one of the greatest pleasures of visiting here, you're going to jump out in the Santa Fe Railyard cultural district and go straight for a lunch of blue-corn burritos on the flower-laden patio at La Choza when you arrive. And then, of course, have a pint or three at the city's best beer house, Second Street Brewery (both are within walking distance of the railway depot).

But for now, gazing out of the train window into a muted rainbow of desert colours, it could be any point in history. Much of the first part of the journey is a ride alongside the Rio Grande, visible out of the train's left-hand windows as a swath of greenery – cottonwood trees giving signs of the only water for miles in any direction. As the train slows through San Felipe Pueblo, a Native American reservation, it passes right next to old mud structures now abandoned and worn from decades of abuse by New Mexico's cold winter winds. The state is home to 19 pueblos – small Native American tribes that have lived in villages from as early as the AD 700s.

A few minutes further north, the train circuits its way through a set of low-lying hills dotted with piñon trees and juniper bushes. These are the Cerrillos Hills, where natural turquoise deposits were discovered first by Native American artisans and later by big-business jewellers, eventually spawning the signature Southwestern fashion style as we know it today.

From here, the Rail Runner takes a straight shot northwards, its tracks straddling Interstate 25 into Santa Fe, concealed like a diamond beneath the Sangre de Cristo Mountains, and suddenly you are no longer in the low desert but creeping your way up into the southernmost tail of the Rockies.

❷ LIFE ON BOARD

Primarily designed as a commuter service, the Rail Runner is a single-class train with no seating assignments. Carriages are bi-level, with the best seats on the upper decks for panoramas of the passing landscape. There are toilets, bike racks and free wi-fi, but no food is sold on board (you can bring a picnic, though alcohol is not permitted).

❸ MAKE IT HAPPEN

On weekdays, trains depart from Downtown Albuquerque approximately hourly during the morning and afternoon commuting hours, and there are limited departures on weekends. Tickets can be purchased online (www.riometro.org), via the Rio Metro Ticketing app or on board with cash or card from a conductor.

Visitors usually travel the route as a day trip; a day pass allows stop-offs. The train connects to the Albuquerque International Sunport airport, making it easy to spend a few days in either city. Northern New Mexico is pretty at any time of year, but the best time to visit is autumn (September–November), when temperatures cool, mountain aspens are painting flames of yellow across peaks and the smell of roasting green chile is in the air. **ME**

CLOCKWISE FROM TOP LEFT: New Mexico Museum of Art; grab a bite in the Santa Fe Railyard District; arriving at Bernalillo Station near Albuquerque. **PREVIOUS PAGE:** An iconic water tank takes centre stage at the Santa Fe Railyard District in New Mexico.

RESERVATION LANDS

As the train enters reservation land, an announcement will warn passengers to put their cameras away. Although it might be tempting to snap a clandestine picture or two, remember that, for Native Americans here, taking photographs of the land or people is a violation of their sacred culture and spirituality.

Grab an upstairs seat for the best views of buttes, mesas and high-desert mountains.

Between Sandia Pueblo and Bernalillo watch for epic views of the Sandia Mountains out of the right-side windows.

Albuquerque   **Montaño**   **Los Ranchos**   **Sandia Pueblo**

© JUSTIN FOULKES | LONELY PLANET

© EFRAIN PADRO | ALAMY STOCK PHOTO

© EFRAIN PADRO | ALAMY STOCK PHOTO

Catch glimpses of the cottonwood-tree-lined bosque from the left-hand windows as the train follows the Rio Grande.

Look out for the crumbling remains of San Felipe Pueblo's historic adobe buildings. Remember not to take photos!

Past Kewa, the train winds through the Cerrillos Hills, where turquoise stone was first mined by Native Americans.

Bernalillo

Kewa Pueblo

Santa Fe

The Serra Verde Express

BRAZIL

START **CURITIBA**

END **MORRETES**

DEPARTS **DAILY**

DISTANCE 42 MILES (68KM)

DURATION **3 HRS 30 MINS**

One of Brazil's most spectacular train journeys, the Serra Verde Express winds its way through dramatic mountain passes covered with tropical rainforest. The half-day trip takes in canyons, jagged mountain peaks and lush lowlands along one of South America's early engineering marvels. The slow-going locomotive allows plenty of opportunities to photograph the cinematic backdrop as it makes a 3064ft (934m) descent while traversing some 30

bridges and chugging through 14 tunnels. Aside from the captivating scenery, the journey provides a fascinating glimpse into the past as it trundles past tiny stations that date back to the late 1800s.

❶ RIDING THE RAILS

The journey starts in the town of Curitiba, an architecturally rich city in the state of Paraná, deep in the south of Brazil. After taking in some of the showcase designs by Oscar Niemeyer, Brazil's greatest architect, it's time to hit the rails for a look at Brazil's wild side. Leaving the urban bustle of Curitiba (population 1.9 million), the Serra Verde Express courses past wide boulevards and open spaces as it heads toward the thick mountains of greenery lying beyond the city's eastern periphery.

Travel on a weekend and a celebratory air pervades the train, with flowing drinks and chattering Brazilian

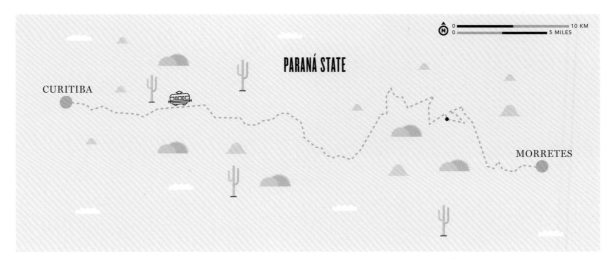

PARANÁ STATE

CURITIBA

MORRETES

and foreign travellers gaping at the impressive views. Of course, the train line wasn't always a ready-made, slow-moving festa. The line was originally built for transporting grain and other products from the hinterland to the port of Paranaguá. Construction started in 1880, and required a Herculean effort of some 9000 workers labouring on three sections simultaneously over the course of five years. Tragically, hundreds lost their lives from diseases such as malaria and typhus during construction.

Through the wide windows of the train cars, you can watch the landscape transition from urban to rural and finally into the dramatic peaks and forests of the Serra do Mar. This green jewel is part of a vast network of mountain ranges and coastal slopes that follow the coastline over 930 miles (1500km), stretching from Espírito Santo in the north, down through Rio de Janeiro, and all the way to Rio Grande do Sul, Brazil's southernmost state. This remnant of Mata Atlântica (Atlantic rainforest) is actually older than the Amazon and evolved independently. It also hosts some of the highest biodiversity levels on earth with many unique species, though sadly only 7% of the forest's original expanse remains.

Those wanting to explore this lush landscape more deeply can disembark from the train at Marumbi Station and follow the trails of the Parque Estadual Marumbi. The 937-acre (379-hectare) reserve is home to waterfalls, grand vistas and colonial trails first blazed back in the 17th century. While a few hikers (mostly Brazilians) disembark here, the majority of passengers continue to the end of the line at Morretes. Slumbering on the banks of the Rio Nhundiaquara, this picturesque colonial town enjoys a fabulous backdrop of Serra do Mar mountains. In Morretes, passengers have a few hours before the train's return.

Since the arrival in Morretes perfectly coincides with lunchtime, Paraná cuisine is the name of the game – in particular, *barreado*, a rich, meat and manioc-flour stew served in a clay pot that's slow-cooked in a wood-fired oven. It goes down nicely with a caipirinha or two.

IMAGE COURTESY OF SERRA VERDE EXPRESS

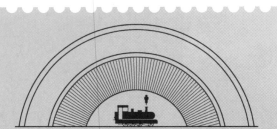

ILHA DO MEL

If you've come this far, it's worth heading to Paranagua (24 miles/39km east of Morretes) and catching a boat out to Ilha do Mel. This small hourglass-shaped island has picturesque shoreline walks, sun-kissed beaches and an 1872 lighthouse affording splendid views. You can overnight in one of many guesthouses on the island.

Hope for a window seat on the left side for the best views of the jagged peaks and forested valleys.

Admire the grand panorama atop the 180ft (55m) Ponte São João (St John's Bridge).

Hold your breath while zipping around the Viaduto Caravalho, a cliff-clinging viaduct set on five soaring masonry pillars.

Curitiba

CLOCKWISE FROM LEFT: Travelling the biodiverse Serra do Mar; engineering wonders; marvellous mountainscapes. **PREVIOUS PAGE:** Passengers enjoy the thrilling ride from Curitiba to Morretes.

❷ LIFE ON BOARD

The Serra Verde Express has three classes. Economy is just a plastic bench seat without any on-board service, while tourist class comes with padded bench seats, a Portuguese-speaking guide and one drink. Executive class has slightly comfier seating, free drinks and a bilingual guide. You can also hire a four-person cabin. There's no air-conditioning but you can open the windows and get a nice breeze.

Travel agents can arrange packages coupled with an overnight stay down on the coast. Several nights a month, you can book a train trip with dinner service.

❸ UPGRADES

The *trem de luxo* (luxury train), which runs only at weekends, has specially outfitted cabins evoking the glamour of the past, with hardwoods and colonial-style decor. Passengers are served a full breakfast, and bilingual guides give background info on the journey.

❹ MAKE IT HAPPEN

Trains depart Curitiba at 8.15am daily. The luxury train departs at 9.15am at weekends. You can book tickets online at www.serraverdeexpress.com.br, but it may be easier to book through a travel agency or at Curitiba Station. Reserve at least three weeks in advance during the summer (December to March).

Some passengers opt for the speedier 90-minute bus for the return journey, but it's more enjoyable to make a day of it and return by train, which leaves Morretes at 3pm. The best time to visit is during the summer or the less busy shoulder seasons (November and April). Many nationalities require a visa to enter Brazil. **RSL**

Photograph the vintage station of Marumbi, gateway to the hiking trails of the lush Parque Estadual Marumbi.

Wander Morretes' cobblestone lanes and enjoy the classic Paraná dish of *barreado* (meat stew) before your return.

Marumbi

Morretes

Cruising the Pacific: the Coast Starlight

USA

START **SEATTLE**

END **LOS ANGELES**

DEPARTS **DAILY**

DISTANCE **1377 MILES (2216KM)**

DURATION **34 HRS**

Trace America's 'left coast' in all its varied splendour. The 34-hour (OK, it's Amtrak, so maybe more) trip between Seattle and Los Angeles curves alongside crashing Pacific waves, cuts through America's lushest agricultural land, and passes below snow-capped mountains and towering redwoods. Of all the Amtrak routes, this one offers the most scenic variety in the fewest hours.

Another reason this train is special: it's the only Amtrak service with a dedicated parlour car, open only to passengers who book sleepers. The parlour conjures old-time rail romance, with wood panelling and soft lighting, plus a special menu and wine-and-cheese tastings.

❶ RIDING THE RAILS

On the second day of the trip from Seattle to Los Angeles, long-haul passengers are settled in. They've picked their favourite seats in the lounge car. They've shared their life stories and personal advice. So it feels comfortable and natural when, sometime after 4pm, everyone looks out the window and conversation stalls. The temporary community of the train hasn't failed; it's just that the Pacific Ocean has appeared.

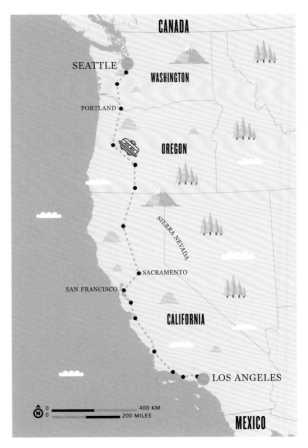

From south of San Luis Obispo to just past Santa Barbara, the ocean is the star. The floor-to-ceiling windows of the Sightseer Lounge car fill with light reflecting off the water – the 'shining sea' of song. In the dining car, strangers' chitchat at the shared tables is broken by meditative silences as the sun sinks lower. In the parlour car, people turn from their convivial cocktail tables, from their glasses of

Lombard Street in San Francisco at sunrise.

wine or their *palomas* (grapefruit and tequila, picked to reflect California's Mexican heritage), and stare out the window.

It's not as if the train hasn't gone through dramatic landscapes already. The first day, starting outside Seattle, the route plunges into deep forest, often

"the real thrill is where it runs at the edge of the continent, where the cliffs drop away to the water"

wreathed in mist. Rangers in the lounge car point out such landmarks as 8366ft (2550m) Mt St Helens, its white peak still jagged from its 1980 eruption, and sometimes leaking steam. The 20-mile (32km) length of Upper Klamath Lake turns dark in the dusk, or reflects the rising moon.

The next morning, tidy suburban tracts of San Jose – Silicon Valley – give way to the equally tidy fields

of California's Central Valley, which grows more than half of America's produce. The train cuts across vast green acres of spiky artichokes and glinting berries, under arcing sprinklers, alongside small armies of field workers. The food in this dining car – the same menu served on every Amtrak train across the country – tastes better, fresher, probably because the produce has travelled to the train from these very lush fields. As the route syncs up with the historic Spanish Camino Real, Franciscan missions, built in the 18th and 19th centuries, pop up in every town with 'San' (Saint) in the name.

But this is the Coast Starlight, after all, and the real thrill is where it runs at the edge of the continent, where the cliffs drop away to the water below. Past Santa Barbara, the train passes just above beaches and little towns – Mussel Shoals, Carpinteria – and the golden-hour light inspires reverie: what if I bought a surfboard and a VW bus? What if I rented a little redwood cabin, sheltered by windswept trees? This view could be mine, every night. America's West

© PATRICIA MARROQUIN | GETTY IMAGES

TIPPING ON AMTRAK

Tip your sleeping-car attendant, especially if he or she brings you a meal in your room (always an option); between $10 and $20 per room at the end of your trip is typical. Also tip your server in the dining car, even if your meal is free; a few dollars per passenger is always welcome.

Seattle's King Street Station, refurbished in 2014, is dazzling, with ornate white tile inside.

Stroll the pretty Pearl District during the hour-long Portland stop – or stay longer for great eats and bars.

Seattle　　　　**Portland**　　　　**Albany**　　　　**Sacramento**

CLOCKWISE FROM LEFT: Golden Gate Bridge; Hearst Castle; the surfing life as lived in LA. **OPENING PAGE:** South of San Francisco, the Coast Starlight hugs America's west coast.

Coast, especially California, the Golden State, has always been a place of dreams, and this train offers them every day.

❷ LIFE ON BOARD

Sleepers are snug roomettes for two (toilets and showers are located downstairs) or larger bedrooms with in-room facilities. Sleeper tickets include all meals in the dining car, as well as local wine tastings (Oregon wines in the north, California wines in the south, naturally) and optional meals in the parlour car. In coach class, seats come equipped with a good recline and footrests, but there is no shower access. Snacks such as sandwiches, pizza and beer and wines are sold in the lounge car, and full meals can be purchased in the dining car. Wireless internet is promised but inconsistent, especially in rural areas.

❸ MAKE IT HAPPEN

The Coast Starlight runs once daily, leaving midmorning and arriving late the next day. Book online (www.amtrak.com), but call the number on the website to request a room on the right side going south or left going north. Book sleepers at least two months in advance, especially for holiday weekends. Coach seats are usually available, though even they may fill at peak times.

To break up the trip, Oakland (for San Francisco) is a good midpoint. You cannot book a layover; you must purchase two separate tickets. If you're travelling only a day leg (Oakland to Seattle, for example), a sleeper is a smaller surcharge and especially good value.

Trains run cold; pack warm layers. In coach, bring a blanket and pillow, and a washcloth if you want to brave a sink bath. **ZO**

Oakland is the gateway to San Francisco, but also an increasingly cool destination in its own right.

San Luis Obispo is the stop for Hearst Castle, newspaper magnate William Randolph Hearst's lavish home.

Admire Los Angeles' 1939 Spanish art deco Union Station, and get tacos at historic Olvera Street.

Oakland   **San Luis Obispo**   **Santa Barbara**   **Los Angeles**

Coast to Coast on VIA Rail Canada

CANADA

START **VANCOUVER**

END **HALIFAX**

DEPARTS **3 PER WEEK**

DURATION **1 WEEK**

DISTANCE **3946 MILES (6352KM)**

Travelling the varied landscapes of the world's second-largest country makes for an epic rail adventure. As you cross Canada between Vancouver in the west and Halifax in the east, you'll chug over the snow-covered Rocky Mountains, across the flat prairies with their carpets of wildflowers, through Ontario's woods and into the diverse metropolises of Toronto and Montréal. You'll travel through historic Québec City and New Brunswick's Acadian communities, before reaching Nova Scotia and the Atlantic Ocean. A journey

on three trains operated by Canada's national rail carrier, VIA Rail, can take you from coast to coast.

❶ RIDING THE RAILS

When you first glimpse the Canadian Rockies from VIA Rail's flagship train, the Canadian, the mountains appear as tiny snow-topped bumps far in the distance. Gradually, as the train approaches, the peaks get taller and taller, with evergreens standing below the rocky summits. If you're lucky, the top of Mt Robson will peek out of the clouds; at 12,972ft (3954m), it's the tallest in Canada's Rockies.

For many travellers, whether you're riding from the east or the west, that first look at the majestic mountains is a highlight of a Canadian rail adventure. Yet, on this extended trip that takes you from Vancouver, BC, across eight of Canada's 10 provinces to Halifax, Nova Scotia, the unfolding landscape changes daily as your train crosses this vast country.

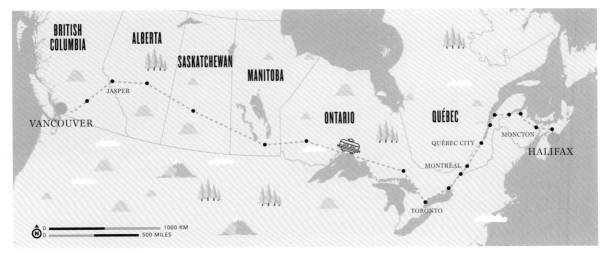

Though there's no single train that goes all the way across Canada, you can easily put together a trip on three VIA Rail routes to travel from the Pacific to the Atlantic (or vice versa). The Canadian is the longest-distance train, operating between Vancouver and Toronto, with four nights and three days on board. From Toronto, several daily trains ply the busy corridor to Montréal, just five hours away. In Montréal, you can catch the Ocean, an overnight train, to complete your journey into Halifax.

Allow about a week to travel straight through, but to really see the country, stop off for at least two or three days at points along the way. Get off in the town of Jasper, in the Canadian Rockies' huge Jasper National Park, to hike through the limestone gorges of Maligne Canyon, take a cruise on scenic Maligne Lake and soak in the natural pools at Miette Hot Springs. In Winnipeg, explore the Forks, where rivers meet and the histories of the indigenous communities and fur-trading voyageurs converged, or visit the francophone St Boniface neighbourhood and learn about the heritage of Canada's aboriginal-French Métis people.

In Toronto, Canada's largest city, you could easily spend a week or more walking along the Lake Ontario waterfront, cycling the nearby Toronto islands, exploring museums and galleries throughout the region, and checking out what's new and cool in the city's varied urban districts. Bilingual Montréal has some of the country's best restaurants, and festivals liven up the streets seemingly every week.

Take a couple of days in historic Québec City (founded back in 1608) and then get off the train again in New Brunswick to see the unusual tides in the Bay of Fundy or explore the region's Acadian culture. In Halifax, wander the colonial-era streets or head for the beach to dip your toes into the Atlantic Ocean. After a journey of nearly 4000 miles (6400 km), you've earned a little beach time.

FREIGHT FIRST

Although passenger service on Canada's cross-country railways is important, freight traffic takes priority on the tracks. VIA Rail trains often stop and wait as freight trains go by, so add time to your itinerary to account for potential delays. You don't want to miss hiking in Jasper, for example, if your train pulls in late.

© AXEL M. MOSLER | COURTESY OF VIA RAIL CANADA

Start your journey exploring the rainforests and beaches in diverse urban Vancouver.

Catch your first glimpse of the snow-topped Rockies as the train nears Jasper.

| Vancouver | Jasper | Edmonton | Saskatoon | Winnipeg |

CLOCKWISE FROM LEFT: Vancouver's art gallery; ice skating in Toronto; riding into the sunset. **PREVIOUS PAGE & OVERLEAF:** The route travels right across Canada's expanses.

❷ LIFE ON BOARD

The three trains that take you across Canada all have different services and amenities. On the Canadian between Vancouver and Toronto, you can choose between basic economy seats and several types of sleeping compartments. Economy seats, which recline, are significantly cheaper, but you'll essentially be sitting up for four nights and three days. Economy tickets don't include meals; bring your own or purchase food from the snack car.

In Sleeper Plus class, you can choose between a berth or a cabin. Each sleeper car has shared toilets and showers. Berths are set up as seats by day, converting at night into one-person upper and lower bunks. A heavy curtain, which you button from inside the berth, provides privacy. Sleeper Plus cabins sleep one to four people, with seating areas that convert into beds and private toilets (but not showers). Note that in the cabins for one, the bed inconveniently folds down over the toilet, so at night, you may find it easier to use the shared facilities down the hall. The Canadian also offers larger Prestige class cabins for two, with a private washroom and a shower. Prestige class travellers have a dedicated concierge, too.

The Canadian travels with its own chefs, and all sleeper accommodation includes meals, snacks, and non-alcoholic drinks (Prestige fares include alcohol as well). In the dining car, staff seat you with other travellers at tables of four, which encourages conversation. Lots of people socialise in the bar car, or hang out in the activity car, which is stocked with magazines and games. Sleeper Plus and Prestige passengers can also take in the views from the Panorama car, with windows above and all around.

Trains on the Toronto–Montréal corridor have economy and business seats; the latter include meals. You won't need sleeper accommodation here.

© STEVE ROSSET | SHUTTERSTOCK

© DAMION RAE PHOTOGRAPHY | 500PX

Gallery-hop and dine out in multicultural Toronto.

Take in Canada's francophone culture in stylish Montréal.

 In Moncton, learn about the Acadians and try the sweet cinnamon pastry known as a 'nun's fart'.

Toronto   **Kingston**   **Montréal**   **Québec City**   **Moncton**

Between Montréal and Halifax, the Ocean has standard economy seats and two-person Sleeper Plus compartments with private toilets; you can also choose a compartment with a private shower. If you're travelling solo, you can book a sleeper compartment for yourself. Sleeper Plus tickets on the Ocean include pre-prepared meals. Economy passengers can buy light meals, drinks, and snacks.

Note that the Canadian does not have on-board wi-fi, and some areas along that route may not have good mobile-phone coverage. Toronto–Montréal corridor trains have wi-fi, as does the Ocean.

❸ UPGRADES

Between Vancouver and the Canadian Rockies, the privately run Rocky Mountaineer offers upscale rail tours combining a train journey with accommodation and activities in Banff, Lake Louise, Jasper and Calgary. Rather than sleeping on the train, you stay overnight in hotels along the way. See www.rockymountaineer.com and pp48–53 for more.

❹ MAKE IT HAPPEN

The Canadian runs three times a week from May to mid-October, twice weekly the rest of the year. Toronto–Montréal trains operate five to six times daily. The Ocean runs three times a week. Book online at www.viarail.ca. Check online for last-minute specials.

The best way to cross Canada is as a one-way trip with multiple stopovers. Break your journey in Jasper, Winnipeg, Toronto, Montréal, Québec City or other locations. The warm summer months (July and August) are peak travel season, but in September and October the weather is mild, attractions may be less crowded and trees take on their autumn colours.

Visitors to Canada need a valid passport and, depending on your nationality, you may also need a visa or an Electronic Travel Authorization (eTA). See www.cic.gc.ca for more information. **CH**

End your trip where many immigrants began new lives – at Halifax's Pier 21, now the Canadian Museum of Immigration.

IMAGE COURTESY OF VIA RAIL CANADA

Halifax

ASIA

AMAZING TRAIN JOURNEYS

The Darjeeling Toy Train

INDIA

START NEW JALPAIGURI (NJP)	
END DARJEELING	
DEPARTS DAILY	DURATION 7–8 HRS
DISTANCE 55 MILES (88.5KM)	

India's narrow-gauge steam railways are the stuff of legend, and the bottle-blue Darjeeling Toy Train is the nation's lead engine. The ride from the Bengal plains to Darjeeling travels past emerald-green tea plantations and precariously balanced, tin-roofed townships, while clouds tumble down the looming massif of Mt Khangchendzonga. Sure, steam engines are now only used for a small section of the route, and most people rumble into Darjeeling by diesel power, but this iconic mountain journey still serves up memories of the Raj, when teatime in Darjeeling was as English as jodhpurs, jungles and pyjamas.

❶ RIDING THE RAILS

The idea of forging a railway line from the plains into the eastern Himalaya would have sent many construction engineers running for the hills. The Darjeeling line climbs from just 330ft (100m) above sea level at New Jalpaiguri (NJP) to over 7220ft (2200m) at Darjeeling, and rises even higher at Ghum, the highest railway station in India at 7408ft (2258m).

To achieve this gain in elevation, engineers were required to construct a staggering 554 bridges, six zig-zags in reverse, and three complete loops, with the

track passing over itself like a Scalextric track at the aptly named Agony Point. And all this through dense jungle and teetering tea plantations.

Railway technology has improved since the Toy Train was inaugurated in 1881, but few of these developments have reached Darjeeling, so despite the change from steam to diesel engines for the main NJP–Darjeeling run, passengers still have to perform the same sequence of stops and starts, forwards and backwards shuffles and dainty pirouettes. No matter – the breathtaking scenery on all sides more than makes up for the snail's pace progress of the journey.

On the way, your neck will be craning as you scan the hills for tea workers and peek between forested hilltops for glimpses of celestial Khangchendzonga (28,209ft/8598m), the world's third-highest summit. The views, of course, depend on the vagaries of the Indian climate; during the monsoon, isolated stations appear out of the gloom like ghost towns, and mists swirl around the train like a phantom army.

Darjeeling's Toy Train still runs on Indian standard narrow-gauge track, just two feet wide and compatible only with miniature engines and kindergarten carriages. When Franklin Prestage made his pitch to build a railway to Darjeeling, his intention was to carry the cream of colonial society away from the baking heat of the plains, and he had no idea that the train would become one of India's biggest attractions for domestic tourists.

Today, the Toy Train sees more Indian travellers than foreign tourists, and a fevered atmosphere often prevails, as children shout excitedly at each passing landmark and sudden glimpses of waterfalls through the greenery. At times, the train almost clips the front of roadside vegetable shops and the backyards of mountain bungalows, sometimes tracing the road, and sometimes losing it in dense vegetation.

As you struggle into the hills, the temperature drops with every foot of increased elevation. Even in the warm spring season, Darjeeling often shivers while New Jalpaiguri cooks in tropical heat. Cashmere shawls and knitted woollen balaclavas are de rigueur, and chai-wallahs at the scattered stations along the route do a lively trade in cups of hot, sweet, warming Indian tea.

The most important thing train enthusiasts should note is that the daily NJP to Darjeeling train is today a diesel service. To experience the atmospheric thrill of trundling behind – or sometimes in front of – one of the railway's original Sharp, Stewart & Co B-Class steam locos, you'll need to board the joy-ride train from Darjeeling to Ghum, which includes a stop at the Batasia Loop, a marvel of engineering with giddying views over dotted hill villages and the snow-frosted massif of Khangchendzonga.

❷ LIFE ON BOARD

Narrow-gauge travel doesn't offer much room for luxe amenities, but you probably care more about the views. Since the abolition of 2nd class, all travellers get a padded reclining seat and supersized windows, so you can make the most of the scenery en route.

© IMAGEBROKER | ALAMY STOCK PHOTO

© ANANDOART | GETTY IMAGES

A LONG JOURNEY

Before the construction of the narrow-gauge railway, the journey from Kolkata to Darjeeling took two weeks, starting with a steam-train journey to Sahibgunj, a steamer trip across the Ganges, a bullock cart to Siliguri, then a two-day trip by horse-cart or palanquin to Darjeeling!

Above Tindharia, the line loops over itself like a snake with indigestion, one of dozens of engineering wonders on the way to Darjeeling.

New Jalpaiguri (NJP)   **Siliguri Junction**   **Tindharia**

FROM BELOW: A rest stop at a hilltop station just outside Darjeeling; arrival at Darjeeling; men in traditional Nepalese dress. **PREVIOUS PAGE:** The fairy-tale train chugs along.

➌ MAKE IT HAPPEN

The train ride from NJP to Darjeeling (No 52541) depends on the condition of the tracks; suspensions due to landslides are not uncommon. The joy rides are usually more reliable.

All travel is in 1st class, and there is usually one daily train each way between Darjeeling and NJP, plus nine daily joy-ride services.

Tickets can be booked in either Siliguri (the nearest town to NJP) or Darjeeling, ideally a day or more before travel. Online bookings are possible through www.irctc.co.in, but finding the joy-ride services (Nos 52591 to 52599) is tricky. You'll need to enter 'DJ' as the origin station and 'DJRZ' as the destination, and select First Class in the class field.

The website of the Darjeeling Himalayan Railway Society (www.dhrs.org) is a mine of information. **JB**

Kurseong hill station sits among sprawling tea gardens, with Hindu temples, Buddhist *gompas* and colonial churches.

Often cloaked in cloud, the pint-sized station at Ghum now houses a museum of railway relics.

The Batasia Loop circles a monument to Gorkhas who fought with the Indian Army.

Kurseong

Ghum

Darjeeling

The Hokkaidō Shinkansen

JAPAN

START **TOKYO**	
END **HAKODATE**	
DEPARTS **DAILY**	DURATION **4 HRS**
DISTANCE 512 MILES (824KM)	

 The shinkansen is Japan's iconic bullet train, long a source of pride for a nation built on engineering.
The Hokkaidō Shinkansen, which began operation in 2016, is the newest – and to date, longest – line. It takes you from Tokyo to Hakodate, the southern port of Hokkaidō, Japan's northernmost and least developed island. Along the way, it runs past picturesque scenes of rural Japan, through mountains and under the sea. The route is only part of it, though: riding the shinkansen – with its food trolleys and staff who bow upon entering and exiting the train car – is a classic Japanese experience.

❶ RIDING THE RAILS

The first thing you need to know about the shinkansen is that you could set your watch by it. It waits for no one. In anticipation of its arrival, passengers form neat, diagonal lines on the platform. Then it glides, nearly soundlessly, into the station. The doors open, passengers file in and before you've had a chance to get yourself settled, it's moving again. You may not have even noticed.

The second thing you need to know about the shinkansen is that it is, somehow, *kawaii* (cute), the same word you might use to describe Hello Kitty (or

any other member of Japan's pantheon of disarming characters). It has an extra-long, sloping nose reminiscent of a platypus. Children love it.

The Hokkaidō Shinkansen, also called Hayabusa (Peregrine Falcon), uses the latest H5 train series, which can travel at up to 200 mph (320 km/h). Within minutes of departure you're out of the city centre, careering through the suburbs, past blocky apartment buildings, and then the exurbs, past family homes surrounded by small farm plots, factories and warehouses. Just when it seems that the spaces between houses is beginning to expand, they start to contract, as the train approaches Sendai, the largest city in Tōhoku, the northern region of Honshū, Japan's main island.

Past Sendai, the train heads deep into rural Tōhoku, considered one of the remotest parts of Japan. In southern Iwate prefecture, about mid-way between Sendai and Morioka, there's a particularly lovely stretch of Japanese countryside, with rice paddies – emerald green in summer, golden in autumn – and traditional wooden farmhouses, called *minka*, identifiable by their massive, sloping roofs. As the train approaches Morioka, hulking mountains appear on the horizon, including the volcano Mt Iwate, nicknamed Nanbu Fuji, because it resembles Mt Fuji.

The Japanese are great tunnel builders, which will soon become apparent. A long spine of mountains runs the length of the country. The shinkansen can only achieve the travels speeds that it does by ploughing right through them. Nearly the entire journey between Morioka and Shin-Aomori is in darkness, with just small, but tantalising, glimpses of forested mountains between tunnels. The crowning achievement is the 33.5-mile (54km) Seikan Tunnel, nearly half of which runs 330ft (100m) under the seabed of the Tsugaru Strait between Honshū and Hokkaidō. (It's bested in length and depth only by the Gotthard Base Tunnel in Switzerland.)

Then, after 20 minutes of darkness, you're among the rolling hills of southern Hokkaidō, trundling along the final leg to Shin-Hakodate-Hokuto. It's the end of the line – for now: work has already started on an extension that will run another 131 miles (211km) to Hokkaidō's capital city, Sapporo, by 2030.

❷ LIFE ON BOARD

The shinkansen has three classes: ordinary, Green (business class) and Gran (1st class). Ordinary is perfectly comfortable, with a 3–2 seat layout; Green

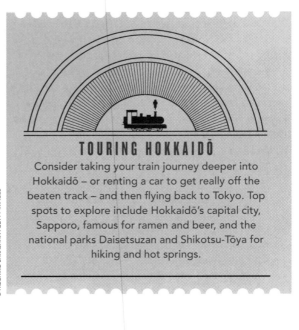

TOURING HOKKAIDŌ

Consider taking your train journey deeper into Hokkaidō – or renting a car to get really off the beaten track – and then flying back to Tokyo. Top spots to explore include Hokkaidō's capital city, Sapporo, famous for ramen and beer, and the national parks Daisetsuzan and Shikotsu-Tōya for hiking and hot springs.

 Pick out your *ekiben* – the boxed lunches (*bentō*) sold at train stations (*eki*) – from kiosks at Tokyo Station.

Sit back in your seat as the train reaches maximum speed just outside of Utsunomiya.

 Take in the views of the northern farm country between Kurikoma Kōgen and Ichinoseki.

Tokyo   **Ōmiya**   **Sendai**

© LOZZY SQUIRE / ALAMY STOCK PHOTO

CLOCKWISE FROM LEFT: The Shinkansen travelling through northern Honshū; in the Gran carriage, free food is made from local specialities; a view of Mt Iwate is a bonus. **PREVIOUS PAGE:** An H5 series Shinkansen bullet train in Hokuto, on Japan's northernmost main island of Hokkaidō.

gives you a little more space with a 2–2 layout; Gran is extra spacious at 2–1. Green and Gran class cars tend to be quieter; Gran goes the extra mile with blankets, slippers and complimentary food made from local specialities. There's no dining car, but train staff come through all classes with food carts regularly, selling sandwiches, crackers, soft drinks and beer. Still, unless you're in Gran, it's better to buy food at Tokyo Station.

❸ OTHER ROUTES

Shinkansen lines run nearly the length of Japan, covering some 1335 miles (2150km). Hakodate is the northern terminus; Kagoshima, on the island of Kyūshū, is the southern terminus. A Japan Rail Pass (www.japanrailpass.net) gives you unlimited use of the shinkansen network for one, two or three weeks – by far the easiest and cheapest way to see the country.

❹ MAKE IT HAPPEN

There are ten to twelve trains a day, departing once or twice an hour in the morning and once every hour or two hours in the afternoon. You can reserve seats online at www.eki-net.com or at a JR East Travel Service Center (www.jreast.co.jp/e). It's possible to request a window or aisle seat when you reserve too.

If you have a Japan Rail Pass, stopovers won't cost extra; otherwise, the single fares between points add up to much more than a direct journey.

Go in June to September for views of green, October to early November for autumn leaves and January to March for snow-covered vistas. July, August and October are peak travel times.

Tokyo Station is large and can be confusing; give yourself plenty of time to figure it out, buy supplies and get to the tracks; trains are *very* punctual. **RM**

Look to your left (on northbound trains) for Mt Iwate as you approach Morioka.

Emerge from the darkness of the Seikan Tunnel into the wide-open landscapes of Hokkaidō.

Morioka　　　　　　　　　　**Shin-Aomori**　　　　　　　　　　**Shin-Hakodate-Hokuto**

The Eastern & Oriental Express

THAILAND, MALAYSIA, SINGAPORE ●

START BANGKOK	
END SINGAPORE	
DEPARTS WEEKLY	DURATION 3 DAYS
DISTANCE 1342 MILES (2160KM)	

Tracing a route between the busy cities of Bangkok and Singapore, the Eastern & Oriental Express is an appealing way to sample the sights of Southeast Asia. Passengers experience a little of everything on the two- to three-night journey: luxurious comfort within finely crafted decor; quality dining with a choice of Asian and European dishes; beautiful scenery as the tropical landscape slips past the train windows; and cultural experiences provided by off-train excursions in both Thailand and Malaysia. If you're happy to dress up for dinner, this rail journey is a genteel way to explore three diverse Asian countries in style.

❶ RIDING THE RAILS

Though it's possible to catch the Eastern & Oriental (E&O) in either direction, there's much to be said for starting your journey at Bangkok's Hualamphong Station. Bustling and atmospheric, this century-old railway station provides an exciting and colourful backdrop for a rail adventure. E&O passengers congregate in a lounge area here, sipping tea before boarding the train.

Though the train's carriages were once part of New Zealand's railways, they've since been thoroughly refurbished and redecorated.

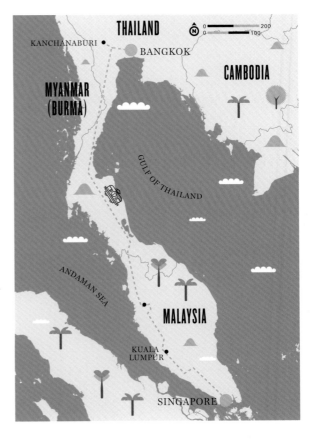

Aboard, there's luxurious decor, with intricate decorative details throughout the dining car, lounge car and piano bar, which are the common domain of passengers. Inlaid wood provides a sheen of elegance, as does Malaysian embroidery and hand-tufted carpets sourced from Thailand.

The individual cabins are similarly pleasing, with timber panelling, art nouveau light fittings, and small but serviceable en suite bathrooms. A final space, the open-sided observation car, comes with its own bar and is a perfect place from which to take photographs unaffected by window reflections.

Dining is a highlight of the experience, though some passengers may be fazed by the requirement to dress for dinner – jacket and tie for men, and similarly elegant outfits for women. It's a requirement that seems to work, however, as this common dressiness adds a touch of glamour to each meal.

Dishes are of a high standard, contemporary and innovative. Given the train carries passengers from around the world, the chefs prepare meals from both European and Asian traditions. For example, a dinner menu may offer a laksa (curry soup with noodles) followed by a choice between braised beef cheek and *ayam rendang biryani* (spicy chicken with rice).

Meals are included in the fare, and comprise afternoon tea, as well as house beers, wines and spirits. Beyond that, passengers can buy more exotic drinks in the piano bar, maybe while crooning along to a Sinatra ditty performed by the resident pianist.

It's not all about on-board luxury. Departing from Bangkok, the first night is spent with the train stationed at Kanchanaburi in Thailand's west. The next morning, passengers can join a tour to the famous Bridge over the River Kwai and learn about the infamous Thai-Burma Railway of World War II; or instead join a local food tour or a cycling tour.

The next day, once the train has passed into Malaysia, there's the opportunity to disembark at the city of Kuala Kangsar. Visiting the Ubudiah Mosque, the Sultan Shah Gallery and the Royal Museum of Perak, passengers learn about the history and culture of this attractive city. Alternatively, there's a choice of two other tours here: one includes a rural village and a rice paddy, the other a plantation and a hilltop hike.

Dinner on the final evening aboard is a highlight, as new acquaintances reflect on the journey and its imminent conclusion. Then the Eastern & Oriental Express slides across the causeway into Singapore's gleaming modern rail terminal, and the dream is sadly over. But you'll always have the memories.

IMAGE COURTESY OF BELMOND

HOTEL OF WRITERS

The Eastern & Oriental Express train shares its name with the Eastern & Oriental Hotel on the Malaysian island of Penang. Established in 1885 during British colonial rule, its elaborate Moorish architecture has played host to many famous authors, including Rudyard Kipling, Noel Coward, Somerset Maugham and Hermann Hesse.

Join travellers, including saffron-robed monks and commuters, at Bangkok's main station.

Visit the Bridge over the River Kwai and reflect on its sombre wartime history.

Take a cycling tour in Kanchanaburi past rice paddies, with a stop at a farm.

Bangkok

Kanchanaburi

CLOCKWISE FROM LEFT: The dining car, where dressing for dinner is de rigeur; taking in the scenery; passing through the pretty River Kwai Bridge Station. **PREVIOUS PAGE:** Live the high life in a luxury cabin.

IMAGES COURTESY OF BELMOND

❷ LIFE ON BOARD

The train is eminently comfortable and the service prompt and efficient, no matter whether you sit in your cabin or join fellow passengers in the common areas. The observation car is great for a breath of fresh air – if you can take the tropical heat.

❸ ALTERNATIVE ROUTES

In the other direction, the Singapore–Bangkok journey offers one less night aboard, and is slightly cheaper. It's also possible to start or end in Kuala Lumpur.

❹ BUDGET ALTERNATIVE

It's possible to travel by rail all the way between Bangkok and Singapore for a fraction of the fare you'd pay to do the E&O trip, though not aboard a single train. For details of how to do it, consult the Man in Seat 61 website (www.seat61.com).

❺ MAKE IT HAPPEN

The Eastern & Oriental express departs approximately weekly, depending on the season. Book via travel agents or www.belmond.com. Most passengers travel one-way, either Bangkok–Singapore or Singapore–Bangkok. The wet season between May and October can be uncomfortably hot and humid, though it's always comfortable aboard.

Entry procedures for Malaysia are handled aboard the train. Most nationalities can enter the three nations visa-free as tourists.

Bring formal wear for evening meals aboard the Eastern & Oriental Express. **TR**

Learn about the royal history of Kuala Kangsar, seat of the Sultan of Perak.

Celebrate your journey with a Singapore Sling at the Long Bar of the Raffles Hotel.

Kuala Kangsar **Kuala Lumpur** **Singapore**

Hong Kong's West Rail Line

CHINA ●

From the urban canyons of Kowloon to the coastal suburb of Tuen Mun, Hong Kong's West Rail (aka 'the magenta line') is a metro ride like no other. Travelling more than 22 miles (35km), it cuts a fishing hook-shaped path through city and countryside. Riders seated on the shiny plastic benches take in the skyscrapers of Tin Shui Wai and the mountain landscape of Tai Mo Shan County Park, the agricultural valley of Yuen Long District and the space-age skyline of Shēnzhèn. All this plus prime people-watching for about US$3.

❶ RIDING THE RAILS

Like most Hong Kong Mass Transit Railway (MTR) stations, vast Hung Hom is filled with shops – bakeries, ramen joints, clothing boutiques – giving it a pleasant scent of cookies and pork. It's also filled with suitcases. Big rolling hard-shells, knock-off Louis Vuittons, and plastic laundry bags stuffed to

START	HUNG HOM
END	TUEN MUN
DEPARTS	DAILY
DISTANCE 22.2 MILES (35.7KM)	DURATION 35 MINS

splitting. Hung Hom is the departure point for trains heading into mainland China, carrying visitors flush with the spoils of Hong Kong shopping trips. People run for their trains, dragging their luggage behind them. Recorded announcements in three languages – Cantonese, Mandarin and English – play on a loop, as yellow-clad MTR employees patrol the concourse. It's chaos, but controlled chaos.

Our destination today is not mainland China, though. It's the far reaches of Hong Kong's New Territories, the mostly rural area in the city's north. To get there we're riding the West Rail, a commuter train line that traverses some of the city's densest urban neighbourhoods and most unspoiled countryside.

After three loud chimes signalling the closing doors, the train rumbles underground for a while. You can't tell, of course, but it's travelling under Tsim Sha Tsui in Kowloon, the teeming peninsula of neon, skyscrapers and squawking taxis that is in many ways Hong Kong's spiritual heart.

The train emerges above ground on the west side of Kowloon, the train car suddenly filled with sunlight. To the east is a blur of residential towers and industrial buildings. To the west is the sea. The train travels along an ocean promenade at Tsuen Wan, where elderly locals practice t'ai chi and toddlers wobble along on plastic scooters. Beyond is the island of Tsing Yi, once a pirate hideaway, its green slopes now lined with high-rise towers and shipyards. Connecting Tsing Yi to the rest of Hong Kong is an impressive cable-stayed bridge, its towers like sails on a giant ship.

Abruptly, the windows go dark again, as the train roars through what feels like an endless mountain tunnel. When it comes out on the other side, the landscape has changed entirely. Now we're in the middle of an enormous flat valley. Gone are the skyscrapers; the buildings that flash by the windows are low-rise 'village houses', built by members of the indigenous groups that inhabit this part of the New Territories. Nearby are several preserved walled villages dating back nearly half a millennium. The best-known is Kat Hing Wai, its thick grey-brick ramparts still home to members of the ancient Tang Clan.

As the train heads into Yuen Long Station, the skyline of the city of Shēnzhèn appears on the horizon, its futuristic towers rising from the green agricultural plain. A sleepy fishing village just 40 years ago, it's now the pulsating heart of China's tech industry.

Equally futuristic is the sight, a bit further on, of Tin Shui Wai, a purpose-built 'New Town' of towering housing blocks so identical they look like a glitch in the matrix. It disappears almost as quickly as it appeared, as the train clacks on to more suburban environs. Coming into Siu Hong you'll pass the Miu Fat Buddhist Monastery Complex, with its huge glass shrine built to resemble a lotus.

MTR

Hong Kong's Mass Transit Railway (MTR) is a marvel of modern efficiency. With more than 124 miles (200km) of rail and 159 stations, its trains are on schedule more than 99% of the time. Each station is a different colour, from pale blues to eye-catching yellows, designed to help illiterate riders get to their destinations.

© JOAN GAMELL | GAMELL | 500PX

☆ Soak up the bustle of energetic Hung Hom Station before your journey.

👢 Weave between the neon lights, taxis and chatty touts of Tsim Sha Tsui, should you choose to disembark.

Watch t'ai chi–practicing grannies, strolling couples and kite-flying kids at Tsuen Wan's promenade.

Hung Hom   **East Tsim Sha Tsui**   **Austin**   **Nam Cheong**   **Mei Foo**   **Tsuen Wan West**

CLOCKWISE FROM LEFT: Shēnzhèn and the Hong Kong skyline; Union Square and Kowloon Station; amid the city's hustle and bustle.
PREVIOUS PAGE: The Hong Kong skyline.

Next up is Tuen Mun, the end of the line. Another New Town, it's a fairly undistinguished jumble of apartment towers, warehouses and malls. But hop off the train and into a taxi, and in 10 minutes you'll be at Sam Shing Hui, a popular local seafood market. Stroll past bubbling tanks of mantis shrimp, alien-like geoduck clams and googly-eyed groupers, taking your pick of what looks good. Cooks at the various seafood stalls will prepare them any way you like.

Fortified, head back to the MTR station for the journey back.

❷ LIFE ON BOARD

This is a commuter metro, so expect hard plastic seats and constant dinging as the doors open and close. That said, it's extremely clean, thanks to strict no-eating and drinking rules. Commuters are not apt to chat, and there's no busking or panhandling, leaving you to gaze out the window in peace.

❸ MAKE IT HAPPEN

Trains depart every three minutes or so from before 6am until after midnight. Buy tickets at the machines in the MTR station, or purchase an Octopus card, a smart card that can be filled with money and used on any form of public transport and in many Hong Kong stores, restaurants and vending machines.

Be sure to avoid travelling during the rush hour, which can last from 7.30 to 9.30 in the morning and from 5 to 7 in the evening. Travelling on a sunny day will offer the best views, but those can be hard to come by some months. And however sunny it is outside, bring a sweater or jacket for the frigid air conditioning inside. **EM**

Zoom through the flat agricultural plains around Kam Sheung Road, home to many indigenous clans.

Admire the glass lotus temple at Miu Fat Buddhist Monastery, especially when it glows at night.

Choose fish from the burbling tanks at the Sam Shing Hui seafood market at the end of the line.

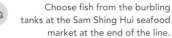

Kam Sheung Road   **Yuen Long**   **Long Ping**   **Tin Shui Wai**   **Siu Hong**   **Tuen Mun**

The Reunification Express

VIETNAM ●

START	HO CHI MINH CITY
END	HANOI
DEPARTS DAILY	DURATION 2 DAYS
DISTANCE 1072 MILES (1726KM)	

Some railways rattle through historic cities; others swoosh beside spectacular coastline. A few have an epic history, one or two are remarkable for the colourful characters on board. The Reunification Express line, also known as the North–South Railway, fulfils all these criteria – Southeast Asia's best-loved railway, its fortunes have waxed and waned with those of the country it traverses. Travelling over a thousand miles from Hanoi in the north to Ho Chi Minh City in the south, there is no more atmospheric way to haul into Vietnam's twin metropolises. And there's no better way of exploring all the glories in between.

❶ RIDING THE RAILS

The story of the North–South Railway is the story of modern Vietnam in microcosm. The railway has its origins in the days of French colonial rule in Indochina – the government promising to build a new 'backbone' that would connect northern and southern portions of their territory. It quickly became caught up in Vietnam's tumultuous 20th-century history. The railway was hijacked by invading Japanese forces in World War II, and soon after formed the front line during the First Indochina War when Viet Minh guerrillas seeking independence from France attacked armoured trains that rolled along the line.

But the most famous chapter in its history came during the Vietnam War, when tanks and artillery were transported along the line, stretches of track were dynamited and countless bridges were bombed. The line was split in two between communist North Vietnam and American-backed South Vietnam. It

"As the neon lights of the city retreat, a mosaic of bucolic landscapes emerges"

became a symbol of national healing and solidarity when the line once again connected Saigon and Hanoi in 1976. Though no particular train officially carries the name, all passenger services along the line have since been known as 'The Reunification Express'.

Ho Chi Minh City is an obvious place to start your journey – though the rather humble-looking station still bears the old name by which the city remains commonly known, 'Sai Gon.' It's set at the heart of Vietnam's most energetic metropolis, close to the principal sights: including the fascinating War Remnants Museum, which displays captured American military hardware from the Vietnam War, and the ornate French-style Ho Chi Minh City Hall.

It's quickly clear there is no better way of studying the soul of Vietnam than by boarding a northbound service from Ho Chi Minh City. For a few miles passengers watch the skyscrapers and neon lights of the city retreat into the distance, and a mosaic of bucolic landscapes emerges: rice paddies, banana groves, pagodas and jagged limestone hills. There's as much colour on board, from the kitchen dispensing piping-hot noodles to the diverse assortment of students, families and suited commuters shuttling on and off at the stations.

Not a few tourists dismount at the raffish seaside resort of Danang and make the short hop onward to Hoi An – a centuries-old trading port, where mustard-yellow merchants' houses look out over the quays. You could easily spend a few days wandering its lantern-lined alleyways and covered bridges, visiting temples where sailors from across Asia once prayed for safe passage on the seas. North of Danang, the line is at its most spectacular. The poetically named Ocean Cloud Pass sees the train

© MATT MUNRO | LONELY PLANET

© MATT MUNRO | LONELY PLANET

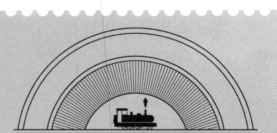

ON TO SA PA

A popular onward route is the Hanoi–Lao Cai line, which snakes northwest from the capital to the verdant mountains along the Chinese border. From Lao Cai, it's a 24-mile (39km) road transfer to the former French hill station of Sa Pa – a breezy town overlooking a landscape of cascading rice terraces.

Go in search of the dining car as the skyscrapers of HCMC disappear from view.

Sunbathe by the South China Sea in resort towns like Nha Trang.

Ho Chi Minh City (Saigon)   **Binh Thuan**   **Nha Trang**   **Dieu Tri**   **Quang Ngai**

CLOCKWISE FROM LEFT: Martyrs' Monument near Hanoi's Hoan Kiem Lake; train drivers enjoy the ride; a woman sells flowers. **PREVIOUS PAGE:** A railway guard on the Reunification Express line.

© MATT MUNRO | LONELY PLANET

skirting cliffs beside the South China Sea, diving in and out of the tunnels as green hills rise above and turquoise waves break far down below.

The royal town of Hue follows soon after – home to fearsome-looking battlements and 19th-century palaces from which a dynasty of kings once ruled over Vietnam. After many hours on board the train, it's a small relief to stretch your legs here, wandering its serene courtyards and gilded throne rooms, and strolling beside moats and beneath ceremonial gateways.

Vinh marks the last big city on the journey north – a handy staging post for those heading to Laos. Keep an eye out as the train crosses the famous Ham Rong bridge soon after at Thanh Hoa – perhaps the most strategically important bridge on the railway during the Vietnam War, it was the target of hundreds of unsuccessful American bombing raids,

contested by countless dogfights in the skies above.

The Reunification Express saves the best for last on its final approach to Hanoi – slicing straight through the chaotic urban sprawl of Asia's most beautiful capital. Rather alarmingly, the tracks form an ad hoc market-turned-pedestrian-walkway when trains aren't running, with stalls and houses standing inches from the rails.

Connecting Vietnam's greatest attractions makes the railway immensely popular with tourists – reliably whisking visitors from the serene pools of Hue to the hectic markets of Ho Chi Minh City, and from the lazy resorts of Nha Trang to the scooter-clogged Old Town of Hanoi. But nonetheless the Reunification Express line is a working railway used every day by ordinary Vietnamese people. True to its name, it still brings together all-comers in this long, slim country.

Take a detour from Danang to the serene lantern-lined streets of Hoi An.

Get your camera ready as the line crosses Ocean Cloud Pass.

Follow in the footsteps of royals among the palaces and fortifications of Hue.

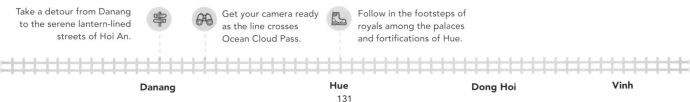

Danang   Hue   Dong Hoi   Vinh

❷ LIFE ON BOARD

Though a number of different types of trains run on the line, classes are broadly divided into four options in ascending order of comfort: hard seat, soft seat, 6-berth hard sleeper and 4-berth soft sleeper. Most foreign tourists opt for soft-sleeper class – this option sees very reasonably priced meals dispensed to your cabin, with a trolley service on hand for snacks and drinks between the meals. Try to bag a seat on the right-hand side travelling north for the best views of Ocean Cloud Pass.

❸ UPGRADES

Privately-run Livitrans and Violette carriages both also run on the Reunification Express line, attached to standard-service trains. Marginally more luxurious than the 4-berth soft sleeper service, they're popular with foreign tourists, offering air-conditioning and complimentary snacks (www.livitrans.com, www.violetexpresstrain.com).

❹ MAKE IT HAPPEN

There are four or five northbound and southbound departures daily, mostly leaving in the early morning and early evening. Different trains have different class options – trains SE1, 2, 3 and 4 are the most comfortable. Bao Lau (www.baolau.com) or 12Go Asia (www.12go.asia) are among the tour operators that can book tickets – in order to stop off in such places as Hue and Danang, you'll need to make multiple bookings. Trains run year-round, but during Vietnamese New Year (Tet) can be incredibly busy.

As Hanoi and Ho Chi Minh City are served by numerous international flights, many visitors fly into one city, make a one-way journey on the Reunification Express and depart from the other. Many nationalities will need to obtain a visa to enter Vietnam. **OS**

Breathe in as the train squeezes through narrow alleyways approaching Hanoi.

Thanh Hoa   **Ninh Binh**   **Hanoi**

Hugging the coast of the South China Sea just north of Hai Van Pass, between Hue and Hoi An.

Mandalay to Lashio

MYANMAR (BURMA)

START **MANDALAY**

END **LASHIO**

DEPARTS **DAILY**

DISTANCE **125 MILES (201KM)**

DURATION **15 HRS**

The Myanmar's colonial-era railways may be creaking under the weight of time, but that's rather the appeal. The hill railway cutting northeast from Mandalay rattles and shakes across the precarious Gokteik Viaduct, defying the centuries above a seemingly bottomless valley, on its way from the British-era hill station of Pyin Oo Lwin to Lashio, the wartime terminus of the Burma Road. To ride these well-polished rails is to travel through time as well as geography, as colonial bungalows, hill-tribe villages and forest monasteries flash by in a sea of jungle foliage.

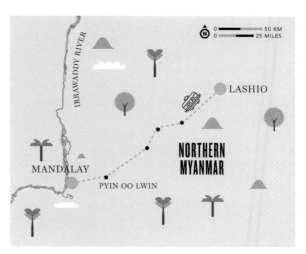

● RIDING THE RAILS

The bone-rattling ride from Mandalay to Lashio begins, as all great rail journeys should, before dawn. Travellers start the day sipping Burmese tea beneath lurid strip-lights, before rumbling out into the darkest-before-dawn blackness. But it doesn't stay dark for long. Sleepy villages and backwater stations tumble by as the light turns slowly grey, then golden, as the sun tips over the horizon.

Sunrise coincides with the departure from the plains to the hills, and the clackety-clack of wheels on rails gets louder as the train starts its slow ascent to Pyin Oo Lwin, erstwhile summer capital of British-

governed Burma. By the time the train rolls into the tin-roofed station at Pyin, passengers are shaken like soda cans by the side-to-side motion of the train and the wind rushing in through the open windows.

Perfect timing, in fact, for a platform breakfast of Pyin Oo Lwin strawberries, samosas, rice wrapped in banana leaves, or *e kya kway* – Chinese-style cruller doughnuts – washed down with condensed-milk-sweetened tea. It would be a shame not to stop for the night to soak up the atmosphere of this British-era fantasy of mock-Tudor mansions, faux-Gothic churches, horse-drawn 'wagons' and rolling flower gardens.

The journey as far as Pyin Oo Lwin is just a warm-up, as far as adventure goes, for the journey onwards towards Lashio. To reach Hsipaw, the next landmark on the journey, the train has to cross a plunging gorge on the Gokteik Viaduct – a marvel of colonial-era engineering 335ft (102m) above the valley floor, made even more remarkable by the fact that it's still standing after more than a century with minimal maintenance.

American engineers erected the 2260ft (689m) span in 1901 using American-milled steel, riveted together into a curving sweep not much wider than the train tracks it supports. The tall struts of this mighty railway bridge loom into view long before the train begins the tentative journey out across the abyss. Don't be alarmed by the apprehensive creep of the train, or the creaks, tings and rattles from below – the bridge was given a clean bill of health a mere 20 years ago, so concentrate instead on the inspiring views.

Chasm crossed, you can sit back and enjoy the scenery, scanning the forests and villages for stepped monastery roofs and golden *zedis* (stupas). From the market town of Kyaukme, the line cuts northeast to Hsipaw, one-time capital of the last Shan sky prince. Now a laid-back provincial town with a low-key traveller scene, Hsipaw is surrounded by teak monasteries, hill-tribe villages and clusters of ruined stupas partly reclaimed by the jungle.

For the last leg, the line brushes the riverbanks, passing scattered forest cascades. The number of foreign passengers drops markedly, and you may be the only tourist disembarking at the dusty platform in Lashio. The Chinese influence on the town is obvious from the black-market imports piled up in the bazaar and the sweeping eaves of the Quan Yin Taoist temple, and the British also left their indelible stamp in the form of churches, mosques, Hindu temples and Sikh gurdwaras. Alcohol is sold locally by the 'peg' (large shot), the perfect way to toast the end of one of Asia's most atmospheric rail journeys.

❷ LIFE ON BOARD

Creature comforts are limited on Burmese trains; it's worth paying the extra pennies for a padded upper-class seat (complete with an antimacassar to keep your hair cream from darkening the upholstery), rather than bumping your saddle-bones on the slatted wooden seats in ordinary class. In either class you get windows that open to the world, offering front-row seats onto the passing scenery.

© THIERRY FALISE | GETTY IMAGES

© ULLSTEIN BILD | GETTY IMAGES

HSIPAW'S SKY PRINCES

Hsipaw was once the capital of an independent princely state, ruled by a *sawbwa* (sky prince), but the kingdom was absorbed into British Burma. After falling foul of the Burmese junta over access to the area's rich gem deposits, the last *sawbwa*, Sao Kya Seng, vanished in 1962, but his descendants still reside in the family palace, a colonial-style mansion.

Mandalay, Myanmar's northern capital, is ringed by sacred Buddhist sites, attracting legions of Burmese pilgrims.

Pyin Oo Lwin is a charming colonial cast-off, stuffed with British-era architecture.

Gokteik Viaduct is a marvel of engineering, balanced precariously over a plunging gorge.

Mandalay

Pyin Oo Lwin

Gokteik

CLOCKWISE FROM ABOVE: Buying some supplies; chilling in a carriage; the Gokteik Viaduct. **PREVIOUS PAGE:** Pyin Oo Lwin Station on the Mandalay–Lashio line.

❸ MAKE IT HAPPEN

The train from Mandalay to Lashio runs once daily year-round, leaving early in the morning and arriving in the evening in both directions. Tickets can be purchased in person at the train stations, ideally a couple of days in advance (bring your passport). In smaller towns, station staff are sometimes reluctant to sell tickets to foreigners; finding the stationmaster will normally help ease things along. A basic meal service operates in upper class; in ordinary class, hawkers buzz along the carriages selling fruit and packed lunches. Confirm train times locally as schedules are often altered at short notice to fit around curfews. **JB**

Once the capital of a Shan kingdom, Hsipaw is now a laid-back traveller centre circled by tribal villages and monasteries.

The British left an intriguing melting pot of Taoist, Christian, Muslim, Hindu and Sikh influences in Lashio.

Nawngpeng   Kyaukme   Hsipaw   Lashio

Baikal–Amur Mainline (BAM)

RUSSIA

START **TAYSHET**

END **SOVETSKAYA GAVAN**

DEPARTS **DAILY**

DISTANCE **2687 MILES (4324KM)**

DURATION **4 DAYS OR MORE**

Here's a question that would confound even ardent railway anoraks. Which line runs through over 2500 miles (4320km) of Siberian wilderness, connects remote settlements where temperatures sink to -60°C (-76°F) in winter and was envisaged as the greatest construction project in the history of the Soviet Union? The Trans-Siberian? Nope, it's the Baikal–Amur Mainline, better known as the BAM – the rogue sibling of the infinitely more famous railway to the south. Built the better part of a century

after the Trans-Sib, the BAM is colder, remoter and traverses scenery that is every bit as spectacular, but its rails are travelled by barely any tourists.

❶ RIDING THE RAILS

The BAM is a journey to be attempted only by black-belt railway fans. Its pleasures, to the eyes of many, verge on the perverse. Lying cocooned in a small cabin for 36 hours straight. Gazing out the window at infinite birch forests without the vaguest indication of human presence. Disembarking at desolate stations where the crippling winter cold can freeze the liquid on your eyeballs. Enduring hangovers of metaphysical proportions after long nights knocking back vodka with fellow passengers.

To fully appreciate the BAM, however, you need to understand its extraordinary and bizarre history. Construction began in the 1970s, ordered by a Soviet leadership keen to open up mineral-rich corners

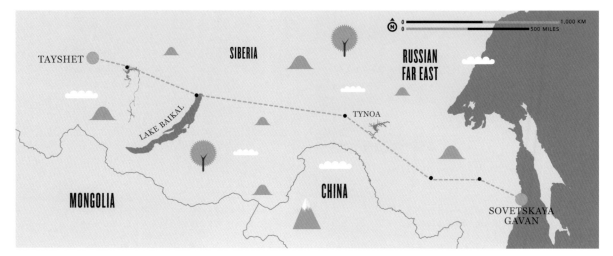

© PHILIP LEE HARVEY | LONELY PLANET

CLOCKWISE FROM RIGHT: Sunset in Siberia; mosaic remnant of the USSR; a Soviet steam engine left to rust; Baikalskoe village near Severobaikalsk.
PREVIOUS PAGE: The BAM presses on.

of Siberia. They planned to create a new communist utopia in the virgin territory of Russia's wild east. But things didn't go to plan: permafrost warped the rails, volunteer railway builders absconded (bathtub-brewed booze is often cited as a factor). Many of the purpose-built model towns along the line are largely uninhabited. To its detractors, the BAM has been a 2500-mile (4023km) white elephant ever since it opened in 1991, after the fall of the Soviet Union. But to its fans, it is a pioneering railway and continues to be a lifeline for some of the most remote communities on Earth.

The BAM begins in earnest at Tayshet, before crossing the top of the Bratsk Dam, home to one of the world's largest hydroelectric power stations. On the morning of the second day, the train hauls into the town of Severobaikalsk, set in a lofty mountain range on the northern shore of Lake Baikal, close to many thermal springs. In winter, you can watch ice fishers driving over the frozen surface of the lake, while in summer it's easy to take a day trip to timber-built fishing villages along the shore.

From Severobaikalsk, the line skirts the northern shore of Lake Baikal on its overnight journey to Tynda, the so-called capital of the BAM. Like other towns along the line, Tynda has a number of Soviet artworks dedicated to the heroics of railway builders – most notably a giant hammer-wielding silver statue that looks as if it might have strayed from the world of Marvel Comics.

The last major city is Komsomolsk-na-Amure, which is set on the banks of the Amur River, not far from the Pacific Coast. It's known for its abundance of neoclassical architecture and its troubled past as a centre of Stalin's gulags – the Soviet prison system that once extended right across the east of Russia. But like all other towns on the BAM, it's not a place

© PHILIP LEE HARVEY | LONELY PLANET

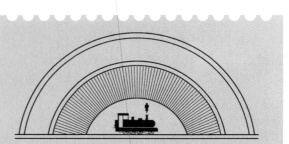

THE RAILWAY OF YOUTH

Constructing the line was largely a project of the Komsomol – the youth wing of the USSR. BAM museums in Severobaikalsk and Tynda give you a sense of what it was like for the ardent young comrades. It wasn't all hard work, though: volunteers also staged rock festivals and sports competitions in their downtime.

Cross the hulking concrete mass of the Bratsk Dam and gaze out at the so-called Bratsk Sea.

Swerve among snowy mountains as you approach the northern shore of Lake Baikal.

Soothe train-weary limbs in the thermal springs outside Severobaikalsk.

Tayshet
Bratsk
Severobaikalsk

for conventional sightseeing, and international visitors are rather thin on the ground.

Like all of the great railways, the true appeal of the BAM is the journey rather than the destination: watching endless birch forests slip past, sharing a cabin with passengers who are genuinely surprised to see outsiders, falling asleep each night to the clanking of the rails and the whistling of the wind.

❷ LIFE ON BOARD

BAM trains are predominantly divided between two classes. In the *kupe* class, carriages are divided into four-berth compartments where the couchettes fold down to form seats during the day. *Platskartny* consists of open-plan dormitory style coaches. Note that Russian Railways' 1st class (*spalny vagon*) is rarely available on BAM services. It's worth bringing an emergency supply of instant noodles, as meal times on the train can be erratic. Always be sure to make friends with the *provodnitsa* – the carriage attendant

tasked with stripping your bedding, serving meals and keeping the samovar hot.

Bear in mind that station signs are generally not marked in Roman letters, so brush up on Cyrillic if you don't want to miss your stop at Северобайка́льск.

❸ MAKE IT HAPPEN

Travelling the BAM requires serious advance planning. Trains are slow, departures are irregular (daily or else less frequent) and to get from one end of the line to the other you'll need to factor in connections between at least three services. Although it's feasible to travel end-to-end on the BAM in roughly four days, it's worth allowing eight days to fully appreciate the stops along the route. BAM runs year-round. In winter, be sure to pack lots of cold-weather clothing.

It's possible to book tickets for the service online through the Russian Railways website (eng.rzd.ru). Many visitors to Russia will need to obtain a visa to enter the country. **OS**

🚊 Admire the bizarre modernist architecture of BAM stations: Tynda's looks a bit like a spaceship.

⭐ Spend hours trying to figure out the heating as the temperature fluctuates between roasting hot and freezing cold.

👢 Wander among the neoclassical buildings of Komsomolsk – a mini St Petersburg on the Amur River.

Tynda   Novy Urgal   Komsomolsk-na-Amure   Sovetskaya Gavan

The Běijīng to Lhasa Express

CHINA

START BĚIJĪNG		
END LHASA		
DEPARTS **DAILY**	DURATION	**40 HRS**
DISTANCE 2330 MILES (3750KM)		

Linking the futuristic architecture and imperial wonders of Běijīng with the dreamlike monasteries and palaces of Lhasa, the Z21 train transports its passengers from the neon lights of urban China to a once-remote land of magenta-robed monks, where the air is heady with the aroma of incense and yak-butter candles. As it chugs westward the train climbs nearly 16,400ft (5000m) on its journey to the roof of the world: the Tibetan plateau, where it glides past grazing yaks, fluttering prayer flags, snow-capped mountains and boundless blue skies. On board, passengers slurp noodles and play cards with their bunkmates.

❶ RIDING THE RAILS

Not far from the city of Lánzhōu in Gānsu Province, the train trundles past jagged, sandstone mountains, their lower slopes carved up into a patchwork of

paddy terraces. Overnight the train has left the bright lights of Běijīng far behind. Here, just south of the Gobi Desert, hamlets of houses with mud walls and tiled roofs are interspersed with stacks of hay bales and ox-drawn carts; only satellite dishes place the scene firmly in the 21st century.

By late afternoon the train pulls into the city of Xīníng, which sits at an altitude of 7464ft (2275m) on the eastern edge of the Qīnghǎi-Tibet plateau. There's just enough time to jump out to buy snacks at the station, inhale the cool, thin air and look out for the traditional clothes and distinctive hats of the city's sizeable Tibetan population. From Xīníng, the climb up onto and across the permafrost-covered Tibetan plateau begins.

The gleaming, state-of-the-art train is well-equipped for the extremities of the journey: the windows have a UV coating to protect passengers from the intensity of the sun's rays at high altitude and oxygen is pumped into the carriages. Each carriage is manned by a

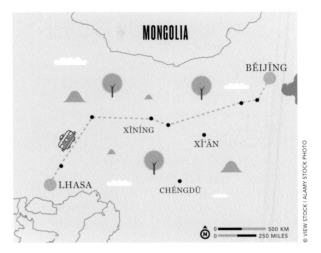

"Stupas surrounded by colourful prayer flags and the white tents of nomads come into view"

uniformed guard, whose peaked cap stays in place throughout the two-day journey. Passengers watch films on their tablets and eat snacks as the train makes its ascent through the desolate, moon-like landscape.

Soon the scenery switches as Qīnghǎi Lake comes into view, the reflective surface of the salt water mirroring the sky. By the time the train pulls into Golmud Station night has fallen. The next section of track was the most challenging to build; construction workers had to contend with low temperatures of -45°C (-49°F), the unstable permafrost surface, and the shortage of oxygen at altitudes of up to 16,400ft (5000m) above sea level. A feat of modern engineering, it is the highest railway in the world. On board, the temperature is kept comfortably warm and the ride is remarkably smooth.

As the train moves through the darkness, the restaurant car fills up. Tasty Chinese fare is served at Formica tables, decorated with a cheery vase of pink plastic flowers. It's a sociable place, where passengers swig beers and chat into the night.

Daylight breaks the following morning to reveal the snow-capped peaks of the Tanggula Mountains as the train approaches the highest point of the journey: the Tanggula Pass, which sits at 16,640ft (5072m) above sea level. As the train descends, yaks can be spotted grazing in the lush green grasslands, and soon gold-topped stupas surrounded by colourful prayer flags and the white tents of nomads come into view. Next the track passes alongside the mesmerising, luminous blue waters of Namsto Lake, a sacred site for people of the Tibet region.

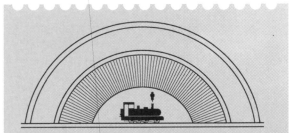

RAILWAY TO THE ROOF OF THE WORLD

Construction of the 710-mile (1142km) stretch of track from Golmud to Lhasa, completed in 2006, posed numerous challenges, being laid on unstable permafrost at high altitude. With the help of bottled oxygen, it took 100,000 engineers and construction workers four years to complete the project, at a cost of US$4.2 billion.

© PHILIP YUAN | SHUTTERSTOCK

Fight through the crowds at frenetic Beijing West Station then watch the city lights disappear into the night.

Gaze at the arid landscape of dusty peaks as the train chugs onwards to Lanzhou.

| Běijīng (West) | Shíjiāzhuāng | Tàiyuán | Zhōngwèi | Lánzhōu |

CLOCKWISE FROM LEFT: The
Potala Palace in Lhasa; the picturesque
landscape of the Nyenchen Tanglha
Mountains. **PREVIOUS PAGE:**
Racing across the Tibetan plateau.

Finally, the train approaches Lhasa, and high above
the city the white and magenta tiers of the Potala
Palace, the former residence of the Dalai Lama, can be
seen. The sight evokes the wonder of this seemingly
fantastical land.

❷ LIFE ON BOARD

The train has three classes: the crowded, 'hard-seat'
compartments with rows of cushioned upright seats;
the six-bed 'hard-sleeper' compartments consisting
of three-tiered bunks with thin mattresses, and the
more luxurious, four-bed compartments of the 'soft-
sleeper' class. Hot water is available for preparing
instant noodles and tea; if you want something more
substantial, the train has a restaurant car.

❸ MAKE IT HAPPEN

Trains depart Běijīng West at 8pm daily. Tickets in
soft-sleeper and hard-sleeper class can be booked
through www.chinatibettrain.com. Stopping for
a day in Xīníng can help with acclimatisation.
The best times to visit Tibet are April to June and
October to February. From late February to early
April, Tibet is usually closed to foreign visitors, due
to sensitive anniversaries, and train tickets can be
hard to come by in July and August.
   In addition to a valid Chinese visa, tourists
require a Tibet Tourism Bureau (TTB) permit to
enter Tibet. To get this you must book a guide for
your trip. Contact a Tibet-based agency four to six
weeks in advance and they will arrange the permit
for you. See www.thelandofsnows.com for the latest
information. **IA**

© HFZIMAGES | SHUTTERSTOCK

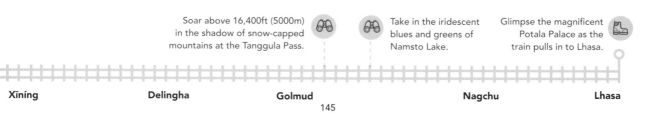

Soar above 16,400ft (5000m)
in the shadow of snow-capped
mountains at the Tanggula Pass.

Take in the iridescent
blues and greens of
Namsto Lake.

Glimpse the magnificent
Potala Palace as the
train pulls in to Lhasa.

Xīníng   Delingha   Golmud   Nagchu   Lhasa

The Death Railway

THAILAND

Thailand's Death Railway is a beautiful line with a dark history. In 1942 thousands of Allied Prisoners of War (PoWs) were brought to Thailand by their Japanese captors and forced to build a railway line through dense jungle into Burma. With meagre rations, arbitrary punishments and brutal working conditions, thousands of British, Australian, Indian, Malaysian and other workers perished – their struggles recounted in such movies as The Bridge on the River Kwai. Remarkably, a portion of the line they built remains in service today, with trains striking west from Bangkok into landscapes of sluggish rivers, rolling hills and thick forests. A ride on the Death Railway is, for many passengers, a tribute to the lives that were lost.

❶ RIDING THE RAILS

Today's Death Railway is a rather unassuming operation – a workaday railway with wooden seats,

START **BANGKOK**	
END **NAM TOK**	
DEPARTS **DAILY**	DURATION **4 HRS 40 MINS**
DISTANCE **120 MILES (193KM)**	

creaking carriages, whirring ceiling fans and notional timetables. The first stretch sees trains departing Bangkok's Thonburi Station for Kanchanaburi town – almost three hours to the west. Tourists are scarce during this section of the trip, with Buddhist monks, students and commuters among those embarking and disembarking at tidy little stations. The view out of the window turns from suburbs to rustic stilt-houses, verdant rice paddies, golden temples and country roads where tuk-tuks race the train beside the tracks.

Kanchanaburi was the staging post from which many prisoners of war were dispatched to labour camps deep in the jungle, and is the place to hop off if you want to learn more about the Death Railway's role in World War II. Close to the station, the excellent Thailand-Burma Railway Centre has exhibits on the line's construction – from its origins as a means for the Japanese to reinforce their front line against the British in neighbouring Burma, to its eventual closure in 1947. Artefacts tell the story of everyday PoW life

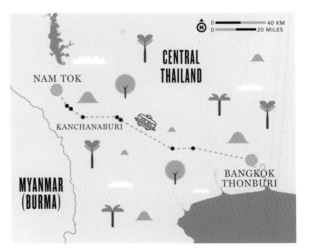

> "This is a railway of paradoxes: of beautiful scenery, tragic history and amazing feats of engineering'

too, from the meagre tools used to excavate cuttings and build bridges, to the secret improvised radios with which service officers tried to stay in touch with the outside world. The neighbouring War Cemetery also bears witness to those who died of exhaustion, malnutrition and disease while working on the line.

Kanchanaburi's headline attraction is the real-life 'Bridge on the River Kwai' – a hulking iron structure on the edge of town, bombed by the Allies during the war. Its connection to the Hollywood film is tenuous: David Lean's 1957 epic movie was filmed entirely on location in Sri Lanka, and is based on a novel written by an author who never came to Thailand. Nonetheless, after crossing the span, the railway becomes more spectacular. Thickly forested hills and limestone monoliths rise up on all sides as the train clatters through shadowy bamboo groves, and the scent of jasmine wafts through open windows.

The grand finale is the Wang Pho viaduct – where the railway shimmies over a rickety bridge, precariously poised between a vertical cliff and the Khwae Noi (River Kwai). The end of the line today is at Nam Tok, two hours on from Kanchanaburi, where everyone dismounts next to a rusting steam engine near a little waterfall. From here, it's also possible to walk along some of the original course of the line northwest to the Burmese border – much of it long since reclaimed by the jungle – or strike out to nearby national parks.

This is a railway of paradoxes: of beautiful scenery and tragic history, and amazing feats of engineering born of great suffering. And though known to many as the Death Railway, this is very much a living line.

THE DEATH RAILWAY IN LITERATURE AND FILM

A somewhat more realistic portrayal than the iconic but flawed *The Bridge on the River Kwai* is fomer PoW Eric Lomax's excellent memoir *The Railway Man*, with a 2013 film adaptation starring Colin Firth. Best of all is Richard Flanagan's outstanding 2014 Man Booker Prize–winning novel *The Narrow Road to the Deep North*.

© DEA I C. SAPPA I GETTY IMAGES

☆ Haul out of Bangkok and bag a seat before the crowds board at Kanchanaburi.

Get to grips with Death Railway history at Kanchanaburi's excellent Thailand-Burma Railway Centre.

 Hop aboard a boat and drift down the Khwae Noi during a stopover at Kanchanaburi.

Bangkok (Thonburi)   **Nakhon Pathom**   **Nong Pladuk junction**   **Kanchanaburi**

CLOCKWISE FROM LEFT: Monks walk the track; the tranquil waters of Kanchanaburi belie a bloody history; the colourful train on a typically rickety bridge. PREVIOUS PAGE: Crossing the famous River Kwai bridge.

❷ LIFE ON BOARD

Bangkok–Nam Tok trains consist of 3rd-class carriages only, but are all comfortable. No on-board food is served, though you may find hawkers selling snacks at some of the busier stations. Be sure to sit on the left-hand side when travelling from Bangkok to Nam Tok – the views are especially good from the Wang Pho viaduct.

❸ UPGRADES

While standard Death Railway trains are no-frills affairs, the Nam Tok line is occasionally visited by the luxurious Eastern & Oriental Express. This private train makes a detour onto the line as part of its journey from Singapore to Bangkok, via Kuala Lumpur (www.belmond.com; see page 117).

❹ MAKE IT HAPPEN

Two trains depart Bangkok Thonburi for Nam Tok daily. Note that Thonburi is not to be confused with Hualamphong – Bangkok's main railway terminus. Bangkok–Nam Tok trains cannot be booked online. It's easy to book a train on the day at Thonburi Station.

It's possible to do the return journey as a day trip, leaving the capital in the (very) early morning and returning in the late afternoon, but if you're not pushed for time, be sure to overnight in Kanchanaburi. The best time to visit is between November and April. Many visitors to Thailand will need a visa to enter the country. OS

Try not to look down while crossing the Wang Pho viaduct, a spectacular example of trestle-bridge engineering.

Go in search of abandoned portions of the line after disembarking at Nam Tok.

Kwai Bridge   Thakilen   Thamkrasae Bridge   Wang Pho   Nam Tok

Colombo to Badulla

SRI LANKA

START	COLOMBO FORT	
END	BADULLA	
DEPARTS	DAILY	DURATION 9-10 HRS
DISTANCE 181 MILES (292KM)		

 One of many unforgettable things about Sri Lanka is the variety and intensity of the colour green. Fortunately for train aficionados, there is no better way to appreciate the country's full verdant spectrum than an all-day rail journey from urban gardens at sea level to tea plantations in the Hill Country via brain-spinning sensory doses of jungle and forest, paddy field and palm tree, mountain and valley, national parks…and human habitation too. This is no showcase for speed or high tech, though. Instead, it is a slow case for enjoying one of the most scenic train trips in the world.

❶ RIDING THE RAILS

From beginning to end, this railway line is historic. Starting at its terminus in Colombo's 100-year-old Fort Railway Station, it traces the tracks of the first train line in the country, which began as a 33.5-mile (54km) stretch inaugurated in 1864. It was extended in stages, and through important railway engineering feats, finally reached Badulla in 1924. It is still in active use today. The journey can be divided into five parts: the flatlands, three climbs, and a descent.

The flatlands: from Colombo to Rambukanna,

travellers adjust to the jouncing clatter of the train, sometimes broken by whistle-stops at little stations.

The climb, part one: after Rambukanna, a single track climbs toward the royal capital and cultural city of Kandy, easing through dozens of cuttings, diving into the first of 43 tunnels and even clinging to a cliff face between Balana and Kadugannawa. The new blue trains travel all the way to Kandy, reversing direction to depart. Older trains discharge Kandy passengers at Peradeniya Junction and then carry on.

The climb, part two: this is when the swirls and whorls of the tea plantations kick in. The train passes through rolling hills atop frozen waves of green flecked by colourfully clad tea pickers. The plantations remain constant companions – best seen from the right side of the train – through such market centres as Gampola and Nawalapitiya on the way to Hatton, the principal tea hub and a gateway to the sacred mountain and pilgrimage site of Adam's Peak. The steepest section is between Galboda and Nanu Oya,

the jumping-off station for visits to nearby Nuwara Eliya, a celebrated upcountry colonial hill station.

The climb, part three: using the highest broad-gauge tracks in the world, the final ascent continues as far as Pattipola, the loftiest railway station in Sri Lanka (6207ft/1892m above sea level) and best point of access to Horton Plains National Park, site of the World's End precipice and views.

The descent: from Pattipola, it is pretty much downhill all the way to Badulla, with astounding views of Uva Province to the north (out to the left) and breathtaking infinity vistas far out to the south from such ridge-top saddles as Haputale. The remarkable Nine Arch Viaduct and Demodara Loop come shortly after departing the Ella Railway Station.

All along the way, thrill-seekers will notice the locals' penchant for hanging out of train cars, especially on sweeping turns or when passing over any of the hundreds of bridges. Taking great care, it is worth a try, especially for photographers staging incredible shots.

It's worth noting that anyone journeying on a ticket covering more than 50 miles (80km) is entitled to break the trip at intermediate stations for 24 hours. There is no penalty other than needing to make new reservations for the next day's train.

❷ LIFE ON BOARD

The most coveted reservations are in the once-daily, 1st-class observation car, where the seats face backward through large rear-facing windows towards the retreating scenery. Although there is no air-conditioning, the side windows open for both ventilation and photography.

The 2nd- and 3rd-class reserved cars of the new blue trains are comfortable and even arguably preferable to the air-conditioned 1st-class cars, whose windows are small and often grubby. Meanwhile, unreserved cars are a true cultural experience – hot and usually packed to the rafters, but great for

meeting locals and hanging out of the doors.

As there is limited or no food on board, local vendors patrol the corridors with such delicious treats as sliced fruit, chilli fritters, papadums, and fresh rice and curry packets.

❸ UPGRADES

Although neither luxury service over this route is currently in operation, both Expo Rail (www.exporail. lk) and Rajadhani Express (www.rajadhani.lk) expect to recommence...eventually. Previously, they attached special carriages to trains operated by Sri Lanka Railways, but marketed their premium services – such as wi-fi (both) and at-seat dining (Expo Rail only) – as separate businesses.

❹ MAKE IT HAPPEN

There are three daily departures before 10am and one in the evening: two modern blue-coloured trains,

ENGINEERING FEATS
Technical achievements include the famous Nine Arch Viaduct at Gotuwala and the Demodara Loop, where the track spirals back under itself to attenuate a steep gradient. The 3819ft (1164m) ascent in 34 miles (54km) from Galboda to Nanu Oya is one of the world's steepest 'adhesion' (ie non-cog) railway lines.

After 2500 years of monarchy, Kandy is the country's final royal capital and its cultural heart.

Hatton is a principal upcountry tea hub, and gateway to Adam's Peak and Sinharaja National Park.

Colombo Fort　　　　**Rambukkana**　　　　**Kandy**　　**Hatton**

one classic set with the rear observation car, and one sleeper.

Reserved seats or berths in all classes and the observation car are available up to 30 days in advance, either directly at stations or, for a fee, via recommended online agencies such as www.visitsrilankatours.co.uk.

It is wise to book well ahead, as the best seats often sell out quickly. Tickets for 2nd- and 3rd-class unreserved cars are available at the station on the day of departure. Should Expo Rail and/or Rajadhani Express reappear, they can be booked online (see Upgrades, facing page).

The blue trains and most sleepers have only limited buffet counters, so although vendors patrol corridors proffering treats, it's a good idea to pack lots of food and water, particularly if you're planning to break your trip with some hiking in the hills. **EG**

CLOCKWISE FROM TOP LEFT: Heading to Kandy through tea plantations; marketing posters make great souvenirs; a pensive passenger looks out. **PREVIOUS PAGES:** A plantation worker picking tea; crossing the Nine Arch Viaduct near Ella.

The highest railway station in Sri Lanka, Pattipola is the jumping-off point for Horton Plains.

Ella is a tourist favourite for hikeable hills, waterfalls and views of the Nine Arch Viaduct.

The Demodara Loop spiral railway is considered a civil engineering marvel.

Nanu Oya　　　**Pattipola**　　　**Ella**　　　**Badulla**

The Nilgiri Mountain Railway

INDIA

START **METTUPALAYAM**

END **OOTY (UDHAGAMANDALAM)**

DEPARTS **DAILY**

DISTANCE **28.5 MILES (46KM)**

DURATION **4.5 HRS**

There's a hint of steam-punk about India's only rack railway, which climbs into the spice-scented Nilgiri Hills on clockwork cogs and pinions. Unesco-listed since 2005, the train journey from Mettupalayam to Ooty (Udhagamandalam) is a tropical classic, sliding through the lush, green highlands where British colonials fled to escape the heat of the plains. What it lacks in Himalayan views, compared with, say, the Darjeeling Toy Train or Shimla's Himalayan Queen, it makes up for in precarious bridge crossings, sweeping vistas, lavish greenery… and the giddy nostalgia of old-fashioned steam power.

❶ RIDING THE RAILS

Beating a trail from the tropical plains to the cool, calm hills of Tamil Nadu, the Nilgiri Mountain Railway ticks all the boxes for a classic Indian train journey. You want steam power? You got it. Mountain scenery? It comes with the territory. Metre gauge? Absolutely. There's even a whiff of spiced Indian chai in the air, from the abundant tea and spice plantations in the Nilgiri Hills.

Covering just 28.5 miles (46km) between Mettupalayam and Ooty, the mountain railway might seem like an awful lot of work for such a short journey, if only from an engineering perspective. The steepest railway in Asia was pushed through dense tropical jungles, with sections of track angled uphill at a grade of 8.33%. Only four railways in the world have a steeper pitch, and none of those had to deal with monsoon downpours, malaria and tigers.

So what was it that drove this particular piece of locomotive madness? The damnable heat, of course. Being more acclimatised to the tepid temperature of summer in Britain, the officials of the Madras Presidency wilted like tea leaves during the hot, sticky monsoon, fleeing for the green cool of the Nilgiri Hills between May and October every year. And to service their insatiable appetite for tea on the veranda, plantations spread around such hill towns as Ooty and Coonoor like algal blooms, producing south India's most refined brews.

Today, you're more likely to be joined on the train from Mettupalayam by legions of newly-weds. Fuelled by more than 200 Bollywood films set in Tamil Nadu's green and pleasant hills, the train ride to Ooty has become a magnet for Indian honeymooners seeking romance in the temperate highlands. Any foreigners along for the ride can expect regular requests to pose for snaps for the wedding album.

Despite the crowds, and the rather smoggy nature of downtown Ooty, there's an undeniable romance to the journey uphill from the plains. From the anonymous junction town of Mettupalayam, the line climbs through increasingly verdant scenery – beginning among palm trees and ending amid tea plantations – and the air becomes pleasantly cooler, as you relive the journey taken by a veritable army of Raj officials and Indian staff.

But what dials the romance up to 10 is the fleet of X Class steam locomotives that push – not pull – the carriages uphill from Mettupalayam to Coonoor. These venerable engines have been in service for close to eight decades, and, although they only serve part of the route, they provide a chugging soundtrack and scent of soot that will have train enthusiasts dropping to their knees in praise. Just one blast of the steam whistle makes the painstakingly slow progress uphill all seem worthwhile.

The steam engines emerge from their sheds like smoking dragons before being hitched to the passenger carriages, but even these mighty locos need help on the challenging mountain inclines. Between the 2m-gauge tracks is a third toothed rail that engages with a cog beneath the train, adding extra muscle to the uphill surge. Stops to check the pinions and refill the water tanks provide extra photo opportunities for rail (and hill) fanatics.

But let's return to the scenery for a moment. Imagine tinkling cascades in jungle glades and hillsides etched into tattoo swirls by emerald tea plantations. Picture narrow, dark tunnels and rushing streams crossed by curving, rusted rail bridges that seem all the more precarious because of the stick-thin, metre-gauge tracks. Then later in the journey, imagine the oohs and aahs as the landscape opens up and the true scale of the Nilgiri Hills becomes apparent.

© CORNFIELD | SHUTTERSTOCK

© RAJESH NARAYANAN | SHUTTERSTOCK

FORGED IN SWITZERLAND

It's rather pleasing to note that India's only cog railway uses bona fide Swiss technology. When the British constructed the rail line to Ooty in 1908, they turned to the industry expert, the Swiss Locomotive and Machine Works of Winterthur, which was the company that built Europe's first mountain-climbing railway in 1871.

Arrive early at Mettupalayam to watch the steam engine being hitched to the passenger cars.

The stretch of track from Kallar to Hillgrove snakes through tunnels and rattles across viaducts, offering ample photo opportunities.

Mettupalayam   **Kallar**   **Adderly**   **Hillgrove**   **Runneymede**

CLOCKWISE FROM LEFT: The Nilgiri Mountain train readies for departure; a would-be passenger without a ticket; your fellow passengers; crossing a bridge through the hills. **PREVIOUS PAGE:** The train passes through a green landscape of jungle and tea plantations.

© ALEXANDRA LANDE | SHUTTERSTOCK

© HEMIS | ALAMY STOCK PHOTO

Locals – and visitors – frequently get carried away by the experience, and whoops, screams and whistles greet every tunnel and emerging vista. At certain times, you will be able to see all the way back down to the plains, with banks of cloud billowing out of mountain valleys like steam from witches' cauldrons. Periodically, the engineers who sit on the covered verandas between carriages will leap out in order to check that everything is still working smoothly with this century-old technology.

Above Coonoor, the dignified steam locomotives are swapped out for diesel engines but, due to the green and gorgeous scenery, you probably won't mind. This is the colonial heart of the Nilgiri Hills, where whitewashed churches and tin-roofed British-era bungalows (an Indian word, in case you were wondering) are scattered like confetti around the bottle-green hills. The British were also responsible

Scenic viewpoints, waterfalls and botanical gardens ring Coonoor, the second city of the Nilgiri Hills.

Lovedale is the highest stop on the route, and home to the famous Lawrence School, attended by author Arundhati Roy.

Coonoor   Wellington   Aravankadu   Ketti   Lovedale

for the stands of tall, straight eucalyptus trees that periodically shade the rail tracks, tapped today for high-grade eucalyptus oil.

After the idyllic scenery all the way uphill, arriving in Ooty can be a bit anti-climactic, but the romance returns once you head into the hills on foot in search of tribal villages, tea plantations and churchyards full of memorials to forgotten empire builders.

❷ LIFE ON BOARD

There are just three or four carriages on the Nilgiri Mountain Railway, so book well ahead, particularly if you hope to secure a seat in the slightly more comfortable 1st-class carriage. This is not one of those luxurious Indian train rides you may have heard about – whichever class you book, you'll get a simple padded seat and windows that open directly on to the scenery, with slightly fewer fellow passengers to share the views in 1st class. There's no food service, so grab yourself some snacks at the station in Mettupalayam or Ooty before you set off.

❸ MAKE IT HAPPEN

One daily train makes the entire trip from Mettupalayam to Ooty, leaving at 7.10am and returning at 2pm. Three additional daily services run between Coonoor and Ooty. Book at least two weeks ahead in the April to June high season or on public holidays, either in person at an Indian railway station, or online via the Indian Railways website at www.indianrail.gov.in. The main difference between 1st and 2nd class is the number of people in each carriage, and the slightly thicker padding on the seats in 1st class. Locals favour return trips, but international tourists usually travel one-way, continuing by bus to Mysuru (Mysore) or Bengaluru (formerly Bangalore). Uphill is the most atmospheric direction of travel. It's a long, slow ride, so bring drinks and snacks. **JB**

The end of the line is the start of rambles to colonial churches, tea plantations and tribal villages in the Nilgiri Hills.

Ooty (Udhagamandalam)

© INDIAPICTURES | GETTY IMAGES

Japan's Post Road Train

JAPAN

Rather than the super-speedy bullet train so often associated with Japan, here is a trundling local railway that puffs its way up into the Japan Alps along the old Nakasendō, or post road. It stops in tiny mountain villages where teetering timber buildings exist as they have since the Edo period, and local craftworkers still hand-make bowls. A Japan Rail Pass offers unlimited travel on this train, meaning you can spend all day, or a couple of days, hopping on and off and exploring this route. Combine it with hiking part of the signposted Nakasendō Way to really get a feel for how travellers and traders plied this route in bygone times.

❶ RIDING THE RAILS

Winding. You feel the mountains rise up next to you almost immediately as the train works its way out of Nagoya's urban sprawl. Tin-topped houses and

telephone poles give way to a river, which you follow most of your way to Matsumoto. The river changes course and names several times but feels a constant companion. You have to relax, because this railway is not your stereotypical Japanese bullet train. Make no mistake: you'll depart and arrive on time, exactly – Japanese efficiency extends to the farthest reaches of its railway network – but that is not the point here.

You've chosen this train because it is slow. It works its way through a landscape that was meant to be walked, or ridden. A landscape it used to take people so long to traverse that they needed dozens of stopovers to get where they were going. Today, these stopover towns themselves are the draw: see an Edo-period village almost perfectly preserved in its teetering wooden state. In some ways, it's the dream for travellers to Japan.

You're here to take your time. Stop-offs are compulsory, so you need to allot the whole day; several days if you've planned well. Don't miss

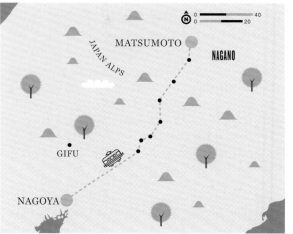

"At sunset, the dark wood eaves begin to glow, reflecting the water of the moat"

Magome, hometown of writer Shimazaki Tōson, who recorded the area's history in his works about the local families. A small museum documenting his life and writing is a charming discovery.

Tsumago is a must-do stop-off for the real architecture hunters, many of its buildings having been restored so perfectly in the last 50 years that it's now designated by the Japanese government as a Nationally Designated Architectural Preservation Site, while laid-back Narai further north up the valley is quieter and you might get lost trying to figure out which calligraphy-clad signs mean 'restaurant' or something else. Local artisans here sell works they make much in the same way that their forebears have for centuries: bowls, chopsticks and other beautifully utilitarian items hearken back to a time when travellers' needs were simple, making for unique souvenirs with real history.

Before reaching Narai, though, a glimpse out of the right-hand windows reveals the Nezame no Toko, a small gorge that wows with its unusual granite rocks. Though completely carved by water erosion, the rocks appear cube-like rather than sinuous. A hike up this rocky ravine is possible by stopping off at Agematsu Station for a couple of hours.

If you've managed to get all this done in one day, and been lulled by the small details of the post towns and bucolic beauty of the route, arrival in Matsumoto will come as a shock. Though it's just a small mountain town, it has a cosmopolitan feeling as soon as you step out of its boutique train station. Don't leave it until after dark – you'll want to stretch

NAKASENDŌ POST TOWNS

During the Edo period, the Nakasendō connected Tokyo (then, Edo) with Kyoto. This train follows a section known as the Kisoji, through the Kiso Valley. Along the route, 'post towns' were established – these official government rest and transit stops eventually expanded to include lodgings, tea houses and shops for civilian travellers.

© VISUALSPACE | GETTY IMAGES

Get an insight into the region's most famous writer, Shimazaki Toson, in the small Magome museum dedicated to his life.

Glimpse perfectly perserved Edo-era architecture in the post road town of Tsumago, a detour from Nagiso.

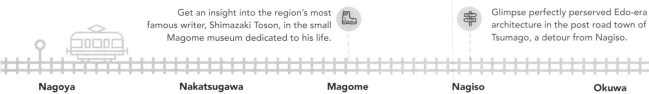

CLOCKWISE FROM LEFT: A picture-postcard view of Tsumago-juku; riding through the Koshin'etsu region; hiking the Nakasendō Way's big trees. **PREVIOUS PAGE:** Matsumoto Castle is Japan's most ancient wooden castle.

your legs after some hours on a circuitous train. Strolling north from the station, it's almost impossible to miss the dark hulk of 16th-century Matsumoto Castle – nicknamed Crow Castle – with its perfectly manicured grounds surrounded by a pristine moat. At sunset, the dark wood eaves begin to glow, reflecting the moat's waters in a magical way that seems to defy its intended colour.

Maybe you'll ride the train south again tomorrow.

❷ LIFE ON BOARD

All trains in Japan are clean, comfortable and efficient, but this is not the flashy bullet train that whisks people across the country at high speeds. Prepare for winding mountain valleys and wide views out of slow-moving (but big) windows. Bring snacks.

❸ MAKE IT HAPPEN

Trains depart very regularly from Nagoya; be sure to only take trains labelled JR Chuo Line. Change in Nakatsugawa for the Kiso Valley post road train.

A Japan Rail Pass (purchase before you leave your home country) allows unlimited train travel, meaning you can ride the entire route, base yourself in very pleasant Matsumoto, then take shorter day trips to explore the post road villages at leisure.

You can reserve a seat with a pass, or purchase a single ticket, beforehand or on the day of travel from machines or offices in any station in Japan.

Any time of the year is beautiful along this route, but autumn (September–November) is the best time to visit, not least to take part in *momijigari*, the Japanese pastime of 'autumn leaf viewing'. **ME**

Keep a look out on the left side of the train for the granite rock formation of Nezame no Toko Gorge.

Stroll the pristine single street of Narai, a village lined with postcard-perfect Edo timber buildings.

Cameras out to catch the sunset over the astonishing Matsumoto-jō, Japan's oldest wooden castle.

Kuramoto   **Narai**   **Shiojiri**   **Matsumoto**

Trans-Mongolian Railway

RUSSIA, MONGOLIA & CHINA

START **MOSCOW**

END **BĚIJĪNG**

DEPARTS **ONCE A WEEK**

DISTANCE **4735 MILES (7621KM)**

DURATION **5 DAYS 7 HRS**

Connecting the capitals of Russia, Mongolia and China, the Trans-Mongolian Railway presents the chance to experience a trio of distinct cultures as well as a diverse range of landscapes. Compare and contrast the awe-inspiring architectural splendour of Moscow's Red Square with Běijīng's Tiān'ānmèn Square, the silver birch forests of Siberia with the arid Gobi Desert where dinosaurs once roamed. A weekly direct service rolls out of Moscow and Běijīng, but to fully experience the three countries on the route you'll need to hop on and off a variety of trains.

❶ RIDING THE RAILS

For centuries before the railway was completed in 1956 there was a well-trodden trade route connecting China, Mongolia and Russia, along which tea flowed west, and furs and other commodities flowed east. Commerce remains a prime concern between these nations, so it's highly likely you'll encounter native businessmen and women on the train as it veers off the main Russian line at Ulan-Ude and continues to Běijīng via Mongolia and its capital Ulaanbaatar. Hence this is a popular route, with demand for tickets on Trains 3 and 4 often exceeding supply.

If your aim is to relax for five days, admire the passing scenery and connect with a varied cast of Russian, Mongolian and Chinese passengers and staff, securing a berth on this Chinese-operated train is highly recommended. However, for many, the Trans-Mongolian's prime attraction is more the route itself. The options for stopovers between Moscow and Ulan-Ude alone are legion, but the one that many rightly opt for is Irkutsk. This pleasant city, combining both historical and contemporary aspects of Russia, is just 43 miles (70km) from beautiful Lake Baikal. Should you pass on the chance to hop off here, the deepest lake on earth will make a showstopping appearance on the way to Slyudyanka: here Baikal is so close to the tracks it's tempting to dash down for a quick dip.

Another highlight of the journey is traversing the vast open spaces of Mongolia. These gently undulating steppes, which stretch to the horizon, are an otherworldly landscape on which the sight of a lone yurt or horseback rider appears heroic. Few people

RIGHT & BELOW: Běijīng's Forbidden; horses swim in the Yenisei River.
PREVIOUS PAGE: Catch a glimpse of the Great Wall through your window.

would sing the aesthetic praises of Ulaanbaatar, yet on a stop in the Mongolian capital you can experience the chants of monks in ancient Buddhist temples or attend the famous summer festival of Naadam with its thrilling contests of traditional archery, horse-racing and wrestling, as well as performances of *khöömei* (throat singing).

Life aboard the train is interrupted twice by the frisson of crossing international frontiers, with the novelty of having the wheels changed at the China-Mongolia border to fit the different track gauge. While this process, lasting several hours, takes place, you can size up the Chinese station at Erlian, a mini-Las Vegas of neon, fairy lights and booming welcome music.

About 50 miles (80km) outside Běijīng the train tunnels through a mountainous landscape of canyons and soaring rocks quite unlike anything else seen on the journey. Cruising into Běijīng's cavernous main station, dating from 1959 and the only one within the old walled city, is only the start of another adventure exploring China's fabled capital.

❷ LIFE ON BOARD

Trains 3 and 4 are Chinese operated, with Chinese locomotives, rolling stock and staff. The main choice of compartment is between deluxe 1st class – roomy, two-berth compartments with showers shared between two compartments; and hard-sleeper 2nd-class compartments (the equivalent of *kupe* on Russian trains), which sleep four people. The latter offer no showers. Toilets, squat as well as Western style, are found in every carriage.

Outside the train attendant's compartment will be a samovar dispensing hot water for drinks and pot-

© TYPEHISTORIAN | GETTY IMAGES

© ZHAO JIAN KANG | GETTY IMAGES

CHANGING TRACKS

Russian and Mongolian trains run on a 5ft (1.5m) gauge, which is slightly wider than the standard gauge used in China. Therefore, when the train arrives in Erlian on the Chinese side of the border with Mongolia, the bogies beneath the carriages must be changed to fit the track.

Tour the wonderful museums and galleries of Moscow before boarding the train at Yaroslav Station.

Look out for a white monument marking the Europe–Asia border post near Yekaterinburg.

Hop off the train at Irkutsk to spend time beside Siberia's amazing Lake Baikal.

Moscow (Yaroslav Station)   **Yekaterinburg**   **Irkutsk**   **Ulan-Ude**

noodle-type snacks. Otherwise, one of the pleasures of the Trans-Mongolian is that you can run a taste test between the Russian, Mongolian and Chinese restaurant cars, which are hitched to the train as it passes through each country. Common opinion is that the Chinese dining car is the best, but the food can be fine and palatable in the other two. You also won't want to miss out on the pleasures of purchasing food and drinks from the locals who wait at station platforms along the way.

❸ ALTERNATIVE ROUTES

For a fully escorted tour along the Trans-Mongolian route, with 1st-class train travel, city tours, a yurt stay and other activities included, look into making the trip with Russian Railways' Imperial Russia service (rzdtour.com/en). Budget travellers can book tickets on the cheaper train services that connect each of the stops along the way.

❹ MAKE IT HAPPEN

Train 3 departs Běijīng every Wednesday, Train 4 leaves Moscow on Tuesdays. For timetables and online bookings see Russian Railways (pass.rzd.ru) or www.chinahighlights.com/china-trains. Tickets can be bought up to 60 days in advance. Go one-way and make some stops, such as Irkutsk and Ulaanbaatar. You can travel the route any time. July and August are popular with tourists so book ahead and use a specialist travel agency to buy tickets. Most foreign visitors require visas to each of the countries; organise this about three months before your visit. For details on Russia, see www.mid.ru/en/main_en; Mongolia, www.mfa.gov.mn; China, www.chinese-embassy.info. **SR**

Make another break at Ulaanbaatar to explore Mongolia's capital and the surrounding countryside.

Look out for views of China's Great Wall between 180 miles (295km) and 170 miles (275km) west of Běijīng.

Marvel at the splendour of Běijīng's Forbidden City, the world's largest palace complex.

Naushki / Sükhbaatar   **Ulaanbaatar**   **Zamyn-Üüd / Erlian**   **Běijīng**

Běijīng to Shànghǎi by High-Speed Rail

CHINA ●

START **BĔIJĪNG**

END **SHÀNGHǍI**

DEPARTS **DAILY**

DURATION **4.5–6 HRS**

DISTANCE **819 MILES (1318KM)**

A train journey in China begins long before hitting the rails. Every step is an eye-opening cultural experience, from buying tickets and navigating hangar-sized stations to settling into one's seat and gaping as the speedometer sometimes surpassing 248mph (400km/h). Engines of China's economic development, high-speed ('bullet') trains power across dozens of routes, but the first and most significant line – that of the world's fastest passenger train – moves more than half a million people a day between the megacities of Běijīng and Shànghǎi.

❶ RIDING THE RAILS

The numbers are practically beyond comprehension. Approximately 2600 high-speed train departures run daily between more than 200 cities spread across 32 of China's 34 provinces. In 2016, these services carried nearly 1.44 billion passengers, up 24% from the previous year. That is more in eight days than the US Amtrak's annual ridership.

China's ability to cycle so many people through its rail system is a big part of what makes the Běijīng–Shànghǎi high-speed train journey so remarkable. This becomes abundantly clear when approaching any main train station in a major Chinese city, but all the

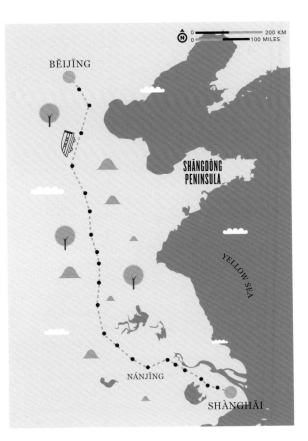

more so at the Běijīng South Railway Station, which at 79 acres (32 hectares) in size is the city's (and one of Asia's) largest. This terminal's 24 platforms can shunt 30,000 travellers an hour toward their destinations from a central waiting area with a capacity of 10,000 people – parents, children, students, retirees, tourists, businesspeople and more. It is a profound understatement to say that one feels small in such a thronging sea of humanity.

RIGHT: The Fuxing streaks through the Chinese countryside. **PREVIOUS PAGE:** Attendants on the Fuxing train service, the world's fastest, which runs between Běijīng and Shànghǎi.

And yet processes move along well – through several levels of ticket and security checks, down vast hallways with clear departure information boards (in English and Chinese) and past dozens of convenience stores, restaurants and coffee shops. Even the boarding happens with good speed, facilitated by reserved seats in plainly labelled carriages that pull up to marked platform locations.

On board, regular announcements in English and Chinese, digital placards identifying upcoming station stops and, especially, current speed are almost as distracting as the outside views.

However, it really is the external world that holds one's attention. First, it flies by at such an alarming clip that the reality of travelling at record-breaking land speeds hits home. Fortunately, the well-grounded weight and smooth thrust of the trains are fantastically reassuring.

Second, the country's accelerated growth finds blunt form in an astonishing number of high-rise buildings clustered at regular intervals among fields and rolling hills. Some of these are new, purpose-built commuter cities developed around China's 'high-speed rail economy', both responding to and supplying the railway system with huge numbers of new riders – an expanded labour pool of working-age Chinese helping drive new investment and technology into less-developed areas of the country.

Responding to these commuters' needs, most high-speed trains on the Běijīng–Shànghǎi line make six or seven of the 20-plus intermediate stops, while still regularly achieving top speeds of 186mph (300km/h). However, the latest generation train, called Fuxing (meaning 'rejuvenation'), is the fastest passenger service in the world, covering the uninterrupted distance between Běijīng and Nánjīng at an average speed of 217mph (350km/h) but getting as fast as 248mph (400km/h) before carrying on to Shànghǎi in a total of just four and a half hours.

❷ LIFE ON BOARD

There are three types of high-speed trains that presently operate on this line, but they all have 2nd class (five across), 1st class (four across) and business-class (three across) seats. They are all comfortable and rotate to face forward, but are roomier the more expensive they get. Business-class seats also recline into flat beds and the price includes complimentary snacks, tea and a tray meal. Power sockets may not be available in 2nd class.

Every train has a buffet car with tables available to all passengers. The buffet sells snacks, soft drinks, beer and meals. All cars also have free boiling water for tea and instant noodle soups.

HIGH-SPEED RAIL ECONOMY

China's ambitious high-speed rail system is critical to a diversified economy after decades of reliance on manufacturing and exports. This new 'high-speed rail economy' emphasises, among other things, tourism and boosting capacity through better networks of large but not oversized cities, including new commuter corridors along rail lines.

Explore Běijīng, an incomparable capital city at the political, economic and cultural centre of China.

Tài'ān is a cradle of Chinese civilisation, with human remains dating back more than 500,000 years.

Běijīng (South)   **Jinan**   **Tài'ān**

❸ ALTERNATIVE ROUTES

As of mid-2017, China's high-speed train system spanned about 13,670 miles (22,000km) of track, or about two-thirds of the world's total. China anticipates 18,640 miles (30,000km) of rail by 2020 and another 8000km (4970 miles) by 2025.

❹ BUDGET ALTERNATIVE

Although high-speed expresses rule the day, slower and cheaper sleepers from Běijīng to Shànghǎi – taking 15 to 20 hours – preside at night. Inexpensive seats exist, but 'hard' (six-bed, open compartment), 'soft' (four-bed, closed compartment) and 'deluxe soft' (two-bed, private compartment) sleeping berths are more comfortable. There are also express sleepers with cosy 'soft' berths for the 12-hour trip.

❺ MAKE IT HAPPEN

There are approximately 40 high-speed departures every day in each direction and tickets can be purchased up to 28 days in advance directly at the stations or 30 days ahead through English-language online agencies, which include ctrip.com and www.china-diy-travel.com.

For purchases at ticket offices, valid identification for all travellers may be required, as will precise train information (departure date and time, train number) and cash if without a Chinese credit card. In major cities, at least one ticket window has an English-speaking sales clerk. For purchases through online agencies, there are small service fees.

Even in summer, extra clothing layers may be necessary on board, as the air conditioning is sometimes very effective. **EG**

Nánjīng is a historical and cultural city that was capital of numerous Chinese dynasties.

Visit Sūzhōu, the Jiāngsū city famous for beguiling gardens, canals, stone bridges, pagodas and more.

End your journey at Shànghǎi, China's most glamorous and futuristic city that hasn't lost sight of its past.

Xuzhou   Nánjīng   Sūzhōu   Shànghǎi (Hóngqiáo)

EUROPE

AMAZING TRAIN JOURNEYS

Settle to Carlisle

ENGLAND

START **SETTLE**

END **CARLISLE**

DEPARTS **DAILY**

DISTANCE 73 MILES (113KM)

DURATION **1 HR 40 MINS**

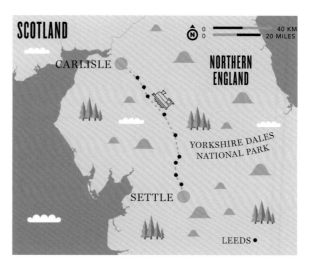

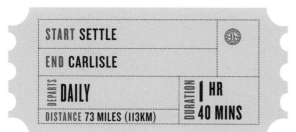

England's Settle-to-Carlisle line has long been synonymous with the fight to preserve beautiful and historic stretches of railway. But this is no heritage line. Proudly part of the British rail network and served by regular mainline trains, the railway enjoys a double life as a frequent host of steam specials and, even rarer, steam-hauled mainline services. Whether you have the whiff of steam in your nostrils or the hard-working growl of diesel-hauled regular trains in your ears, the views from the carriages are pretty much unmatched on the English railway network. Passengers can feast their eyes on mile after mile of magnificent Yorkshire Dales and North Pennines scenery, interrupted only by stations so sweet you would expect to find them pictured on a box of biscuits.

❶ RIDING THE RAILS

Not every day offers a chance to take a ride along a national treasure. It tells you something about the place the Settle-to-Carlisle line has in the hearts of the British public that its full reopening in 2017, after a partial closure due to a landslip, was a national event. To much media fanfare, the Flying Scotsman steam train ran along the line and there was a feeling that all was once again well in the world. Remarkably, though, you won't feel like you're surrounded by legions of tourists on any stretch of the journey. In fact, the most striking thing about the Settle-to-Carlisle line is how wild and remote the terrain is that it passes through. This is upland England in every way, where glorious open moorland is populated by hardy sheep, and dramatic views stretch for miles over rocky hillsides.

On departure from Settle, the line passes into high, open country marked by the famous fells of what Yorkshire devotees refer to as God's Own Country. The peaks of Pen-y-Ghent and Ingleborough are impressive guardians of the railway, easily spotted on either side of the line around Horton-in-Ribblesdale. Another mountain top, Whernside, stands sentinel by the Ribblehead Viaduct, the line's biggest drawcard for visitors. For a proper view, get off the train and walk beneath the line. Or, if you're caught short, the 'loo with a view' at Ribblehead's Station Inn frames the viaduct through a small window.

The Settle-to-Carlisle line owes its existence to the Midland Railway, which, in competition with other railway companies, decided to construct its own route to Scotland in search of lucrative cross-border traffic. Though the Midland is long gone, its stamp can still be seen along the line. Look out for the handsome 'Derby Gothic' station buildings and elaborate wrought-iron all painted in the distinctive cream and red of the Midland.

The line was threatened with closure by British Rail in the 1980s, and it was the determination of the Friends of the Settle to Carlisle Line that kept it open. Doff your cap respectfully to the Friends at the statue of Ruswarp, the loyal dog of former Friends secretary Graham Nuttall at Garsdale Station, near the line's high point at Aisgill Summit. Better still, join the Friends (www.foscl.org.uk) on one of their excellent guided walks showcasing the history of the railway and the beautiful scenery around it.

The line is wonderful all through the year, though the weather can be wild at any time. Being on board as rain lashes the windows adds to the experience, though the colours visible from the line in autumn make this arguably the best time to travel. Should you be lucky enough to traverse this high country when there's snow on the ground then you're going to get a different perspective again.

North of Kirkby Stephen the line enters the idyllic Eden Valley. This is a contender for one of England's most underrated areas, mainly due to its proximity to the more famous, and neighbouring, Lake District. The line enters the valley around the headwaters of the Eden and continues northwards through more superb countryside, broad and lower-lying than the Dales high country preceding it and with distant views of the Cumbrian mountains.

Services trundle onwards through the market town of Appleby, the starting point for the Pennine Cycleway's northern section, a superb multiday adventure of a ride over an area known as England's last wilderness, which finishes at distant Berwick-upon-Tweed. Appleby also hosts an annual Horse Fair

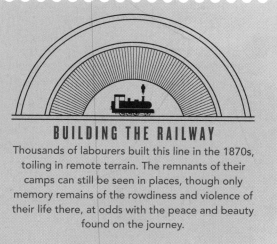

BUILDING THE RAILWAY

Thousands of labourers built this line in the 1870s, toiling in remote terrain. The remnants of their camps can still be seen in places, though only memory remains of the rowdiness and violence of their life there, at odds with the peace and beauty found on the journey.

Admire the floral delights at Horton-in-Ribblesdale Station, then strike out for a stroll over Yorkshire's Three Peaks.

Marvel at the Ribblehead Viaduct, one of the great views of northern England, preferably as a steam train thunders over.

Ponder the signaller's life as you pass Blea Moor signal box, a mile's walk from the nearest road.

Settle   **Horton-in-Ribblesdale**   **Ribblehead**   **Dent**

CLOCKWISE FROM LEFT:
Ribblehead Station; know your direction
of travel; the line crosses a village in the
Eden Valley; Blea Moor signal box.
PREVIOUS PAGE: Full steam ahead.

every June, drawing a huge gathering of gypsies and
travellers from around the UK.

Staying on the train you'll pass through the red-
sandstone-built villages of Armathwaite, Lazonby
and Langwathby, before reaching journey's end at the
historic border town of Carlisle. Scotland is a short
hop away on the west coast mainline from here, but
the town's castle, cathedral and colourful borderland
history demands a diversion off the rails.

❷ LIFE ON BOARD

Though a superbly scenic journey, Settle to Carlisle is
served by regular trains. Commuters, families, hikers
and photographers will jostle for the best seats on
busy days, but off-peak you can expect to have a quiet
journey with only the tinkling of the refreshments
trolley disturbing you.

Admire the fortification at
Appleby Castle, just south
of the town itself.

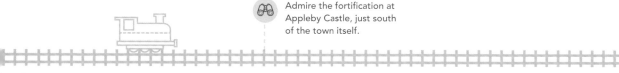

Garsdale   Kirkby Stephen   Appleby   Langwatchby   Lazonby & Kirkoswald

❸ ALTERNATIVE ROUTES

Accessed via Keighley, a stop on the Leeds-to-Carlisle service that runs through Settle, is the Keighley & Worth Valley steam railway which stops at Haworth, home to the Brontë Parsonage. Elsewhere, curving off from the Settle-to-Carlisle line, the Bentham Line runs from Leeds to Morecambe and on through Dales and Forest of Bowland scenery to Heysham, for ferries to the Isle of Man. Alternatively, The Cumbrian Coast Line chugs across viaducts and alongside expanses of sand on its way from Morecambe to Carlisle.

❹ UPGRADES

Should you fancy a steam train excursion over the Ribblehead Viaduct, find details of day trips at www.uksteam.info. For a different view of the line, stay in cosy converted station buildings at Kirkby Stephen or the Railway Master's house at Ribblehead Station (www.sandctrust.org.uk/stayatastation).

❺ MAKE IT HAPPEN

Unless you've already had the pleasure of venturing into the Yorkshire Dales National Park, a ride on the Settle-to-Carlisle line will begin at either Carlisle, a busy stop on the West Coast Main Line, or Leeds, a two-hour journey from London and the best mainline connection from the south. It's also where through trains on the Settle-to-Carlisle line start. Leeds is well connected to Manchester and Liverpool. From Carlisle, you can continue on to Glasgow and into Scotland, or across to Newcastle via the North Pennines.

   Trains depart up to eight times a day in both directions, seven days a week. Book ahead for the best fares or you can buy tickets in advance or on the day at Northern Rail (www.northernrailway.co.uk) or any station in the UK. The line is busiest at weekends and during school holidays. For further information, visit www.settle-carlisle.co.uk. **TH**

EDDIE HYDE | EDHYDE357 | 500PX

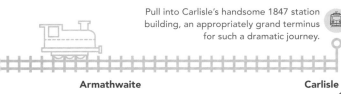

Pull into Carlisle's handsome 1847 station building, an appropriately grand terminus for such a dramatic journey.

Armathwaite   **Carlisle**

Crossing the Arten Gill Viaduct by steam on the Settle-to-Carlisle line.

The Glacier Express

SWITZERLAND

START ST MORITZ	
END ZERMATT	
DEPARTS DAILY	**DURATION** 8 HRS
DISTANCE 180 MILES (290KM)	

No wonder the Swiss are a nation of rail fanatics, with such bang-on-time, ludicrously scenic trains. But if they could pick one definitive ride, the honour would surely go to the Glacier Express. This eight-hour journey from ritzy St Moritz to Matterhorn-topped Zermatt unzips the lovely Alpine terrain in the country's south, corkscrewing up to wind-battered mountain passes, teetering across 291 bridges and rumbling through 91 tunnels. The slowest express train on the planet, it intentionally moves at a snail's pace so as to big up those out-of-this-world views of meadows, forest, falls and mountains – all glimpsed through panoramic windows, natürlich.

❶ RIDING THE RAILS

Boarding the Glacier Express at St Moritz Station is reminiscent of a more graceful age of travel when such journeys were the preserve of the truly wealthy. Liveried chauffeurs drop off smartly dressed passengers, the porters are dapper and the bright-red trains so impeccably polished that they gleam. The sense of excitement on the platform is palpable and justifiable – this is, after all, one of the world's greatest train journeys, and where better to begin than in the birthplace of Alpine tourism?

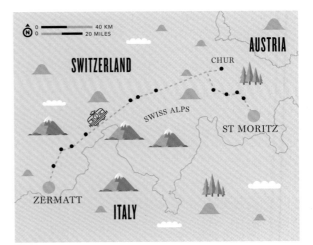

That the Swiss like to do things properly is no secret: trains are timed to the millisecond and journeys are never just about getting from A to B. But the Glacier Express goes a step further by presenting Switzerland in a nutshell. As soon as you've taken your seat, you'll be glued to your window for eight hours, as landscapes unfold cinematically. Doe-eyed cows graze in meadows that spread out like velvet carpets, the green froth of fir-cloaked hills rises up to jagged peaks topping out around the 13,125ft (4000m) mark, and the glacially cold Rhine and Rhône rivers roll past dark-timber hamlets, castles and church spires. Each new view elicits little shrieks of wonder.

Then there's the added engineering factor. Consider that the Glacier Express was first launched as a steam train back in 1930 and you'll see those crevasse-spanning bridges, rollercoaster tracks up to high mountain passes and tunnels in a whole new light. If the journey seems impressive now, back then it must have seemed nothing short of a miracle.

CLOCKWISE FROM RIGHT: The impossibly beautiful Landwasser Viaduct; marvelling at the Alpine vistas.
PREVIOUS PAGE: The Matterhorn.

The journey can also be made in winter and there is a particular magic when snow polishes the mountains pearly white in the sun. From St Moritz, the scene is immediately spectacular as the train makes a steep, looping descent on the narrow-gauge Albula Line, a Unesco World Heritage Site. The 38-mile (61km) stretch of track between St Moritz and Thusis cuts through high Alpine country, trundling helter-skelter into tunnels and across ravine-traversing bridges.

It's a fitting prelude for the view that graces a thousand postcards: the Landwasser Viaduct. Rising 215ft (65m) above a river of pure turquoise, with cliffs and forest sheering above it, the curving single-track, six-arched viaduct has everyone grappling frantically for their cameras. The vista is a ready-made Christmas card when the snow is falling.

On the train rolls, shadowing the Hinterrhein River and castle-crowned hillsides before reaching the glacier-gouged Ruinaulta gorge near Flims, stippled with limestone turrets and pinnacles. The babble of several languages – French, Swiss German, Italian and Romansch – often fills the carriage around Chur, Switzerland's oldest city, and in Disentis, topped by a Benedictine monastery. Then the steep rack-and-pinion gradients begin as the train climbs up and up to the Oberalp Pass, the highest point at 6670ft (2033m), where gnarled mountains rise above the source of the Rhine at nearby Lai da Tuma.

Mooching along at an average speed of 24mph (40km/h), the Glacier Express is in no hurry – and why would you want to rush? Soon after the lovely Alpine town of Andermatt, it scoots into the Furka Base Tunnel, emerging in the glacier-encrusted Rhône Valley, where log-built chalets are dwarfed by 13,125ft (4000m) peaks. St Niklaus is like a drum roll for the ultimate view in Switzerland. As the train clatters up to Zermatt at 5250ft (1600m), the anticipation

© MIKHAIL LEONOV | GETTY IMAGES

© ALESSANDRO COLLE | GETTY IMAGES

THE MAGIC OF MATTERHORN

Zermatt's Matterhorn Museum does a grand job of telling the tale of the Matterhorn and the farming village at its foot, connected only by mule track to the valley below until 1891 when the railway arrived. The mountain was first summited by Edward Whymper in 1865 – an achievement marred by a rope-breaking tragedy.

Book a seat in the all-window panoramic carriage for knockout mountain views.

Draw breath as you cross the curving, six-arched Landwasser Viaduct, with the river but a splash below.

Hop off for a hike through the limestone wonderland of the Ruinaulta gorge.

St Moritz   **Filisur**   **Thusis**

builds and gasps fill the carriage. And suddenly there it is: the Matterhorn, an almighty fang of a 14,692ft (4478m) peak and the ultimate Swiss icon.

❷ LIFE ON BOARD

The landscapes might be wild but the train itself is highly civilised. Meals are brought directly to your seat – enjoy a glass of Swiss wine and regional specialities, such as *Bündnerfleisch* (air-dried beef) and *Gerstensuppe* (barley soup), as you chug through the Alps. Seat reservations are obligatory.

❸ BUDGET ALTERNATIVE

If the Glacier Express is beyond your budget, save francs by opting to take the hourly local trains covering the same route (minus the panoramic carriages). They are slightly quicker and cheaper. Visit www.sbb.ch for details. All discount travel cards (such as the Swiss Travel Pass and Half Fare Card) are valid.

❹ MAKE IT HAPPEN

There are one to three trains daily year-round, except late October to early December, when there is no service. Tickets can be booked at glacierexpress. ch or through tour providers. Reserve your seats as soon as you have firm dates. Upgrading to 1st class is expensive (almost double the 2nd-class fare) but means fewer crowds and greater comfort.

The one-way journey is impressive whether you begin in St Moritz or Zermatt. You can hop on and off as you like, or break the journey down into shorter sections. It's beautiful year-round but go in winter (December–April) for the full-on snow-globe effect. **KC**

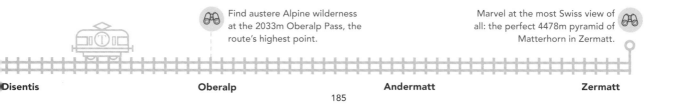

Find austere Alpine wilderness at the 2033m Oberalp Pass, the route's highest point.

Marvel at the most Swiss view of all: the perfect 4478m pyramid of Matterhorn in Zermatt.

Disentis　　　　　　　Oberalp　　　　　　　Andermatt　　　　　　　Zermatt

Bilbao to Ferrol on the FEVE

SPAIN ●

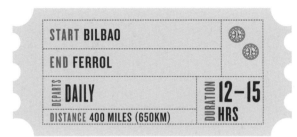

START **BILBAO**

END **FERROL**

DEPARTS **DAILY**

DISTANCE **400 MILES (650KM)**

DURATION **12–15 HRS**

If you're not in a rush, a trip on Europe's longest narrow-gauge railway might be just the ticket. The FEVE is a trio of lines that carve an improbable route across the north of Spain from Bilbao (Basque Country) to Ferrol (Galicia), stopping at more than a hundred stations along the way. Bypassing sprawling suburbs and holiday resorts, this determined little train hauls itself through rough-hewn tunnels, chugs up steep ravines and ducks beneath the legs of motorways. Beautifully isolated and content with its
own slow progress, it immerses its passengers in an astonishingly green region of untamed mountains, hearty regional dishes and warm, authentic people.

❶ RIDING THE RAILS

Your journey begins in Bilbao, a gritty industrial port with an artistic heart. Before you embark, take time to explore the city's jigsaw of medieval and avant-garde architecture, as 15th-century Gothic meets the mercurial, titanium plates of the Guggenheim. *Pintxos*, the Basque take on tapas, are fundamental to daily life here, and the ideal way to soak up a boozy lunch with *kuadrilla* (Basque for 'your tribe').

Right from the off, your journey takes an ambitious route. Railway engineers usually pick the path of least resistance, building tracks along river valleys and natural contours. The determined FEVE, on the other hand – unmarked on most Spanish railway maps, despite being a division of the state-owned Renfe

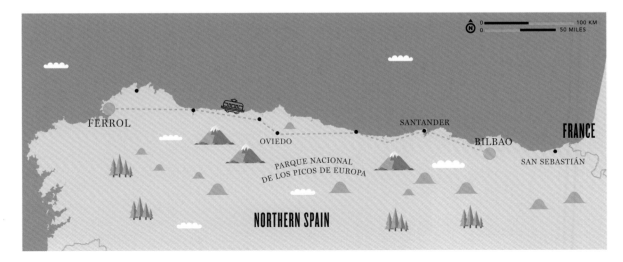

Operadora – takes an altogether more rambling route along the Atlantic coast, stopping at stone platforms in the middle of meadows and fading yellow station buildings with cracked tile maps.

Constructed in 1965, the FEVE is a local train for local people. Passing through cities, you share the carriage with commuters who tap away on their phones. But soon you'll be joined by villagers on their way to the butchers or taking their dog to the vet. For rural communities, this is a chance to dip into the culture and facilities of nearby towns, and to catch up on gossip along the way.

Leaving Bilbao, take a seat on the right, facing backwards, and watch the suburbs retreat as the line meanders inland before towering cranes and a sprawling estuary announce your approach into Santander. With its grand belle-époque facades, breezy avenues and tree-shaded plazas, this characterful Cantabrian capital is made for warm, easy days.

An hour along the line, tranquil Cabezón de la Sal takes its name from its former Roman salt markets. Narrow streets thread past ancient *casas señoriales* (noblemen's houses), their ancient balconies now draped with drying clothes.

Passing into Asturias, seek out Ribadesella, a down-to-earth seaside town nestled in the sweeping S of the River Sella. Here, expert *escanciadores* (cider pourers) decant the local tipple and you can tuck into piles of mussels outside unpretentious promenade cafes. Follow this with a stroll along an avenue of ornate Indiano mansions, built by rich Spanish mariners returning from the Americas.

The Picos de Europa – limestone peaks eroded into vertical flutes and caves – paint a ragged line against the horizon as the FEVE takes an even wilder route. Red-roofed homesteads and *hórreos* (granaries resting on stone pillars) dot the fields; canoeists navigate rapids on the river below; locals quaff homemade cider on platforms. It's about now that you realise you're falling for the charms of this unassuming little train, which steadfastly resists the acceleration of modern life, completely unperturbed by the *autovía* (freeways) that have sprung up around it.

Asturias is renowned for its cave-matured cheeses and robust, hearty dishes, such as *fabada Asturiana*: a stew made with *fabes* beans, spicy sausage and black pudding. You can stuff your bag with vacuum-packed ingredients from one of Oviedo's many delicatessens. Heading west after this, the route (quite frankly) starts to show off, passing under leggy road bridges, cutting across deep valleys and pulling into tiny platforms in the middle of nowhere. Spindly eucalyptus trees tickle the windows as you approach Galicia's unspoilt coast, where it's tempting to jump off at one of the tiny stations. From Loiba, it's a 1-mile (2km) walk to the dramatic Praia do Picón, where you can recline on the 'most beautiful bench in the world' and watch waves crash into the tilted granite cliffs.

On your approach to Ferrol, the Rías Altas – the eastern half of Galicia's north coast – teems with tidal fjord-like rivers where few tourists stray. Locals say it's so peaceful here that even chestnuts fall asleep.

PICOS DE EUROPA

These mountain peaks beckon as you pass through Asturias. Griffon vultures and golden eagles ride the thermals, wolves and brown bears roam wild, while hikers follow paths hewn into the rock. The FEVE passes through the foothills; jump off at Infiesto, Arriondas, Ribadesella or Llanes, where local buses can take you into the interior.

Step over the 'clints' and 'grykes' of the Acantilados de Castro Arenas – an area of limestone blow holes near Ribadesella.

Bilbao   **Santander**   **Cabezón de la Sal**   **Llanes**   **Ribadasella**

FROM LEFT: Wandering one of central Bilbao's pedestrian streets; the exterior of the city's main train station. **PREVIOUS PAGE:** The limestone landscapes of the Picos de Europa.

© NORADOA | SHUTTERSTOCK

❷ LIFE ON BOARD

There is nothing fancy about the FEVE; it's a local train for local people. However, the seats are comfortable, the views are magnificent and you will often have a whole carriage to yourself. There's no buffet cart, but that's all the more reason to hop off and enjoy the myriad local specialities. Pack snacks and be prepared for unreliable services. If a train doesn't show up, trust that a bus or taxi will soon show up to take you on your way.

❸ UPGRADES

The luxurious El Transcantábrico train-hotel traverses the entire northern coast of Spain on a seven-night trip, which includes daily excursions. Passengers on this service can expect leather seats, massage showers,

a library, a club car and gin & tonic on tap. For full details visit www.renfe.com/trenesturisticos.

❹ MAKE IT HAPPEN

Trains run three times daily from Bilbao to Santander; hourly between Santander and Cabezón de la Sal; and twice daily from Santander to Oviedo, and Oviedo to Ferrol. The FEVE system is independent from the main Spanish railway system (Renfe), often with a separate station. Check times at www.renfe.com then buy tickets at the station.

A FEVERail Card allows unlimited travel for 30 days, but it's often equally as cheap to buy one-way tickets as you go. Allow four to seven days for a leisurely trip. Travel in July and August to enjoy warm, dry days, or March to May, and September and October in order to avoid crowds. **JK**

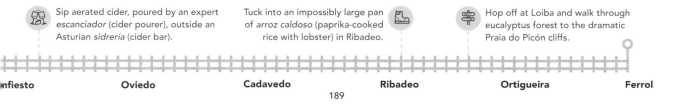

Sip aerated cider, poured by an expert *escanciador* (cider pourer), outside an Asturian *sidrería* (cider bar).

Tuck into an impossibly large pan of *arroz caldoso* (paprika-cooked rice with lobster) in Ribadeo.

Hop off at Loiba and walk through eucalyptus forest to the dramatic Praia do Picón cliffs.

nfiesto   Oviedo   Cadavedo   Ribadeo   Ortigueira   Ferrol

Trans-Siberian Railway

RUSSIA

START	MOSCOW
END	VLADIVOSTOK
DEPARTS	DAILY
DISTANCE 5752 MILES (9258KM)	DURATION 7 DAYS

It takes towering ambition to construct a railway across the largest country on Earth. The completion of Russia's Trans-Siberian route in 1916 made that dream a reality, kindling an infectious passion for train travel between Moscow and the far-eastern port of Vladivostok. Today, the romantic allure of the Trans-Siberian Railway remains undiminished. Connecting some of Russia's most fascinating cities, spanning mighty rivers and running across mountains, taiga (forests) and vast steppes (grasslands), this is an epic journey. The surprise is that it also provides an intimate insight into Russian culture and hospitality.

❶ RIDING THE RAILS

There is no single train service called the Trans-Siberian. Instead, there's a variety of routes tethering European Russia to the Russian Far East and inner Asia, traversed by a host of trains. Russian Railway's premier service is the Rossiya, which is described here; Rossiya No 1 heads west from Vladivostok, No 2 goes east from Moscow.

Before you climb aboard, a quick reality check. There are some striking glimpses of bucolic landscapes and urban environments to be seen out of the train windows. However, for the most part, the background to a Trans-Siberian journey will be seemingly endless vistas of silver birch trees, passing

freight trains and prosaic farmland. For some, all this will be mesmerising, for others, by the sixth – or even the second – day of this nearly week-long odyssey they will be hungering for other distractions.

Fear not – the true magic of a Trans-Siberian journey is what goes on inside the train. From the moment of embarkation, when the smartly uniformed carriage attendant (*provodnitsa* if female, as they often are; *provodnik* if male) stands proudly by the train to check your ticket, to parting handshakes and hugs with the new friends you've made along the way, the essence of the trip is one of personal connections. Imagine the journey as an overland cruise where you are thrown into very close proximity with fellow passengers for up to a week, should you choose to make the 5752-mile (9258km) journey non-stop.

Most travellers do break the journey, which is a recommended move, given the amazing sights to see along the way. Top of the list is crystal-clear and azure-blue Lake Baikal. The world's deepest lake is best accessed from Irkutsk, a city once known as

the Paris of Siberia, where you can still tap into the history of Imperial Russia. Other potential pit stops include Nizhny Novgorod with its stone kremlin overlooking the mighty Volga River; Novosibirsk, Russia's third-largest metropolis, offering a fine selection of museums and entertainments; and Ulan-Ude for a taste of Mongol-Buddhist culture and the surreal sight of a 25ft (7.7m) sculpture of Lenin's head.

Whether you choose to break up the journey or not, the chances are that, pretty soon after settling into your compartment, you will find yourself striking up a conversation with one of your fellow passengers, who may be a businessperson on their way to Tyumen, a grandmother visiting her daughter in Moscow, or a sailor returning to port in Vladivostok. Whether they speak your language or not, most Russians, contrary to popular stereotypes, are friendly and will make every effort to communicate – a process that will become easier on both sides should a certain bottle of the national spirit be introduced into the process. Tea and biscuits work as well.

© TIM PILE | ALAMY STOCK PHOTO

© TINA MANLEY | ALAMY STOCK PHOTO

TRANSCONTINENTAL TRAVEL

Look out for a white monument as you pass through Vershina Station, marking the border between Europe and Asia. If you miss it, get off at Yekaterinburg where you can take a taxi to one of two other monuments. Note that the official start of Siberia is still 160 miles (260km) beyond Yekaterinburg.

Admire the mighty Volga, Europe's longest river, as you pull out of Nizhny Novgorod.

Pause at historic Yekaterinburg, assassination site of Russia's last tsar and birthplace of Boris Yeltsin.

Moscow (Yaroslav)   **Yekaterinburg**   **Novosibirsk**

CLOCKWISE FROM LEFT: The line runs alongside Lake Baikal; Vladivostock Station; a farmhouse near Lake Baikal.
PREVIOUS PAGE: The Trans-Siberian powers through the Russian tundra.

© RAFFAELLO FERRARI | GETTY IMAGES

At meal times, you could trot along to the restaurant car, but the most fun is to be had sharing an improvised picnic at the table in your compartment. Such meals are often made up of, or supplemented by, provisions bought from local vendors on station platforms. Sharing fresh berries and sweet chai (tea) with Ludmilla or smoked omul (a fish native to Lake Baikal) and a beer with Vladimir as you swap photos and stories of home, families, your travel plans and dreams: these are the memories that a Trans-Siberian journey is made of.

❷ LIFE ON BOARD

Most long-distance trains in Russia, including the Rossiya, offer three classes of carriage, all of which have air-conditioning in summer and heating in winter. First-class or SV (short for *spalny vagon*, or sleeping wagon) carriages are divided into nine compartments, each sleeping two. The most common choice for Trans-Sib travellers is the 2nd-class *kupe* (short for *kupeyny*, meaning 'compartment') carriages, where the compartments each sleep four people. *Platskarny*, or 3rd-class carriages, don't have compartments; instead there are 54 narrow bunks arranged in three tiers along one side of the train, and above and below the windows on the other side, with the corridor down the middle.

There are modern toilets at both ends of each carriage, where you will also find the *provodnitsa*'s cabin, outside of which will be a samovar ever ready to dispense hot water for drinks and snacks, such as pot noodles. What you won't find is a shower (although if you charm the *provodnitsa* and tip her, say, R200, she may arrange for you to have the key to the staff shower cubicle in the service wagon).

Take a break at Irkutsk to spend time beside the Siberia's amazing Lake Baikal.

Marvel at Russia's longest rail bridge, a 1.6-mile (2.6km) double-decker span, as you pull into Khabarovsk.

Krasnoyarsk   **Irkutsk**   **Ulan-Ude**   **Khabarovsk**

❸ ALTERNATIVE ROUTES

Two alternative Russian epics are the Trans-Mongolian branch of the Trans-Sib and the Branching off from the primary Trans-Sib route at Tayshet is the lesser-known Baikal–Amur Mainline (BAM), a project of the Soviet era. This alternative route passes few towns of historical interest on its way to Russia's far-eastern port of Sovetskaya Gavan (where you could board a ferry to Sakhalin Island). However, it does stop at Severobaikalsk at the northern tip of Lake Baikal and tunnels of up to 9 miles (15km) long run through the mountainous heart of Siberia (see page 139).

❹ UPGRADES

For those seeking a higher level of comfort than that provided by Russian Railway's Rossiya service, there are several options, of which the Golden Eagle (www.goldeneagleluxurytrains.com) is the most luxurious and expensive. Alternatively, Tsar's Gold is a more affordable premium train that can be booked via several specialist Trans-Sib tour operators.

❺ MAKE IT HAPPEN

The Rossiya No 2 leaves Moscow on odd-numbered days (except the 31st) whereas the No 1 departs Vladivostok on even-numbered days. For exact timetables and online bookings visit the Russian Railways website (pass.rzd.ru). Tickets can be purchased up to 60 days in advance. Go one-way but do make at least a couple of stops, such as Yekaterinburg and Irkutsk.

Travel the route any time. July and August are very popular with foreign tourists, so you'll need to book well ahead. Winter is quieter and delivers the snow-covered Siberia that many dream about.

Nearly all foreign visitors to Russia require a visa. It's wise to start organising this about three months before your visit. See www.mid.ru/en/main_en for

© DEMERZEL21 | GETTY IMAGES

Snap a selfie at Vladivostok to commemorate the epic journey you've just completed.

Vladivostok

One of the journey's most anticipated sights, the ancient Lake Baikal is the deepest in the world.

East Coast Main Line

ENGLAND & SCOTLAND

START **LONDON**

END **EDINBURGH**

DEPARTS **DAILY**

DISTANCE 393 MILES (632KM)

DURATION **4 HRS 20 MINS**

The East Coast Main Line, along with its west-coast rival, is one of Britain's two great spines of tracks, snaking between London's Kings Cross terminal and the sunken cutting of Edinburgh Waverley. In between is 393 miles (632km) of fast running, with blink-and-you'll-miss-it highlights along the way. This route is the historic path of the Flying Scotsman service linking the Scottish and English capitals, with frequent fast services calling at towns and cities in between. With York, Durham and Newcastle as convenient stopping points, the East Coast Main Line can form the basis of a multi-day British itinerary. With more planning, some of the UK's unknown pleasures lie a short detour from the line.

❶ RIDING THE RAILS

Dodging the queues for Platform 9¾ photos reminds visitors to London's King's Cross that this is Harry Potter territory. But an East Coast journey is no retro Hogwarts Express. Though recent renovations at King's Cross, like those at its neighbour St Pancras, may have restored a touch of glamour to northward departures from the capital, this is a modern, fast railway. InterCity 225 trains pick up speed through north London neighbourhoods, passing Arsenal Football Club's stadium and Alexandra Palace, standing sentinel on the flank of the city's northern heights. The railway rides high above Hertfordshire on the Welwyn Viaduct, then settles into its high-speed rhythm alongside rolling pastoral scenery that characterises most of the journey.

The most notable staging post on the route comes after two hours at York, where impressive walls bear

RIGHT & BELOW: York Minster; Alnwick Castle. **PREVIOUS PAGE:** Bamburgh Castle.

witness to millennia of history. Here Constantine the Great was proclaimed Roman Emperor on the death of his father in AD 304 and Vikings led by Ivar the Boneless attacked in AD 866. York's medieval streets and imposing minster are a delight to explore, though passing through here without visiting the National Railway Museum would be to miss one of the world's finest transport heritage centres. Famous locos, including the Mallard and the Duchess of Hamilton, gleam in the engine shed along with a replica of the Rocket, the steam engine that started it all.

Back on the rails, attentive travellers should sit up at Darlington, one end of the Stockton-to-Darlington line, the world's first public railway to use steam locomotives. Twenty-four miles on from here is another great icon of the line, Durham's Norman-era cathedral. With its adjacent castle, it offers a suitably

dramatic welcome to the northeast of England. The largest city in this proud region, Newcastle-upon-Tyne, is the next stop en route, with the line curving over the Tyne giving great views of the eponymous bridge.

Between Newcastle and the Scottish border is the highlight of the line and one of Europe's most scenic stretches of track. North of the village of Alnmouth it hugs the Northumberland coast, with beaches, rocky coves and the North Sea on one side, and swaying cornfields on the other. Those low-lying patches of land out to sea are the Farne Islands, home to seals and puffins, and the pilgrim magnet of Holy Island, linked to the mainland by a tidal causeway. Just before Berwick-upon-Tweed, the train crosses the Royal Border Bridge and, shortly after, you're in Scotland. From here the line continues through rural Borders country with the odd glimpse of the sea, including Bass Rock in the Firth of Forth, before approaching Edinburgh. The train pulls in beneath the castle and the Old Town, offering a final feast for the eyes before passengers enter Edinburgh Waverley.

SEASIDE NORTHUMBERLAND

The sea, a castle, a beach, all flashing by at high speed, with London hours behind but Edinburgh fast approaching – the Northumberland stretch of the East Coast Main Line is arguably Britain's most scenic inter-city stretch of railway.

Pose for pictures at London King's Cross' Harry Potter highlights.

Spot the prototype tracked hovercraft monorail preserved at Railworld, Peterborough.

Revel in the historic views of York's minster and city walls.

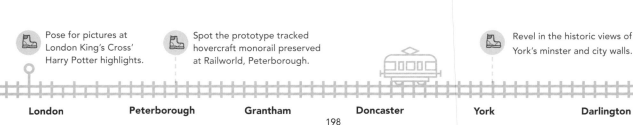

London   **Peterborough**   **Grantham**   **Doncaster**   **York**   **Darlington**

❷ LIFE ON BOARD

The fast and frequent services that travel up and down the East Coast Main Line are heavily used, especially at peak times. A seat reservation is a must in standard class if you don't want to join the huddled masses grabbing a seat where they can. An upgrade to 1st class offers a larger seat, free hot food during the week and a little more space and calm in which to enjoy the journey.

❸ ALTERNATIVE ROUTES

Other mainline scenic delights in the UK include the West Coast Main Line's run through the Lune Gorge in Cumbria and the breathtaking seafront sprint taken by local and high-speed services at Dawlish in Devon on the Great Western Railway.

❹ MAKE IT HAPPEN

Fares are priced for demand, with peak-time services making far more of a dent in your daily budget than quieter trains. To get the best value, be flexible about when you travel and avoid commuter times. Tickets generally go on sale three months in advance, though some tickets are available before that.

Although it's not essential, advance booking online (at www.nationalrail.co.uk) can save you a lot of money, as well as stress, on any of the UK's main railway lines. On some trains you might find that advance fares in 1st class make this a more affordable option than you think.

You should plan to arrive in good time for your departure, both to get through what can be a crowded concourse area to your train at King's Cross and to stop by London's best Harry Potter store. **TH**

Watch a magnificent stretch of castle-studded coastline unfold between Alnmouth and Berwick-upon-Tweed.

Relish one of Scotland's finest scenes as the line cuts through the heart of Edinburgh.

Durham   Newcastle-upon-Tyne   Berwick-upon-Tweed   Dunbar   Edinburgh

Le Petit Train Jaune

FRANCE ●

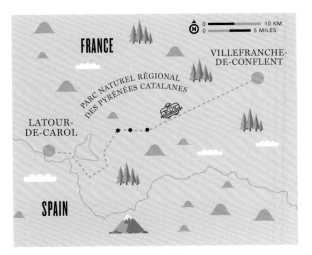

START	VILLEFRANCHE-DE-CONFLENT
END	LATOUR-DE-CAROL
DEPARTS	DAILY (IN SEASON)
DISTANCE	39 MILES (63KM)
DURATION	4 HRS 30 MINS

Since 1910, the dinky, sunflower-yellow carriages of the Ligne de Cerdagne have been rattling and clattering their way through the rolling forests and saw-toothed mountains of the Pyrenees, and they have secured a special place in the hearts of many French travellers. Affectionately known as the Canary, or Le Petit Train Jaune (Little Yellow Train), this mountain railway is frequently cited as the most scenic in France, but it's definitely not a luxury service – it's a rollercoaster ride on which you will feel the wind in your hair and the chill of the mountain breeze as you ratchet your way up to the highest train station in France. On y va!

❶ RIDING THE RAILS

Le Petit Train Jaune looks for all the world like something that's tumbled out of a child's toy box, but don't be fooled by its pint-sized dimensions: this little train is a lot tougher than it looks. Many of the original choo-choos that came into service in 1910 are still chugging along, trundling along the same stretch of track for more than a hundred years, although more recently they've been supplemented by a couple of modern, air-conditioned trains. For purists, though, the only way to ride the Petit Train is aboard one of

the original carriages – complete with their wooden seats, little windows and iconic red-and-yellow livery, inspired by the *sang et or* (blood and gold) colours of the Catalan flag.

The train begins its journey in the walled town of Villefranche-de-Conflent, an old pilgrimage waypoint high up in the French Pyrenees. Ringed by stout, ramparted walls devised by the great medieval military architect Vauban, the town makes a fittingly pretty place for the Petit Train to begin its journey. With a rumble of its engine and a shrill toot-toot of its horn, it crawls out of Villefranche and before long is whizzing through sweeping Pyrenean scenery, surrounded by rolling mountains, rushing streams and deep, densely wooded valleys.

Though the narrow-gauge train never goes more than about 34mph (55km/h), it feels as if it's travelling much faster – especially if you've bagged a seat on one of the open-topped carriages, where the wind is guaranteed to play havoc with your hairdo. From

"The Train Jaune inches along canyons, hurtles over gorges and teeters past dizzying cliff edges"

here, however, you're also certain to get a grandstand view of the scenery. Hilltop villages cling to the steep mountain slopes and golden church towers stand out like signposts against the clear blue sky.

The Ligne de Cerdagne was originally devised to connect the high mountain settlements and the lower foothills of the Pyrenees. Prior to its construction, the only way to reach many of the area's rural villages was on foot or by donkey, following the twisting tracks trodden by generations of shepherds and hill farmers. The railway was a laudable but challenging project to complete, and required no fewer than 19 tunnels and 650 bridges due to the tough mountainous terrain. Although the first section of track from Villefranche

to Mont-Louis was opened in 1910, the final section up to Latour-de-Carol wasn't completed until 1927. Snowfall can often cover the track during winter, and the train is even equipped with its own custom-made snow plough.

However, the difficulties of its construction are exactly what makes this such a thrilling train ride. Along its 39-mile (63km) route, the Train Jaune inches along canyons, hurtles over gorges and teeters past sheer, dizzying cliff edges that would make most modern railway engineers turn pale and tremble.

It also crosses two landmark viaducts: the Pont Gisclard, France's only railway suspension bridge, which hangs 260ft (80m) in the air above a wooded gorge, and the equally impressive Viaduc Sejourné, a double-tiered wonder that took 1500 workmen more than three years to build. Usually, the train slows down as it crosses these bridges to allow passengers to savour the experience and appreciate the precipitous views – and since the line is electrified, with power supplied by a hydroelectric dam higher up the Têt

© BART DUBELAAR | GETTY IMAGES

THEM'S THE BRAKES

The Train Jaune is possibly the only train in the world which has three independent braking systems: standard mechanical brakes, Westinghouse air brakes and electric rheostat brakes. This ensures that it's practically impossible for the train to experience complete brake failure – a comforting fact, given the gradients and mountainous terrain.

Wander the lanes of the lovely walled town of Villefranche-de-Conflent.

Snap a picture as you rattle over the double-tiered Viaduc Sejourné.

Hold your breath as you cross the gravity-defying Pont Gisclard.

Villefranche-de-Conflent

Mont-Louis la-Cabanasse

CLOCKWISE FROM LEFT: Le Petit Train Jaune; the streets and skyline of Villefranche de Conflent; tasting that fresh mountain air.
PREVIOUS PAGE: Crossing one of the 650 bridges en route.

Valley, there's no rumbling diesel engine to disturb the vast, airy mountain silence.

About halfway along the journey, the Little Yellow Train crawls up through the fortified town of Mont-Louis-la-Cabanasse before reaching its highest point at Bolquère-Eyne – which, at a lofty 5223ft (1592m), is also the highest station on all of the French rail network. At the top, passengers step out to stretch their legs and pull on jackets to combat the chilly mountain air; even on the sunniest days, temperatures on the summit are several degrees lower than in the surrounding valleys. Some people head off to explore the many hiking trails that criss-cross the plateau; others decide to stop at one of the traditional bistros in Mont-Louis-la-Cabanasse or Font-Romeu to feast on some *garbure* (mountain stew) and *aligot* (mashed potato), washed down, *naturellement*, with a *pichet* or two of red wine.

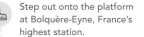

Step out onto the platform at Bolquère-Eyne, France's highest station.

Bolquère-Eyne

Font-Romeu

RIGHT: There are many tunnels on the
39-mile journey, too – 19 in total.

Many people terminate their journey here, but purists
continue another 16 miles (25km) or so further west
to the Train Jaune's last stop at Latour-de-Carol, just
a scant mile or two from the Spanish border. Here,
it's possible to connect with the mainline high-speed
services to Toulouse and Barcelona – but if you catch
the early train, there's time to enjoy a leisurely lunch,
have a wander around town and catch the train back
in time for dinner in Villefranche.

It's a fine idea: the Petit Train Jaune is one of those
rare railway journeys that's well worth doing twice.

❷ LIFE ON BOARD

The Train Jaune is a no-frills service, but its simplicity
is all part of its charm. Depending on the time of
day, the line runs either old-fashioned vintage cars or
more-modern air-conditioned ones; look for *ancien* or
moderne on timetables, or ask station staff when you
book. On the vintage trains, there are a maximum of
six carriages; usually a couple are open-top and the
rest are covered. Seats are wooden, so be prepared for
a numb bum after three hours of travel. Most of the
22 stations along the line are *arrêts facultatifs*, or
request stops – if you want to get off at one, you need
to let the driver know well in advance.

❸ MAKE IT HAPPEN

Le Petit Train Jaune runs year-round. There are
usually between five and seven trains a day in
summer, with a reduced service in winter. The train is
operated by TER, the regional subsidiary of France's
national train operator, SNCF. Tickets can be booked
at www.voyages-sncf.com. Depending on the season,
two or three trains a day run from Villefranche-
de-Conflent (which is indicated on timetables as
Villefranche Vernet-les-Bains) all the way to Latour-
de-Carol; the rest only go as far as Font-Romeu. **OB**

Look out over the Pyrenees
towards the Spanish border at
Latour-de-Carol.

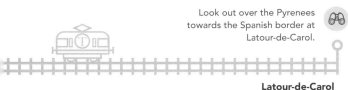

Latour-de-Carol

Belgrade-to-Bar Railway

SERBIA & MONTENEGRO ●

START **BELGRADE**

END **BAR**

DEPARTS **DAILY**

DISTANCE 296 MILES (476KM)

DURATION **12 HRS**

Dramatic is the operative word for this route, which rumbles over unsullied, mountainous landscape from the Serbian capital to Montenegro's Adriatic coast. During the 12-hour journey, the train disappears into the Dinaric Alps, charges through canyons, teeters on stilted bridges spanning river gorges and skims atop an ancient, tectonic lake. Like the region it serves, the railway, which chugs across the heart of the Western Balkans, eludes most tourists' maps. The reward for treasure-hunting travellers, who are informed (or lucky) enough to know where to dig: an embarrassment of authentic culture and pristine geographic riches at every bend.

❶ RIDING THE RAILS

Though the Belgrade–Bar line doesn't have a sexy moniker like the Royal Scotsman or Rocky Mountaineer, the 'Yugoslav Flyer' would be apt. When construction began on the 296-mile (476km) railway in 1951, the Socialist Federal Republic of Yugoslavia was in its infancy: a tenuous post-World War II cadre of states on the Balkan Peninsula's western half. By the time the route opened in 1976, complete with 254 tunnels and 234 bridges winding down from the

Pannonian Plain to the island-studded Adriatic Sea, the country was a geopolitical force and a synapse between the West and the Soviet Union.

Yugoslavia has since splintered into seven nations. The railway, thankfully, endures, connecting Serbia to Montenegro with a brief blip across Bosnia & Hercegovina's eastern border. But the line's existence represents more than just a continued,

CLOCKWISE FROM RIGHT: View from the train in the mountains of Montenegro; old clock tower, Bar.
PREVIOUS PAGE: Riverside Belgrade.

now-international, transport option. These tracks are the Balkans – and a lifeline to a swath of land where cultures have intertwined for centuries. Here, where East meets West, the train takes adventurers across vistas criss-crossed by Greeks and Illyrians, as well as the Roman, Byzantine, Ottoman and Austro-Hungarian Empires. Along the way, visitors have a window onto a living museum exhibit frozen in time.

This sensation begins even before stepping onto a carriage. At the confluence of the Sava and Danube Rivers, Belgrade's crenelated railway station is a faded Habsburg-yellow throwback, opened in 1884. Before boarding the weathered but comfortable cabins, it's not a stretch to imagine 19th-century travellers making the same pre-voyage preparations – water, bread, cheese; flask of *rakija* (schnapps) – when this

was a key stop along the Orient Express. Then, within an hour, the tangle of urban metal and concrete unravels, and the countryside spreads out in all directions. Emerald-green hummocks play leapfrog until they dive out of sight over the horizon.

'I had no idea what to expect,' said passenger and UK native Colin Smith. Outside the window, an old couple leaned against pitchforks next to haystacks. Behind them, vegetable gardens and plum trees aproned a stone farmhouse. 'But I'm surprised by the beauty, mountains, steep ravines and endless drops.'

Like any great entertainer, the railway saves superlatives for the finale. As the sun sets, the tracks levitate atop the 1637ft/499m-long, 650ft/198m-tall Mala Rijeka Viaduct, one of the planet's highest railway bridges. Then the train glides over the Balkans' largest lake, Skadar, which straddles the Montenegro–Albania border. Finally, it pulls into Bar – home to the world's oldest olive tree, more than 2000 years old – where the Adriatic's salty air stamps the route's end... but the beginning of your Balkan odyssey.

© MILA ATKOVSKA | SHUTTERSTOCK

© SASHKO | SHUTTERSTOCK

ONE RIDE, THREE COUNTRIES

The train was built to service one country, Yugoslavia. Today, visitors cross three borders: Serbia, Montenegro and Bosnia & Hercegovina. This is exciting for travellers seeking to add a new country to their CV. However, be warned: there is no stop in Bosnia, nor are passports stamped.

Experience Belgrade's shabby-chic train station, opened in 1884, and once a main stop on the Orient Express.

At Topčider Station glimpse the locomotives where Yugoslav leader Marshal Tito's famous Blue Train is stored.

Belgrade　　　　　　　　　**Požega**　　　　　　　　　**Užice**

❷ LIFE ON BOARD

The carriages are worn, and overdue a makeover, but comfortable. Though there is a dining car on many trains – on all during high season (June to September) – it is a good idea to purchase water, snacks and more substantial sustenance from the Belgrade Station bakery next to the ticket window before boarding. Not only will the croissant, sandwich or *burek* (a filo pastry filled with meat) be less expensive, fresher and of better quality, you'll avoid the wait for lunch on the train and be able to relax with your meal without leaving your cabin. Also make sure you pack wipes. Toilet paper, and bathroom cleanliness, are, unfortunately, not guaranteed.

There are 1st- and 2nd-class options on the train but, with regards to regular seating, this is largely a matter of semantics. Not only are the compartments similar in quality, but it is common – and acceptable – practice for passengers holding 2nd-class tickets to sit in 1st. Class differentiation is more pertinent to night-train passengers, who can choose between levels of exclusivity and compartments that have two or three beds, or couchettes with four to six.

❸ MAKE IT HAPPEN

The line runs twice per day, in both directions, one in the morning and one in the evening. Book tickets at the station a day in advance. Reservations are essential and purchased in addition to the ticket.

The best way to experience the journey is one-way from Belgrade, ending your journey on the Adriatic Coast. The early train from Belgrade, in summer, provides epic sunset views through Montenegro's Dinaric Alps, across Lake Skadar and to the Adriatic. Sit on the right side of the train for the best views.

For most countries, valid passports are all that's needed for travel. For up-to-date timetables and further information visit srbvoz.rs. **AC**

Bathe in a Dinaric Alps sunset while crossing the Mala Rijeka Viaduct, one of the world's highest railway bridges.

The Balkans largest lake – the ancient and tectonic Lake Skadar – straddles the Montenegro–Albania border.

Luxuriate in Bar, home to the world's oldest olive tree (more than 2000 years old), along Montenegro's Adriatic coast.

rijepolje　　　　　Podgorica　　　　　Sutomore　　　　　Bar

Bernina Express

SWITZERLAND

START CHUR

END TIRANO

DEPARTS DAILY

DISTANCE 96 MILES (156KM)

DURATION 4 HRS 30 MINS

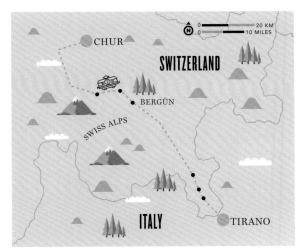

We can wax lyrical about the glacier-capped mountains, waterfall-draped ravines, jewel-coloured lakes and endless spruce forests glimpsed through panoramic windows on Switzerland's Bernina Express but, trust us, seeing is believing. Rolling from Chur in Graubünden to Tirano in northern Italy in four too-quick hours, this narrow-gauge train often tops polls of the world's most beautiful rail journeys. Beyond the phenomenal Alpine landscape, the railway itself is a masterpiece of early 20th-century engineering, taking 55 tunnels and 196 bridges in its stride. The section known as the RhB Albula Line is listed by Unesco World Heritage – and with good reason.

❶ RIDING THE RAILS

So you've reserved your ticket for the Bernina Express? Wise choice. You're in for a four-hour treat where your nose (and probably your camera lens) will be pinned to the window. Regardless of the time of year, this rail journey bombards you with natural beauty. In spring, the contrast between the stark, still-snowcapped Alps and mellower Italian climes erupting with flowers is perhaps most striking. In summer everything has a green lustre and cows swing their bells on the high pastures, while autumn is a

paintbox of ochres and auburns. Winter? Well, it's a full-blown fairy tale, with fir forests rising to ragged mountains frosted white with snow.

As for the railway itself, it's like an impeccably looked-after Hornby train set come to life, with its red paint job and scale completely disproportionate to the epically wild landscapes it passes through. At times, the loops, spiral viaducts and sheer inclines with gradients of up to 7% make it every bit as exhilarating – if not quite as fast – as a rollercoaster. And it's one of the world's steepest railways: climbing all the way up to 7392ft (2253m) without a cogwheel track.

The train begins in Chur, Switzerland's oldest city, inhabited since 3000 BC, which has an intact medieval Old Town and a liberal scattering of galleries. Catching the early morning (8.30am) Bernina Express here means you'll be in Italy in time for lunch. Cool, huh? Through the window, you'll snatch glimpses of the milky grey-green, fast-flowing Plessur River, a tributary of the Rhine, flanked by

"The showpiece of the railway, towering Landwasser Viaduct makes passengers draw breath"

forests of fir and pine. The train clatters onwards through valleys and meadows, and past castle-topped crags and the grey, moraine-streaked Plessur Alps, which top out around the 9850ft (3000m) mark. Thusis, at the foot of the fin-shaped peak of Piz Beverin, is both the start of the Unesco-listed Albula Line and the gateway to the Viamala gorge.

The Hinterrhein River thrashes a path through this narrow gorge, where massive high cliffs rear up on either side. The Viamala struck fear into the hearts of early travellers through the Alps, but crossing it by rail now is a piece of cake. Going strong since 1903, the single-track Albula Line connects Thusis and St Moritz, ascending about 3300ft (1000m) in the

act. As the ride becomes increasingly dramatic, an attentive hush often falls over the passengers, now intent on trying to capture the moment with cameras or smartphones. And never more so than when the ravine-spanning Solis Viaduct slides into view – it's an 11-arched limestone wonder rising 292ft (89m) above the turquoise Albula River.

But if you think that's impressive, it's really just the prelude for the most photogenic of moments. Beyond the dinky hamlet of Tiefencastel, where a frescoed, bauble-domed church stands sentinel on a hill, you reach the Landwasser Viaduct, the showpiece of the Rhaetian Railway. Towering 213ft (65m), the gracefully arched viaduct causes passengers to draw breath because of the way it curves between wooded crags above a distant slither of river, before ducking into a tunnel and emerging in the Engadine Valley.

Around the prettily frescoed village of Bergün, at the foot of the Albula Pass, the scenery is lovely beyond belief: this is Parc Ela, Switzerland's largest nature park spreading across 212 sq miles (548 sq km).

© JUSTIN FOULKES | LONELY PLANET

© JUSTIN FOULKES | LONELY PLANET

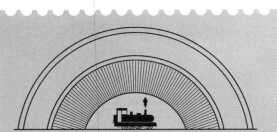

HIKING TO ALP GRÜM

If you fancy stretching your legs and taking a closer look at the tremendous landscapes of the Bernina Pass, jump off for the 3-mile (4.9km) hike from Ospizio Bernina to Alp Grüm, which skirts iridescent Lago Bianco, dips into forest and then opens up arresting views of the Poschiavo Valley and Palü Glacier.

Grab a window seat to ooh and ahh over the sensational views on the Unesco World Heritage–listed Albula Line.

Feel the excitement mount as the train reaches the Landwasser Viaduct's almighty arches.

Swoon over the flower-freckled meadows, pine forests and glacier-capped mountains in Parc Ela.

Chur **Tiefencastel** **Filisur** **Bergün/Bravuogn**

CLOCKWISE FROM LEFT: The Bernina Express barrels through Switzerland; crossing two of several picturesque viaducts. **PREVIOUS PAGES:** There's good reason this is rated one of the most beautiful rail journeys.

© ROBERTO MOIOLA | SYSAWORLD | GETTY IMAGES

Forests and luxuriously green meadows cloak the lower reaches while clouds cast shadows as they scud across the jagged heights. It's a wonderful snapshot of the Alps as they were before the dawn of tourism. Between Preda and Spinas the train scoots into the Albula Tunnel, another marvel of rail engineering dating to 1903; a new tunnel is set to replace it in 2021.

Now the Bernina Express enters the Upper Engadine proper, a long, high Alpine valley that follows the course of the Inn River. The Bernina Line takes over now, with some real treasures in store. The rugged Bernina Range dominates the resort town of Pontresina (the more relaxed sister of St Moritz) and you'll soon clasp eyes on the mighty Morteratsch Glacier, a 4-mile (7km) superhighway of crevassed blue ice; and 13,284ft (4049m) Piz Bernina – the route's namesake and crowning glory is the highest mountain in the Eastern Alps.

The vertiginous tracks continue and the train hauls its way up to Graubünden's highest station at the Bernina Pass, Ospizio Bernina (7392ft/2253m), on the shores of minty-blue Lago Bianco reservoir, which is framed by bald, rocky peaks. Should you fancy staying the night at the mountain refuge, there's some enticing hiking in the area.

From Ospizio Bernina, the train begins a gradual 5984ft (1824m) descent to Tirano at 1407ft (429m), pulling into Alp Grüm at 6860ft (2091m). Here you'll snatch a glance of the hairpin-riddled road that wriggles down through the broad, Italian-speaking valley of Val Poschiavo, bounded by high, densely forested mountains, which runs all the way to the border. Keep an eye out for the glinting Palü Glacier en route to Poschiavo, where the medieval Old Town has Italianate good looks thanks to its shuttered, pastel-painted houses.

Be floored by the sight of Piz Bernina and the Morteratsch Glacier in the Engadine.

Marvel at the astonishingly turquoise Lago Bianco from the route's highest station, Ospizio Bernina (7392ft/2253m).

See the road twist spectacularly down to the Val Poschiavo from Alp Grüm.

Ospizio Bernina

Alp Grüm

Poschiavo

Skirting the shores of mountain-rimmed Lago di Poschiavo, the train reaches its final climax: the astonishing Brusio spiral viaduct, which corkscrews down to Tirano. The scenery now gives way to orchards and campaniles, and when you step out of the train at Tirano, there's no mistaking you are in Italy. Yet you know that just over those brooding mountains lies Switzerland.

❷ LIFE ON BOARD

The train interior is very comfortable and panoramic windows ramp up those fabulous views. There's no restaurant but there is a refreshment trolley serving drinks and snacks, or you're welcome to bring your own picnic on board.

❸ BUDGET ALTERNATIVE

Ordinary SBB trains travel the same route as the Bernina Express (minus the panoramic windows) and give you more choice of times. You don't need any seat reservation for these, just the basic ticket, which will be slightly cheaper than snapping up the 2nd-class option on the Bernina Express.

❹ MAKE IT HAPPEN

The service departs daily. Advance tickets can be booked online at www.rhb.ch or www.sbb.ch. Securing a ticket a couple of days ahead is usually fine, but the sooner the better during the peak summer season. For a little more space, fewer passengers and even bigger windows, upgrade to the 1st-class carriage. For the best views, sit on the right-hand side of the train when going south and the left going north. Between early July and late October, the Bernina Express has open-air scenic carriages between Davos Platz and Tirano. These provide plenty of all-round views, fresh air and opportunities for photographs. **KC**

Le Prese   Tirano

Venice Simplon-Orient-Express

UK, FRANCE, SWITZERLAND, AUSTRIA, ITALY ●

START LONDON

END VENICE

DEPARTS I TO 6 PER MONTH
DISTANCE 1300 MILES (2090KM)

DURATION 2 DAYS

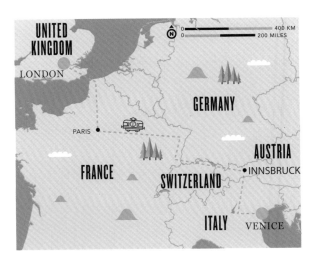

Is anything in travel more romantic than the Orient Express? The promise of travelling from London to Venice cocooned in luxury, twinkly dining cars a-chink with fine china and silver cutlery, is surely one that endures in the hearts of all rail enthusiasts – though adventurers would probably have loved one of the original services from 1889 even more: a through-train that connected Paris with Istanbul in 67½ hours. That, and the Orient Express' various other 20th-century routes, are sadly long gone, but the Venice Simplon-Orient-Express offers a tantalising sample of the original on a trip that is surely the best journey back in time ever. But at more than £2000 for 24 hours on the rails, is it worth it?

❶ RIDING THE RAILS

Your 21st-century taste of the belle-époque high life begins not in one of the iconic Orient Express carriages but in an elegant restored Belmond British Pullman train, which chugs out of London's Victoria Station towards Folkestone in a satisfyingly pomp-filled fashion. It's a lovely way to start the journey, watching smudgy London disappear from view as you sink into a plush armchair in one of the open-plan saloons. Or perhaps you've taken your seat in

one of the four-seat compartments at the ends of the carriages (request one when you book if you want the privacy, though part of the fun is getting to know your fellow passengers). Brunch with a Bellini sets the tone for the afternoon to come as you pootle through the rolling Kent countryside towards Folkestone West. Here the trip back in time hits a rather startling bump when you're transferred to coaches for the Channel Tunnel crossing on a car-carrying Eurotunnel train.

Once through the tunnel, though, the journey proper begins with a transfer to Calais Ville and one of the original 1920s' Orient Express sleeping cars. The wow factor begins the moment the stately royal-blue and gold-trimmed carriages hove into view, and is seriously ramped up when you're introduced to what's inside them. Carefully restored single, twin and double compartments or interconnecting suites all sport beautiful wooden marquetry upholstered in a vaguely Oriental style, and are lit to convey a genuinely thrilling sense of the route's early 20th-

CLOCKWISE FROM RIGHT: Be sure
to partake in on board pleasures; Piazza
San Marco in Venice. PREVIOUS PAGE:
A gondolier for hire.

century heyday, when the glamour of the service
fitted the spirit of the times, when commercial planes
had yet to provide a faster alternative for the nobles,
diplomats and assorted starlets whizzing across a war-
scarred Europe.

As pristine stewards in uniforms matching the
train's livery skilfully make you feel at home, you
start to take everything in – the impossibly plush
upholstery, the baby grand piano in the bar, the
stunning art deco design of the champagne bar, even
the different mosaics on the floors of each bathroom
– and the years flip backward like one of those movie
sequences. Outside, Vimy, Arras and Longeau roll by;
inside, you wouldn't be surprised to see Hercule Poirot
blundering through the dining car hot on the heels of
suspicious-looking types up to nefarious deeds.

As evening turns to night you find yourself listening
to the pianist and wondering if previous real-life
passengers such as Leon Trotsky, Mata Hari, TE
Lawrence or Leo Tolstoy were treated to the same
tune (they weren't – the original Orient Express
had no bars, just a restaurant and the sleeping
compartments). The sense of being transported to
another century mounts as you dress for a suitably
upscale modern-European four-course dinner,
and when you come back to your cabin to find it
transformed into the sweetest bedroom imaginable,
the price tag really does seem worth it.

© MATT MUNRO | LONELY PLANET

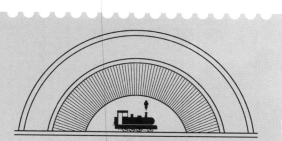

INSIDE OUTSIDE

While this is one rail experience that's more about
the train than the journey, don't discount the latter.
Waking up in your cabin to the sight of the majestic
snow-capped peaks of the Alps is truly magical,
and the route continues to offer treats as you head
through northern Italy's Dolomites and the rustic
towns and villages of Piedmont and the Veneto.

Wake up to the train skirting
picture-postcard Lake Zurich – it
passes close to the water.

❷ LIFE ON BOARD

Refreshment options consist of three restaurants and two bars; you'll be allocated a restaurant for dinner by your steward, but can always request a different one if you have a favourite. Continental breakfast and afternoon tea are served in your compartment; lunch and dinner in the dining cars.

❸ BUDGET ALTERNATIVE

Taking the Eurostar to Paris can be a snip, with special offers from £29 one way. Onward high-speed TGV trains to Turin or Milan are frequent and can be had for even less, with a simple change to the Frecciarossa high-speed train to Venice. But even more fun is to trace the journey of the original Orient Express from Paris to Istanbul, poring over the multitude of separate trains and linking them together according to your preferences. Sleeping cars may not be as fancy, but the romance of the rails is still very much there. And if you want to put on a posh frock and sip Prosecco in the snack bar of your modern train, we're not about to stop you.

❹ MAKE IT HAPPEN

There are one to six trains per month from March to November. Tickets can be booked directly with operator Belmond (www.belmond.com), or at www.railbookers.co.uk. Reserve your cabin as soon as you have firm dates. The London-to-Venice route is the most popular but the return journey takes in more spectacular scenery. The best time of year to go is October when cabins are cosy and the snowy mountains are photogenic. There are no showers on the train, so you might want to bring deodorant. But don't bring jeans or trainers; the dress code is smart-casual during the day, and proper dressing up for dinner; period costume is a popular option. **SB & YZ**

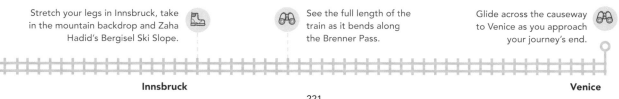

Stretch your legs in Innsbruck, take in the mountain backdrop and Zaha Hadid's Bergisel Ski Slope.

See the full length of the train as it bends along the Brenner Pass.

Glide across the causeway to Venice as you approach your journey's end.

Innsbruck

Venice

Heart of Wales Line

WALES & ENGLAND ●

START	SWANSEA	
END	SHREWSBURY	
DEPARTS	DAILY	DURATION 4 HRS
DISTANCE 121 MILES (194KM)		

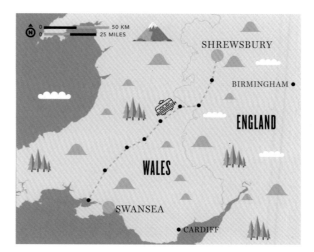

 Winning the prize for the line with the most nightmarish-to-pronounce station names in Britain, this is Swansea to Shrewsbury the slow and, frankly, surreal way. This one-carriage train traverses track through Wales and England that might easily have been consigned to a museum or an out-of-print book but that has somehow defied time and logic to survive as a passenger route. Expect a spectrum of scenery, alternating from the sand-edged estuaries of South Wales, via bucolic farming towns and tracts of forest and hill country you probably never knew existed, through to one of England's prettiest medieval cities. This four-hour, 34-station zigzag passes almost no major sights or settlements, but a very high concentration of spectacularly zany ones.

❶ RIDING THE RAILS

Swansea might not seem the immediately obvious spot to begin an enthralling journey account, but Wales' second-biggest city does sit within stunning surroundings, most notably the fairy-tale sandy strands that grace the Gower Peninsula. Truth be told, though, gorgeous scenery flanks the whole Heart of Wales Line, and in most of it you will have

just sheep, cows and wheeling red kites to contend with as you explore.

Views are instantly alluring as you embark on the first stage of the trundle, where you cross the wide, lovely Loughor Estuary, full of silvery sandbanks and chattering seabirds, with the north of the Gower Peninsula visible across the water. After Llanelli the line then bisects undulating emerald-green farming land and former coal-mining communities before reaching the first worthwhile stop, Llandeilo. This brightly painted arts-and-crafts town shelters beneath dramatically perched Dinefwr Castle, erstwhile home of the Princes of Wales. Ten miles southwest is the National Botanic Garden of Wales, its gargantuan domed greenhouse and the intuitively landscaped grounds forming one of the country's foremost horticultural hotspots.

The route touches outstanding areas of natural beauty. Llandeilo and Llandovery lend close-at-hand access to the north-westerly Brecon Beacons, while

OPPOSITE & BELOW: Station at LLandrindod Wells; sheep shearing, Welsh style, at the Royal Welsh Show. **PREVIOUS PAGE:** Some of the Cynghordy Viaduct's 18 arches, built in 1867.

Llandovery and the subsequent seven stops until Builth Road abut the Cambrian Mountains, an area so isolated it also hails by the somewhat comical moniker 'Desert of Wales'.

A number of rivers rise near here and the gradients rise too: the line climbs to 820ft (250m) near the remotest station, Sugar Loaf. Striking viaducts at Cynghordy and again at Knucklas were among the constructors' solutions for navigating the troublesome topography, and there are six tunnels along the railway altogether.

Four old spa towns lie along this leg of the line: Llanwrtyd Wells, Llangammarch Wells, Builth Wells and Llandrindod Wells. Their serendipitous haughty Victorian architecture hints at their former function, but today they are better known for some of Wales' quirkiest and most quintessential festivals, including the World Bog-Snorkelling Championships (Llanwrtyd Wells) and the Royal Welsh Show (Builth Wells).

The railway winds towards England and Shropshire in between the ruddy uplands of the Radnor Forest, a one-time royal hunting ground. The most beguiling of several stops hereabouts is upmarket Church Stretton, nestled under the ridge of Long Mynd, and a popular hiking base.

And so the four-hour ride rumbles to a fittingly photogenic finish in medieval Shrewsbury, famed for its timber-framed buildings, many of which are over half a millennium old. A sense of sophisticated urbanity as you wander through the town's history is, conversely, your last impression of a train ride that for most of its length has been as randomly rural as railways in Wales or England get.

REQUEST STOPS

The Heart of Wales Line might have 34 stations, but lots are request stops only. If you are getting off at any of these, notify the conductor as soon as possible and, ideally, several stops before your disembarkation station. If you are getting on, stand in a prominent place on the platform and give a distinct hand signal to the oncoming train.

Before leaving, linger on the Gower Peninsula's enticing beaches, easily reachable from Swansea.

Alight at Llandeilo for the National Botanic Garden of Wales, home of the planet's biggest single-span glasshouse.

Disembark at lonely Sugar Loaf Station for a walk or picnic around the iconic nearby knoll of the same name.

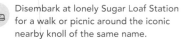

Swansea   Llandeilo   Sugar Loaf   Llanwrtyd

❷ LIFE ON BOARD

The thrills on this railway are all outside the windows. The locals who use the train's one carriage would argue it's certainly better than none at all. But get a boisterous group boarding and there is no escape to the quiet coach. Most Heart of Wales passengers go out of their way to be friendly. With mobile phone reception disappearing on whim and any sort of snack trolley well and truly absent, striking up small talk with a farmer, a rugby-match-watcher or a hiker is the best way to while away time on the line. It is rare indeed to make the whole journey without acquiring new friends or trading tales en route.

❸ ALTERNATIVE ROUTES

Routes also run between Swansea and Shrewsbury via the Welsh Marches Line. The trip is an hour quicker,

has a catering trolley, and is also pretty, but lacks the charm of the Heart of Wales Line because it's a main-line train that runs past most idiosyncratic backwater stations without stopping.

❹ MAKE IT HAPPEN

The end-stations are well connected. Swansea has direct trains to Cardiff and London while Shrewsbury is linked directly to Aberyswyth, Manchester and Birmingham. Any of the UK's nationwide train-booking websites (such as www.nationalrail.co.uk) will let you purchase tickets for any journey along this route. However there is little point in doing so: the train is seldom full and you can buy a ticket at the station just prior to departure. Ticket prices also remain the same whether purchased in advance or on the day. If you live in one of the regions the route runs through, consider purchasing the HoWL Card that offers up to a third off journey fares. **LW**

Break the trip at a Mid-Wales country retreat such as Lake Country House Hotel and Spa by Llangammarch Wells.

Check out gloriously situated Church Stretton, at the foot of the Shropshire Hills.

Wander the medieval streets and 'shuts' (passageways) of Shrewsbury, at journey's end.

Llangammarch   Builth Road   Church Stretton   Shrewsbury

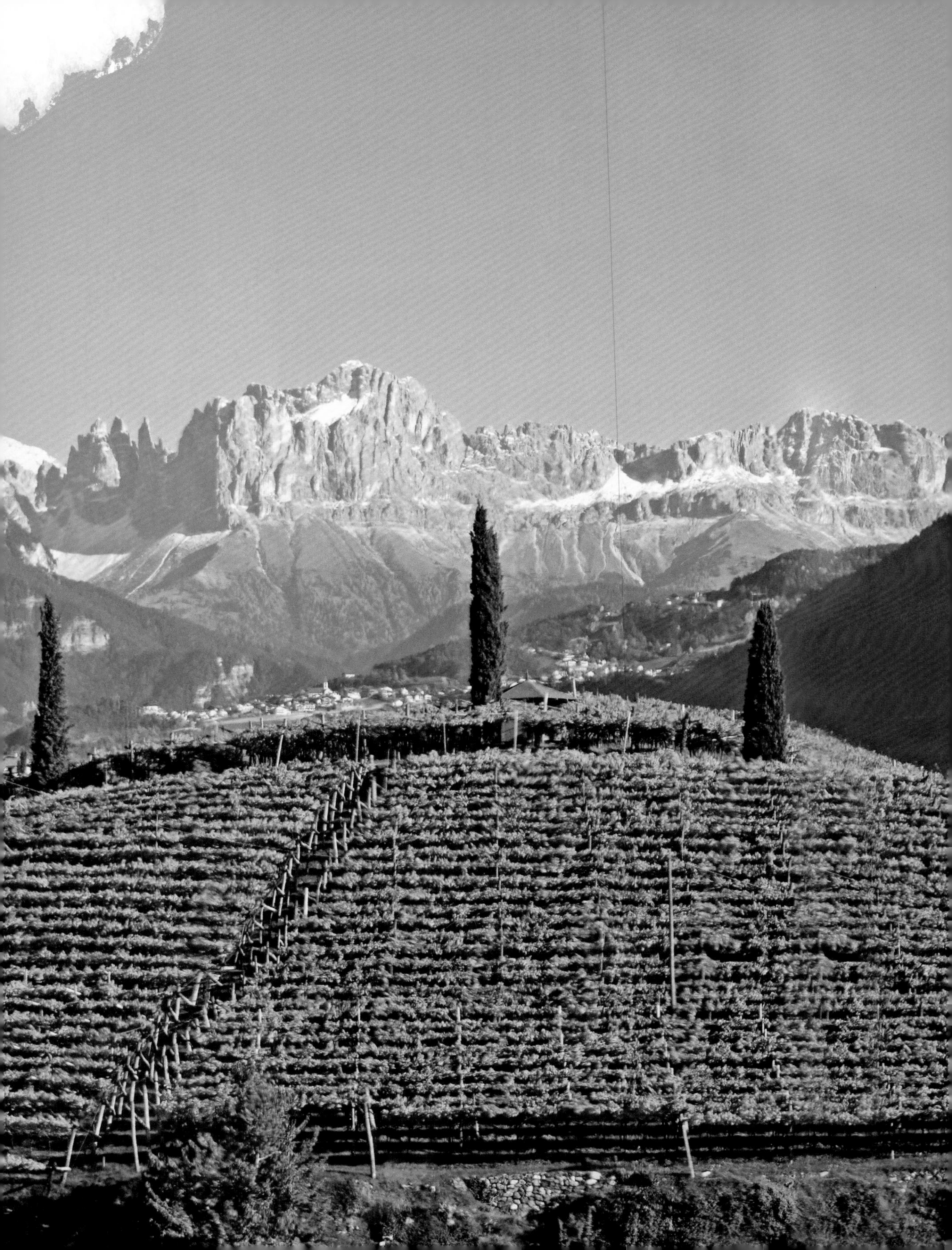

Munich to Venice on the Brenner Railway

GERMANY, AUSTRIA, ITALY ●

START **MUNICH**

END **VENICE**

DEPARTS **DAILY**

DISTANCE 350 MILES (563KM)

DURATION **6 HRS 30 MINS**

The Brenner Railway is attractive for two key reasons: mountains and wine. There may be more technically astonishing high-altitude trains, but this was the first to cross the Alps, in the 1860s. On a surprisingly speedy day trip, you pass through three countries – Germany, Austria and Italy – and descend from the snow line to sea level. The Austrian-run dining car serves hearty, seasonal mountain dishes, as well as impeccable Tyrolean wines. You're rarely far from highways, but the view, especially through the vineyards, is still stunning. Bonus: great European cities – Munich and Venice – at either end.

❶ RIDING THE RAILS

At first glance, Europe seems pretty orderly: people speak French in France, German in Germany, Italian in Italy. But look a little more closely and there are odd corners where history and borders are less consistent. One of those places is Italy's majority-German-speaking Südtirol, also known as the Alto Adige. And the train that serves it, the Brenner Railway, links this region to its past.

A project of the Austrian Empire, the train connected the empire's centre and its port in Venice. But no sooner had the line opened than, in 1866,

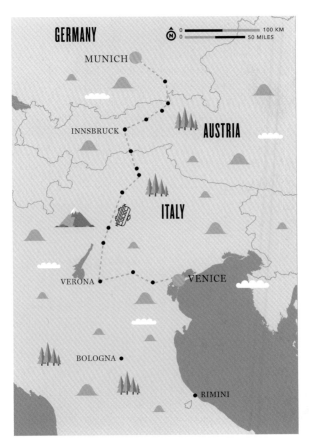

Venice gained its independence. In the aftermath of World War I, a treaty ceded the southern portion of the historic crownland of Tyrol to Italy. While the governments negotiated, the people largely stayed where they were, speaking the languages that they had always spoken – and the train continued to chug along, connecting mountain villages and vineyards, the Alps and the Adriatic.

RIGHT & BELOW: Munich skyline; Ponte Pietra in Verona. **PREVIOUS PAGE:** South Tyrolean vineyards in Italy.

Today's trains begin the journey further north, in Munich, and the route is typical enough for the first half. In the Munich Hauptbahnhof, you can buy a mini-keg of Pilsner. Crossing into Austria at Kufstein, you almost immediately see a 14th-century castle fortress, its round white tower jutting from the hilltop above town. And heading out of Innsbruck, with the rugged Alps wreathed in clouds, the train heads into spiral tunnels and other engineering tricks to ascend nearly 3000ft (915m) in 45 minutes.

Where things get complicated is at Brenner Pass, the border between Austria and Italy. The first clue is the station sign, extra-long to accommodate the bilingual town name: Brenner – Brennero. A monument to Carl von Etzel, who built the line, calls him both *erbauer* (builder) and *costruttore*. Across the road is a *rosticceria*, but everyone on the street is speaking German. This bilingualism continues all the way downhill, and the region is named Südtirol and Alto Adige almost interchangeably. Out the train window, however, the landscape is unified in a single purpose: wine. As the train rolls on, the vineyards tick by, mesmerisingly tidy green rows that dead-end against vertical limestone mountainsides.

Over white tablecloths in the dining car, a late lunch reflects the scenery and history of the Brenner Railway. There's an Austro-Hungarian vibe in the red-pepper-paste sandwiches, goulash and apricot crepes with chocolate sauce. In the fresh sheep's-milk cheese drizzled with pumpkin-seed oil, you taste the wealth of the Alps. And, of course, there's wine: Zweigelt, Grüner Veltliner, Riesling – grape names well known and used on both sides of the Brenner Pass.

By the time the meal is done, Europe is predictable again. From Trento on, the station names are Italian only. The vast plain of the Veneto stretches to the sea, and the train skims across the lagoon to Venice, once an outpost of a multilingual empire.

© MICHAEL FELLNER | GETTY IMAGES

© ALXPIN | GETTY IMAGES

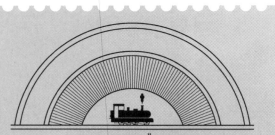

SINGULAR SÜDTIROL

A particularly wealthy part of Europe, Südtirol has relative autonomy within Italy. It also forms a Euroregion (a transnational government) with Austria's Tyrol and Italy's Trentino province. Its official languages are German and Italian, and in some municipalities, Ladin, a Romance language related to Swiss Romansh.

Dress for Munich's beer halls with lederhosen from the Karstadt department store.

Stop off to ski in Innsbruck, the largest winter resort in the Alps.

Stretch your legs at 4498ft (1371m) Brenner Pass, the highest point on the trip.

Munich   **Kufstein**   **Innsbruck**   **Brenner/Brennero**

❷ LIFE ON BOARD

Coach class consists of either open cars or six-seat compartments. An upgrade to 1st class (about €10 extra, which includes a seat reservation) offers roomy leather seats, again in either open seating or compartments. In between the two sections is a full-service dining car.

❸ ALTERNATIVE ROUTES

The route goes through Verona, a major rail hub (and a scenic city in its own right). There, it's possible to change for trains that reach across northern Italy; in summer, some trains continue onwards to Bologna and the beach resort of Rimini. For a short trip with the best mountain views, ride Innsbruck to Brenner, which takes about 45 minutes.

❹ MAKE IT HAPPEN

The Munich to Venice EuroCity runs once a day on weekdays; on weekends, two other trains also run through. At other times, you must change in Verona. Book your ticket with either Deutsche Bahn (DB) (www.bahn.com) or ÖBB (www.oebb.at). The DB website has a better interface for reserving seats.

Although the train is rarely crowded, it's wise to book ahead (and pay the small fee in 2nd class) to guarantee a window seat. Southbound from Munich, sit on the right side; northbound, sit on the left. The route is beautiful all year round, though the vineyards are at their most lush during late summer. If you want to stop off for a hike in the mountains, May to October is the safest time to do so. Winter's frequently overcast skies can be challenging for photographers, but it's dramatic in the pass. **ZO'N**

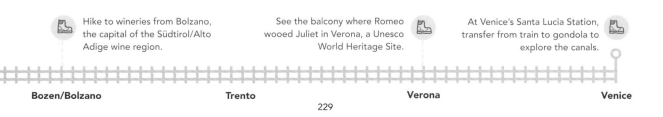

Hike to wineries from Bolzano, the capital of the Südtirol/Alto Adige wine region.

See the balcony where Romeo wooed Juliet in Verona, a Unesco World Heritage Site.

At Venice's Santa Lucia Station, transfer from train to gondola to explore the canals.

Bozen/Bolzano **Trento** **Verona** **Venice**

Fort William to Mallaig by Jacobite

SCOTLAND ●

START **FORT WILLIAM**

END **MALLAIG**

DEPARTS **VARIES** (CHECK WEBSITE)

DISTANCE **42 MILES (67KM)**

DURATION **2 HRS**

This trip is smug revenge towards Beeching, the man British train-lovers blame for the closure of thousands of supposedly surplus-to-requirement UK railway stations and lines during the 1960s. Here, in the Scottish Highlands, wheezing, wondrous steam locomotives from the 1930s or '40s haul glamorously old-fashioned carriages through a magical middle-of-nowhere without a puff of post-Beeching British Rail austerity in sight. Instead, the view is quite literally storybook perfect: this is the line the Hogwarts Express chugs along in the Harry Potter films, after all. Then there are the superlative-inducing natural assets: Britain's highest peak, Scotland's third-biggest body of water and a forest, mountainside, loch-side or seaside panorama to 'ooh' over at every turn.

❶ RIDING THE RAILS

Arrive at the platform in Fort William early: here is your first chance to see the gorgeous vintage locomotive you will be riding as it shunts into life. The Jacobite, as this venerable steam train and the tracks it travels on are called, is the most romantic means of getting between here and the fishing port of Mallaig on Scotland's west coast.

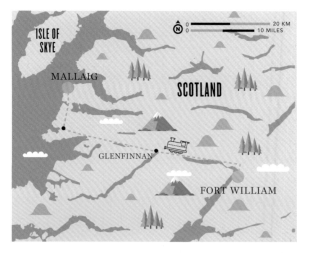

Standing at this station in somewhat grey Fort William is as unexciting as this trip gets: great news, because with vast Loch Linnhe on one side and Britain's loftiest mountain, Ben Nevis, sheering away on the other, this start point is by no means terrible.

As the crow flies, Mallaig is not that far distant; what stretches out this journey are the snaking lochs cutting so deep into this most westerly clump of the Scottish mainland they almost render it an island. The line initially negotiates the head of Loch Linnhe; then in order appear lochs Eil, Shiel, Eilt, Ailort, Nan Uamh, Nan Ceall and Morar. So extensively and dominantly do these lochs rent the region that the railway feels many times longer because of the kinks it makes to navigate them all.

After Loch Eil comes one of the most vegetated sections of the voyage, with the train bursting out of the trees near Glenfinnan to enthrall the Harry Potter fans on board as it rumbles over the astounding 21-arch viaduct where it masqueraded in films two and

RIGHT & BELOW: The Jacobite steam train cuts an elegant dash through Scotland; vintage British Railways insignia. **PREVIOUS PAGE:** The locomotive passes over the Glenfinnan viaduct.

three as the Hogwarts Express. A 25-minute halt at Glenfinnan Station follows, where there's a museum and gift shop at hand.

This whole region, now known as Lochaber, was instrumental in the Jacobite Uprising of 1745 and several poignant Jacobite-related sights lie hereabouts. The Glenfinnan Monument commemorates where the uprising's leader, Charles Edward Stuart (Bonnie Prince Charlie), raised his standard, the Prince's Cairn near Beasdale Station marks where he left in defeat for France a little more than one year later.

Unsurprisingly, this cinematic landscape inspired the setting for more than one blockbuster movie. After the line reaches Britain's most westerly station, Arisaig, you can behold some of the dreamlike beaches used in the filming of cult comedy-drama flick *Local Hero*.

After skirting Britain's deepest inland loch and Scotland's third greatest by volume, Loch Morar, the Jacobite trundles onwards to its terminus in the quaint fishing town of Mallaig. Once Europe's busiest herring port, it is now gaining a name for its fine fresh-seafood restaurants. Most enticingly for travellers here is the possibility of switching transport modes from rail to sea: ferries run from the harbour to Skye and the lesser-visited Small Isles, such as Rùm, Eigg, Canna or Muck.

❷ LIFE ON BOARD

The best 1st-class seats are in environs evoking an antiquated saloon (cosy lamps, armchairs). Another 1st-class option are the 'Harry Potter' seats in the compartments as glimpsed in the movies. All 1st-class seating has increased legroom and complimentary hot drinks are served. A snack trolley services 1st and

THE JACOBITE UPRISING

A fair few places in the Highlands claim association with the 1745 Jacobite Uprising, the final attempt to restore a Scottish king to the Scottish throne. But it was at Glenfinnan that Bonnie Prince Charlie first raised his standard, and the uprising only proceeded because of the support of the surrounding region's MacDonald and Cameron clans.

Grab a window seat and gawp at the vistas: there is no mediocre mile.

Clatter across the glorious Glenfinnan viaduct, imprinted on collective memory courtesy of the Hogwarts Express.

Fort William

Glenfinnan

standard class; added extras such as the 'Jacobite High Tea' are available to buy. It is debatable whether the 1st-class frills are worth the price jump for a ride just two hours long. It is easy to get immersed in the Harry Potter hype, but the Highland scenery unfolding outside is the real star of this show-on-rails.

❸ BUDGET ALTERNATIVES

One road and one set of tracks connect remote Mallaig to Fort William and the rest of Scotland, so unless you're continuing by sea from there, it is useful to bear the other service on this railway in mind for your return. The Abellio ScotRail (www.scotrail.co.uk) calls at all points, not just Glenfinnan and Arisaig, and for less than half the price. The four-times-daily service opens up a new world of back-of-beyond stations with the great outdoors pressing invitingly from the platforms: *fàilte* (welcome) to Banavie, Corpach, Loch Eil, Lochailort, Beasdale and Morar.

❹ MAKE IT HAPPEN

Booking the Jacobite in advance will not lower costs but will help garner the seats you want for this popular run. For optimum choice, especially if there are several in your party, book two or more months ahead via www.westcoastrailways.co.uk/jacobite. Consider whether you want to go both ways on the Jacobite, or take the boat from Mallaig to one of the islands, or return on the Abellio ScotRail service, which stops at all those smaller stations the Jacobite steams past. You can reach the start of the ride at Fort William via a riveting rail adventure too, by taking the overnight Caledonian Sleeper (www.sleeper.scot; see p248) from London Euston. **LW**

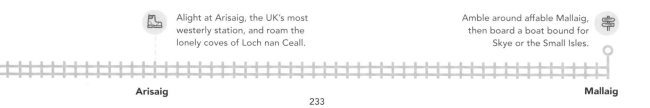

Alight at Arisaig, the UK's most westerly station, and roam the lonely coves of Loch nan Ceall.

Amble around affable Mallaig, then board a boat bound for Skye or the Small Isles.

Arisaig

Mallaig

Nova Gorica to Jesenice

SLOVENIA

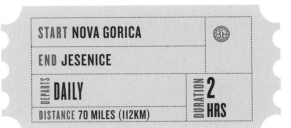

START **NOVA GORICA**

END **JESENICE**

DEPARTS **DAILY**

DISTANCE 70 MILES (112KM)

DURATION **2 HRS**

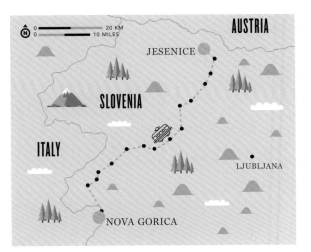

Here is a near-perfect railway adventure that most people have never heard of. Then again, you could be forgiven for missing it. The Bohinj Railway, after all, connects two places whose significance can be lost to modern travellers. Europe's shifting borders and politics may have rather marooned this line, but that, arguably, only adds to the appeal. An unassuming regional train rattling out of a faded-grandeur halt on the Italy–Slovenia border doesn't even hint at what's to come. The journey is a spectacular tour of Slovenia's upland highlights, climbing through mountain towns and villages along the Soča River, passing through superb Alpine scenery close to Lake Bohinj, and on past world-famous Lake Bled.

❶ RIDING THE RAILS

The Austro-Hungarian Empire left a knot of railways that look curious to modern eyes, radiating out of Vienna to important parts of this lost kingdom. The Bohinj, or Transalpina railway, which stretched all the way to the now Italian port city of Trieste is still in service today between Jesenice and Nova Gorica in Slovenia, from where passengers can stroll into the historic Italian city of Gorizia.

The feeling of unlocking a lost part of European history starts with a stroll across Piazza della Transalpina (or Trg Europa in Slovenian) outside Nova Gorica Station, where you will cross the now-open frontier between Italy and Slovenia. The border is marked by a plaque on the floor of the square, and information boards note how different this crossing was until comparatively recently. Enter the imposing station building, which feels too large for the regional service you're about to board, reflecting the historic importance of the line and the location. The unassuming two-carriage service will probably be waiting on the platform.

Soon after departure the train crosses the Solkan Bridge, a mighty 279ft (85m) span viaduct over the Soča River. This is the largest stone railway bridge in the world, and an absolute beauty to ride over or gaze at from a hike nearby. This dramatic piece of railway architecture is a taste of things to come. From here, the train climbs, slowly and steadily, past small towns

and villages where a few passengers get on and off,
passing hydroelectric works and gushing rivers, and
on into the Julian Alps. In winter there'll be plenty
of snow around, in summer the smell of high Alpine
pasture wafts in through the window. At any time you
may find the hills and mountains cloaked in cloud,
but this adds to the sense of drama. Stations including
Podbrdo and Most na Soči, surrounded by river and
reservoir, come and go, with the views getting ever
more striking.

If much of the trip is gloriously unfamiliar, the
end of the 4-mile (6km) Bohinj Tunnel heralds the
railway's arrival in Slovenia's tourist heartland. There's
no glimpse of the beautiful Lake Bohinj that gave the
tunnel its name, but after an idyllic riverside section
the train arrives at Bled Jezero Station, up the hill

from Lake Bled, and shortly after leaving here the
picturesque island Church of the Assumption and
Bled Castle can be seen. The railway then crosses the
Vintgar Gorge, where green water rumbles through
a narrow canyon. The gorge itself warrants a detour
for a better look and a view of another impressive
railway bridge. Podhom is the best halt for the gorge.
After a short final burst the train arrives at Jesenice,
close to the Austrian border. The station is another
reminiscent of having been a grander stop in the
past, and most passengers hurry on to connections
along the mainline. You might feel that staying on for
another ride on this near-secret service is a better idea.

❷ LIFE ON BOARD

With blissfully few distractions and little chance of
even having anyone sitting next to you (bar, perhaps,
a snoozing Slovene), this two-hour trip offers the
prospect of nothing too taxing. There's only one class
– 2nd – which offers comfy seats and room to stretch

© MAX PAOLI I GETTY IMAGES

© ALEKSANDARGEORGIEV I GETTY IMAGES

A STROLL ABOVE THE SOČA

Sabotin Hill (1998ft/609m), a hike from the Nova
Gorica or Solkan stations, overlooks the city, Soča
River and surrounding countryside. Beyond here are
the Julian Alps, the Gorizia Plain and the Adriatic
Sea. The hill still bears the scars of fierce fighting
during World War I, with bunkers and tunnels
dotting the hillside.

Stroll across the frontier between
Gorizia and Nova Gorica, once a
fortified crossing, to catch your train.

Traverse the breathtaking
Solkan Bridge over the
Soča River.

Pause at Most na Soči to
explore the river and
lakeside scenery.

Nova Gorica   **Solkan**   **Kanal**   **Most na Soči**

out. Grab a coffee or a beer at Nova Gorica's station bar before you go.

❸ ALTERNATIVE ROUTES

Most railway journeys in Slovenia have their scenic moments. The lovely trip from Ljubljana to Sezana and on to Villa Opicina in Italy makes for the perfect complementary trip. From Villa Opicina you can hop on a historic tram down the hill to Trieste.

❹ LUXURY ALTERNATIVE

The Museum Train steam special plies the route in summer, offering a whole day out along the line, including lunch in the winelands of the Goriška Brda region. You will need to book this service in advance, unlike the regular train. See www.slo-zeleznice.si.

❺ MAKE IT HAPPEN

With the exception of the steam special, there's no need to book ahead for this trip. Buy your tickets when you arrive at Nova Gorica or Jesenice. Check train times at www.slo-zeleznice.si.

Some services on the line originate and terminate in Sežana, which is about an hour southeast of Nova Gorica. From Sežana you can pick up the onward route to Trieste described above – though you should check connection times first. As the region's main air hub, Trieste is well served by budget airline routes from across Europe, and regular buses link the airport with the Italian city of Gorizia, adjacent to Nova Gorica. At the other end of the line, connections can be made from Jesenice to Villach, Salzburg and Munich to the north, and south to Ljubljana, Zagreb and Belgrade. **TH**

Emerge from the Bohinj Tunnel into the heart of the Julian Alps.

Catch a glimpse of picture-perfect Lake Bled's church, castle and bright-blue water.

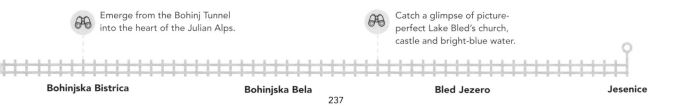

Bohinjska Bistrica   **Bohinjska Bela**   **Bled Jezero**   **Jesenice**

Cannes to Menton

FRANCE

START	CANNES
END	MENTON
DEPARTS	DAILY
DISTANCE 34 MILES (55KM)	DURATION 1 HR 20 MINS

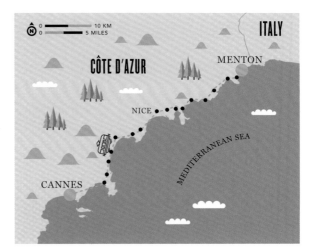

It's the stuff that travel dreams are made of. A slow train skirting the French Mediterranean coast, through towns whose very names resonate with glamour – Cannes, Antibes, Monaco. On one side of the tracks lies that sparkling sea; on the other, dramatic cliffs interspersed with the gorgeous coastal towns of the French Riviera. The journey is a languorous 34 miles (55km) of railway bliss. But you can make a long day of it, hopping on and off to explore a street market, linger at an outdoor terrace, take a breath of history and get a taste of luxury.

❶ RIDING THE RAILS

For more than a century, the Côte d'Azur has been a playground for wealthy sunseekers and a pilgrimage place for artists – painters such as Matisse and Picasso were attracted by the stunning luminosity created here by the meeting of land, water and sky.

If you're journeying from Paris, you'll approach Cannes from the west, signalled by clusters of palm trees and wrought-iron balconied apartment buildings. It's a gently curved 2-mile (3km) stretch of white sand, serried with summer umbrellas and lined with ritzy hotels and luxury boutiques. This is as close as France gets to LA. Disembark to soak up the

accumulated glamour of La Croisette, the legendary seafront boulevard where each May the world's movie stars (and hordes of star-struck onlookers) gather for the famous film festival.

Ten minutes later you'll pull into the wide bay of Antibes, where the train runs alongside joggers and walkers enjoying the town's long promenade. It's an ancient town with Greek origins and imposing 16th-century ramparts, but it's the superyachts of 'Millionaire's Quay' in Port Vauban, Europe's biggest marina, that will first catch your eye. Vieil Antibes, south of the station, is a labyrinth of cobblestoned streets and flower-bedecked squares – among them sits the Musée Picasso, a 14th-century château and the artist's studio when he lived here in 1946.

The train continues east, yards from the glittering sea – you're just steps away from dipping your toes in the waves. Wet them for real in Nice but wait until after lunch. Every day except Monday is market day in the Côte d'Azur's unofficial culinary capital. Make

RIGHT & BELOW: The Prince's Palace, Monaco; apéritifs at sunset. **PREVIOUS PAGE:** The beautiful town of Menton offers more traditional surrounds.

a beeline for local specialities such as *pissaladiére*, a tart of caramelised onions and anchovies, and *socca*, a warm chickpea flatbread. Restaurants line the market street: try *petits farcis* – little stuffed tomatoes, eggplants and zucchinis – and wash them down with some Provencal rosé (ice cubes optional).

The approach to Villefranche-sur-Mer is breathtaking: a wide, sheltered bay, a jumble of huddled buildings painted bright pastel yellows, oranges and reds tumbling down into an azure harbour, speckled with white boats. Cradling Villefranche, the coastline curves out to the

extravagantly pointing finger of Cap Ferrat, a glamorously old-school celebrity hotspot.

Beyond Beaulieu-sur-Mer, something of a mini-Monaco with its own casino, walls of rock rise precipitously out of the sea. One moment you're on tracks that sit directly above the rocky coastline, almost in the ocean, the next you're tunnelling into the forbidding cliffs. Catch a glimpse of villas perched up high, opportunistically grabbing a hitch in the steep ascent to find a perch.

A glittering underground station serves the principality of Monaco. It's only a 15-minute walk from there to the Casino de Monte Carlo if you fancy some bling-gazing and luxury-car spotting. Climb 'The Rock' to the Prince's Palace, and take in views of the harbour and some of the most exclusive seafront property in Europe.

Twenty minutes further along the tracks is Menton, a welcome breath of down-to-earth Frenchness, where glitz gives way to earthier, agricultural delights. Charmingly old-fashioned, Menton is France's premier

© IGGI FALCON | GETTY IMAGES

TRAIN DES MERVEILLES

The wild mountains and valleys inland of the Côte d'Azur create a landscape that's as beautiful as its coast. The 'Train of Wonders' leaves from Nice Ville, taking two hours to climb the mountainous terrain towards Italy through viaducts and tunnels, stopping at villages lakeside and mountain-perched, to reach the medieval fortified village of Tende.

© S-F | SHUTTERSTOCK

Stop at Cannes to soak up some movie-star glamour, whether it's festival time or not.

An ancient town, medieval streets, modern luxury: see why Picasso fell in love with Antibes.

Schedule yourself to hit Nice, the Cote d'Azur's culinary hotspot, for lunch.

Cannes   **Antibes**   **Nice**   **Villefranche-sur-Mer**

citrus-growing region, with an IGP (Indication Géographique Protégé) to prove it. If you can time your visit for the Fête du Citron in March, you'll see enormous, unlikely monuments (Mary Poppins, for example) constructed from oranges and lemons, and locals dressed in wild costumes for a mid-afternoon street parade. All in the name of fruit, and without a superyacht in sight.

❷ LIFE ON BOARD

Seats are comfortable, with tray tables and (usually) electrical outlets. You can reserve the seats you want – side by side, or a set of four seats facing each other. (Solo seats are available in 1st class.) The bar car offers coffee, beer and wine, sandwiches and snacks, and a full French-style *formule* with a bistro-style main course, dessert and drink.

❸ MAKE IT HAPPEN

Although it's connected to the main line from Paris (Paris to Cannes takes about six hours), this is a local route on the TER Provence Alpes Côte d'Azur network, with departures roughly every 30 minutes. There's no need to book tickets ahead if you're travelling only this route; if you're taking the train down from Paris, book as far ahead as possible (within three months) to get the cheapest rates.

If you're travelling in one direction, Cannes to Menton for example, you can simply buy a one-way ticket for this route and hop on and off at will. If you want to travel backwards and forwards (eg Cannes-Menton-Cannes), then buy a one-day pass for the département Alpes-Maritime. Tickets and passes are available online at www.ter.sncf.com/paca or at stations along the route. **JE**

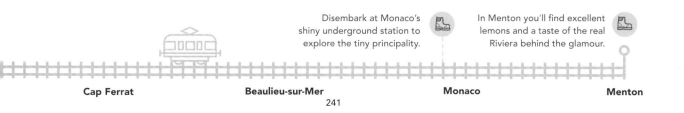

Disembark at Monaco's shiny underground station to explore the tiny principality.

In Menton you'll find excellent lemons and a taste of the real Riviera behind the glamour.

Cap Ferrat   **Beaulieu-sur-Mer**   **Monaco**   **Menton**

The Bergensbanen

NORWAY ●

START **OSLO**	
END **BERGEN**	
DEPARTS **4 PER DAY**	DURATION **6 HRS 30 MINS**
DISTANCE **308 MILES (496KM)**	

This astonishing train is one of the wonders of 19th-century railway building, and yet outside Norway hardly anyone knows about it. In just over six hours and 300 miles (490km) of travel, it covers the spectrum of Norway's natural splendour: climbing canyons, crossing rivers, burrowing through mountainsides and traversing barren icescapes. All aboard for the Bergensbanen: a main line into Norwegian nature.

❶ RIDING THE RAILS

Norway's stunning landscapes are undoubtedly the country's greatest asset, but when it comes to building a railway, they present a formidable challenge – so the decision to construct a line between Norway's two main cities in the late 19th century was fraught with difficulty. It's just 190 miles (306km) as the crow flies from Oslo to Bergen, but in between lies a topographical minefield of mountains and fjords, lakes and valleys, glaciers and gorges – not to mention the sprawling mountain plateau of Hardangervidda, which stays snowbound for much of the year.

Construction began in December 1875, but the line wasn't finished until 1909 – a testament to the massive challenges that were involved. When the first train finally rolled into Oslo's Central Station on 27 November 1909, King Haakon VII described it as 'our generation's masterpiece' – and more than a century later, the Bergensbanen railway remains a great source of national pride.

However, most of the sightseers and commuters who clamber onto the trains at Oslo's Central Station never give the railway's history a second thought. To them, it's simply the most convenient way of getting from A to B – as fast as flying, once you factor in airport waiting times, and often a good

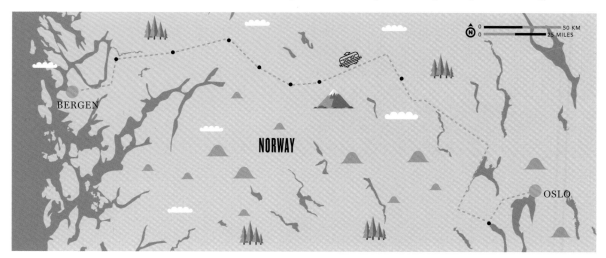

deal cheaper too. And like most things in Norway, the Bergensbanen tends to run with clockwork-like efficiency – up to four times a day, the train hauls its sleek, shiny, steel carriages out of the city, past the weatherboard houses of suburban Oslo and out into the glorious green Norwegian countryside.

After departure, pine forests and steel-grey fjords fill the train windows, and everyone settles back into their seats to enjoy the view, sipping hot coffee and nibbling on cinnamon buns as the scenery flashes past. Towns come and go – Asker, Drammen, Viskersund, Flåm – and the train blurs in and out of tunnel after tunnel; there are 182 in all on the Bergensbanen line, including one that's more than 6 miles (10km) long. And then, past the town of Nesbyen, the train begins to climb.

The crossing of the Hardangervidda plateau between Geilo and Finse is the most memorable section of the Bergensbanen. Climbing to an altitude of 4058m (1237m) – four times the height of the Eiffel Tower – this wild, stark mountain plateau is blanketed with snow for much of the year, and it's not unusual for the Bergensbanen to find itself swallowed up by fog or marooned in a sudden, unexpected snowstorm. But the train takes it all in its stride; it runs in all but the worst weather, chugging past icy lakes and stacked-up snowdrifts that linger long into summer.

Few places in Europe feel quite as harsh and inhospitable as Hardangervidda: members of Captain Robert Falcon Scott's last expedition trained here in 1912, and George Lucas used it as a location for the ice planet of Hoth in *The Empire Strikes Back*. In winter, it's pretty much as close as you'll get to the polar ice-cap without actually travelling there. Lonely shacks dot the white-capped hillsides and, sometimes, herds of wild reindeer wander past, pausing to watch the train rush by, their breath pluming frost into the mountain air.

Over the plateau, the train descends rapidly down the mountainsides as it plummets into the west fjords. At Myrdal, the Flåmsbana branch line ratchets down

© JUSTIN FOULKES | LONELY PLANET

© JUSTIN FOULKES | LONELY PLANET

CYCLING THE RALLARVEGEN

The Rallarvegen, or 'Navvies' Road', is a 50-mile (80km) trail that runs down the mountains from Haugastøl to Flåm. Originally used as an access road by the builders of the Bergensbanen, it's now been turned into a fantastic – if challenging – long-distance cycling route, usually open from around May to October. Bikes can be hired.

Take a day to explore the art museums and impressive architecture of Oslo.

Gaze over the arctic landscape of Hardangervidda between Geilo and Finse.

Oslo　　　　　　**Drammen**　　　　　　**Nesbyen**　　　　　　**Geilo**

CLOCKWISE FROM LEFT: Gabled shopfronts in Bergen; the town's harbour in the snow; welcome aboard; a solitary farmhouse in Hardangerfjord. **PREVIOUS PAGE:** The Bergensbanen cuts through Norway's epic landscape.

© JUSTIN FOULKES | SHUTTERSTOCK

to the fjordside town of Flåm – at a gradient of 5.5%, it's the steepest standard-gauge railway in Europe, and many passengers disembark from the Oslo–Bergen train in order to experience it.

Those who stay on the Bergensbanen continue their journey into fjord country. The train descends into fields, fruit farms and apple orchards, backed by sheer mountains wreathed in cloud and the silver-blue sweep of the fjords. This is the classic landscape of Norwegian postcards: lush, grand and improbably green. Passengers scurry between either side of the train, keen to capture as many of the views as possible – but in truth, no photograph can do justice to Norway's landscapes, so the best thing to do is just sit back and let the scenery do the work. At the town of Voss, the train veers west, tracking the edge of the fjords all the way to Bergen's elegant station, built in 1913 in classic Jugendstil style.

© ANDREAS KLEIBERG

Look out for the landmark Finse Tunnel, the line's highest point at 4058ft (1237m).

Make a stop at Myrdal and enjoy a scenic detour on the historic Flåmsbana railway.

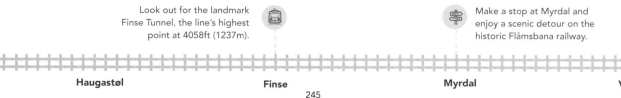

Haugastøl   **Finse**   **Myrdal**   **Voss**

OPPOSITE: Oslo's Opera House, designed by architects Snøhetta, opened in 2008.

A short walk away along the harbourfront, passengers climb aboard the historic Hurtigruten ferry service, which has been shuttling passengers up and down Norway's coastline since 1893. But in its own way, the Bergensbanen deserves to be just as feted: for natural majesty, there are few train journeys in the world that can match it.

❷ LIFE ON BOARD

The Bergensbanen is essentially a commuter service, so don't expect the Orient Express. It's still a comfortable train on which to travel, though: the seats are spacious and comfortable, large windows make the most of the views, and free wi-fi and a well-stocked cafe make the journey pass even faster. For more space, you can upgrade to 'Komfort' class, which offers larger seats, power outlets and complimentary tea and coffee. There are even play areas for children in the family carriage. The overnight trains have sleeper compartments.

❸ MAKE IT HAPPEN

There are up to four daily trains between Oslo and Bergen in both directions. Bookings are made directly through the railway's website (www.nsb.no). For the cheapest 'Minipris' fares, you'll need to buy in advance and be flexible with your travel times; travelling early or late in the day and avoiding busy commuter trains usually bags a big discount. Fares rise and fall according to demand: book well ahead for any trip during the school holidays and around national days.

There's plenty of space for luggage on each Bergensbanen train carriage. Bikes and ski equipment can also be carried on most trains, but you'll need to specify this at the time of booking and pay a supplementary fare. Special assistance is available for travellers with reduced mobility. **OB**

Wander around Bergen's bright-coloured weatherboard houses and lively fish market.

Dale   Bergen

London to Fort William on the Caledonian Sleeper

ENGLAND & SCOTLAND

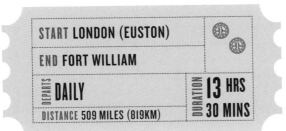

START **LONDON (EUSTON)**	
END **FORT WILLIAM**	
DEPARTS **DAILY**	DURATION **13 HRS 30 MINS**
DISTANCE **509 MILES (819KM)**	

 Segueing from the sooty suburbs and crowded concrete-lined cul-de-sacs of central London to the crisp air and soaring vistas of the Scottish Highlands, via one overnight train journey, epitomises the romance of rail travel. It's just a pity that the whole experience – from buffet-car banter and single malt nightcaps, to being lulled into la la land by the rhythm of the rails, and waking to breakfast in bed with the view of towering granite peaks – feels like it's over in a flash.

❶ RIDING THE RAILS

Forget the kerfuffle around platform 9¾ at London's Kings Cross Station – the mythical (but massively marketed) departure point for the Hogwarts Express of Harry Potter fame – for many people, the proper magic happens a few hundred metres west, twice a night, six evenings a week.

Here, from the real platforms of Euston Station, the iconic Caledonian Sleeper trains begin an overnight adventure along the West Coast Main Line from the busy British capital to the historic cities, castles and quiet corners of Scotland.

The Sleeper experience encompasses several services, with some taking the low road (to Scotland's

main cities of Edinburgh and Glasgow) and others the high road, transporting travellers into a craggy landscape dramatically defined by the towering peaks and lonely lochs of the Scottish Highlands.

Leaving London together, there are three Highland Sleeper routes – all spectacular – but Britain's ultimate rail escapade is the sensational service to Fort William: the Deerstalker.

CLOCKWISE FROM RIGHT:
Glenfinnan Valley near Fort William;
alongside the waters of the Monessie
Gorge; crossing the River Clyde at
Crawford. **PREVIOUS PAGE:** Step off
the Sleeper into the Scottish Highlands.

Escaping the neon glare of the British capital earlier than its Lowland sibling, the train races through the suburbs of the Big Smoke, quickly getting up to speed while passengers invade the lounge car to sip and nibble as Middle England passes in a blur.

The complexion of the crowd changes with the season, but it's ever eclectic, with huddles of happy hill walkers embarking on holiday adventures, long-distance business commuters attempting to work, train enthusiasts effervescent with excitement, and garrulous gaggles of Scottish MPs and football fans.

The locomotive legs it past Liverpool and Lancaster at 80mph (129km/h), galloping through the gap between the Lake District and Yorkshire Dales national parks. Long before the border, the gathering gloom typically transforms carriage windows into black mirrors, and even the most committed barflies swap buffet car for bunk. But regardless of whether you've drunk a dram or not, sleep comes easily when your cradle is rocked by the rattle-and-hum of the rails.

During an unadvertised service stop at Edinburgh in the wee hours, the Highland Sleeper mother serpent splits three ways, but most travellers snooze right through the shuffling and shunting this involves. And then, while passengers slumber on, the Deerstalker stealthily sets off into the inky darkness, with a couple of carriages in tow, wending around the curvaceous bends of the West Highland Line.

In midsummer, the Scottish night is a fleeting affair, with the sun dipping beneath the hills for just a few short hours, and morning arriving early and at express speed. But even before the first blush of dawn begins to colour the heather-bearded hillsides a fiery red, the train starts stopping at stations including beautiful Bridge of Orchy and super-remote Corrour – site of a memorable scene from the film *Trainspotting*.

Then, hot on the heels of daybreak, come stewards serving breakfast in bed, which usually features something hearty (such as creamy porridge followed by Ayrshire bacon) that lets you know you've arrived in Scotland even before you've glanced through the porthole at the suddenly sunlit lochs and glens.

Rolling over deer-rich Rannoch Moor, passengers stalk the landscape with their eyes, longing to spot the antlers of a stag. And then, suddenly, you're at the foot of Ben Nevis, Britain's highest mountain, towering above the deep dark waters of Loch Eil.

The Caledonian Sleeper dream finishes at Fort William, but this isn't the end of the line. Stay on track and extend your railway odyssey to the fishing village of Mallaig, travelling via the great Glenfinnan Viaduct (see page 231), which stars so brilliantly in the Harry Potter films (and knocks the measly modern Platform 9¾ sign into a cocked sorting hat).

BACK TO THE FUTURE

Overnight trains have rolled between London and Scotland for 140 years. The current Caledonian Sleeper service was recently taken over by Serco, which has invested £150 million and promised a new fleet of rolling stock for 2018, including compartments with double beds and showers.

Order haggis, neeps and tatties for dinner, long before you've even left England – because you can.

Let yourself be rocked unconscious by the rhythm of the rails, while motorists muddle along the M6.

Wake up beyond the border to enjoy an ever-so Scottish breakfast in bed.

London (Euston)   **Crewe**   **Preston**   **Helensburgh Upper**

❷ LIFE ON BOARD

There are three classes: 1st, standard and seat-only. Solo travellers with 1st-class tickets sleep in single-berth cabins, while standard-class tickets require you to share a two-berth cabin with someone of the same sex. Standard compartments feature bunk beds, a sink and wardrobe. Couples and families can share standard-class two-berth cabins or interconnecting 1st-class cabins.

If a full berth ticket is beyond your budget, cheaper seat-only options are available. Seats recline and there's a buffet service, but you can't access the lounge car.

A comprehensive menu of hot meals (featuring fine Scottish produce), sandwiches, and a full bar of wines, craft beer, malt whiskies and cocktails, as well as soft and hot drinks, is served on board, despite the late departure.

❸ ALTERNATIVE ROUTES

After the Highland Sleeper train splits at Edinburgh, and the Deerstalker wends west, the other two sections travel away on separate adventures. One ambles along the east coast to Aberdeen, while the other sidles round the Cairngorm Plateau to Inverness.

❹ MAKE IT HAPPEN

Lowland and Highland Sleeper services run twice a day, six times a week (no trains on Saturday) from London's Euston Station. It's possible to buy tickets online (www.sleeper.scot) up to 12 months in advance, and they are cheaper the further ahead you book. Those with children can secure decent discounts by buying family tickets. Friday nights are the busiest, and June is the most popular month. **PK**

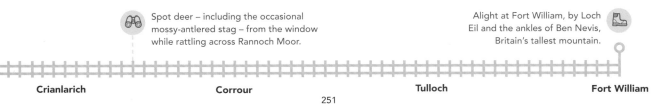

Spot deer – including the occasional mossy-antlered stag – from the window while rattling across Rannoch Moor.

Alight at Fort William, by Loch Eil and the ankles of Ben Nevis, Britain's tallest mountain.

Crianlarich   Corrour   Tulloch   Fort William

Cologne to Mannheim

GERMANY ●

START **COLOGNE**

END **MANNHEIM**

DEPARTS **DAILY**

DISTANCE **149 MILES (238KM)**

DURATION **1–3 HRS**

For a journey through deepest Europe, board a southbound train in the German city of Cologne. After a few miles the track begins to follow the Rhine, and passengers get a premium view of the finest stretch of this mighty river. What unfolds is one of the continent's great railway journeys, stopping at ancient villages and passing under hilltop castles with the vast Rhine waterway as a constant companion. There's so much history, myth and legend that you'd be forgiven for needing a drink – which is another reason to come here, as this is one of Germany's key wine-growing areas.

❶ RIDING THE RAILS

Cologne's Hauptbahnhof is conveniently located next to the city's magnificent cathedral, an appropriately grand starting point for a trip down one of Europe's most scenic main lines. The Rhine becomes visible at several points between here and Koblenz, but these first glimpses are just tasters. The most notable next stop is at Bonn. The city can seem a footnote in this journey, with more exciting things to see upstream, but for 41 years it was the capital of West Germany and many important national and international institutions remain based here. It is also the joint seat of the German government (with Berlin), and the birthplace of Beethoven. Rail buffs should consider another halt at Königswinter, home to the Drachenfels rack railway to the top of the eponymous mountain.

Koblenz marks the confluence with the Moselle, marked in Koblenz by the vast Deutsches Eck statue, a reconstruction of the 19th-century monument to German unification. From here the line enters its most celebrated section. If ever there was a time to stop fiddling with a phone and look around you, this is it. Mile by mile the Rhine narrows, and its banks become studded with vineyards, old towns and castles. To the west are Boppard, St Goar and Bingen, the home of medieval composer, abbess and general polymath Hildegard. On the opposite bank are Braubach, St Goarshausen and Rudesheim. But a look back at the water and the rails will remind you this isn't an outdoor museum. The non-stop procession of trains, cars and boats going about their business adds a bustling, workaday element to the spectacular

CLOCKWISE FROM RIGHT: Cologne's handsome skyline; Rhineland vineyards; racing through the town of Oberwesel.
PREVIOUS PAGE: Riverside Bacharach.

scenery along what has been a key transport route for millennia. Here, like nowhere else, does Europe get on with its business, unfussy beneath the weight of its own history. That said, this most romantic stretch of the Rhine draws the crowds in summer. If you can't beat them, join them by picking a town or two to

pause in and try a few varieties of local wine. Opposite St Goar, looming seemingly into the middle of the river, is Lorelei rock, mythical home of sirens and an inspiration to writers and poets for centuries. It's worth getting off the train here to gaze at it for a while, otherwise it is gone in a flash. River authorities have had the decency to mark the rock with a highly visible sign. The treasure of the Nibelungs, according to the legendary chronicle of their downfall immortalised by Wagner in his Ring Cycle, is also reputed to be buried nearby.

The Rhine spreads out as it exits the gorge past Bingen, and the final run from Mainz into Mannheim feels a little like the end of a rollercoaster. It's a chance to breathe out, but also a moment to think about the wonders that may have passed by quickly. The historic honey-pot of Heidelberg, on the banks of the Neckar River, is a short journey on from Mannheim. Should you stay with the Rhine, a few hours on an ICE (Intercity Express) will take you to Basel, Switzerland. Wherever you go, don't be surprised if you're still dreaming of the Rhine Valley for a long time afterwards.

© GEORG WAGNER

© INSTAMATICS | GETTY IMAGES

© MATTHIAS HAKER PHOTOGRAPHY | GETTY IMAGES

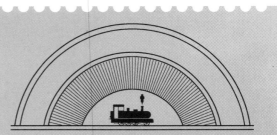

THE MIGHTY RHINE

At 760 miles (1230km), the Rhine is the second-longest river in central and western Europe, after the Danube. Lake Toma in Switzerland is generally accepted as the source. It flows through Switzerland, Germany and the Netherlands before forming part of the Rhine-Meuse-Scheldt delta and flowing into the North Sea.

Start your journey in the shadow of the mighty Kölner Dom, the largest Gothic church in northern Europe.

Check out the confluence of the Rhine and the Moselle at Koblenz's Deutsches Eck statue.

Lose track of how many castles you've seen in the past hour between Koblenz and Rudesheim.

| Cologne | Bonn | Koblenz | Boppard | Oberwesel |

❷ LIFE ON BOARD

You will experience German trains of all types en route, from regional shuttle services stopping at the smallest of halts to high-speed express trains. Facilities will vary accordingly. One of the charms of travelling the Rhine by rail is hopping on and off trains, buying tickets on board like locals, and stopping where you please.

❸ ALTERNATIVE ROUTES

Trains also run along the Moselle Valley from Koblenz, hugging the river for several scenic sections and stopping at Cochem and Trier, one of Germany's oldest cities. A pleasant detour from the Rhine is to take the nearby Vulkan Express service from Brohl to Engeln in the Eifel Mountains.

❹ MAKE IT HAPPEN

Trains run regularly along this main line. Book tickets at www.bahn.de. Ideally you can travel one-way down the western bank, and the other way on the east – trains head along both sides from Koblenz. It won't take much more than two hours to make this journey whichever train you choose, and services are frequent, so get out and explore your surroundings whenever the whim takes you.

Two notes of caution: many of the faster Intercity Express (ICE) trains heading south from Cologne travel via Limburg instead of going along the Rhine. Take care that your service is travelling via Bonn, Koblenz and Mainz to be sure of a river view. Secondly, booking ahead for ICE services is necessary in order to get the best fares. Or better still, just kick back and take the slower services. **TH**

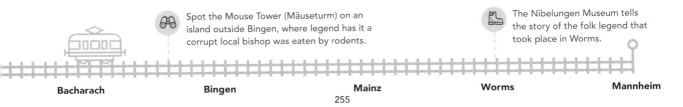

Spot the Mouse Tower (Mäuseturm) on an island outside Bingen, where legend has it a corrupt local bishop was eaten by rodents.

The Nibelungen Museum tells the story of the folk legend that took place in Worms.

Bacharach   Bingen   Mainz   Worms   Mannheim

Inlandsbanan

SWEDEN ●

How many railways are there in the world where the driver might, if the mood suddenly seizes, stop the train so everyone can get out and pick berries? Or halt so that their passengers can nip out for a swim in a nearby lake, or so they can watch a moose stomping about a woodland glade? Believe it or not, this is not uncommon behaviour on the Inlandsbanan – the 'Inland Railway' – the line that traverses the pristine forests of the Swedish interior. Bafflingly slow and willfully eccentric, it is one of Europe's most warm-hearted railways.

❶ RIDING THE RAILS

If film-maker Wes Anderson were ever to build a railway, chances are it would look quite a bit like the Inlandsbanan. It consists of a single-track line, dotted with chocolate-box stations, served by once-a-day, single-carriage red trains (which run only in summer).

START **MORA**

END **GÄLLIVARE**

DEPARTS **DAILY** (IN SEASON)

DISTANCE 800 MILES (1288KM)

DURATION **2 DAYS**

Devised in the early 20th century as a pioneering line that would open up Sweden's northern wilderness, the Inlandsbanan was threatened with closure in the 1990s due to it only ever attracting a tiny number of passengers. In recent years, however, it has experienced a renaissance with tourists for whom its quirkiness is its essential appeal. Its idiosyncrasies are many and varied. You can eat grilled fish in lineside restaurants while your train patiently waits for you to finish your meal. You can enjoy long conversations with the driver in the cab while looking out for bears crossing the line ahead.

Whereas Sweden's lively cities and island-dotted coasts are familiar to many tourists, the interior of the country is largely terra incognita – and a ticket on Inlandsbanan is an excellent way to strike into the unknown. Most northbound passengers jump aboard close to the southern end of the line in Mora – a handsome town poised on the leafy shores of Lake Siljan. Not far away is the village of Nusnäs, the spiritual home of the Swedish Dala horse, busy with the workshops where these tiny carved-timber horses are whittled into shape.

From Mora, the route takes you deep into a landscape of spruce and pine forests – the territory of wolves, bears and moose. Sometimes the train screeches to a halt to let off a hiker in a lonely corner of the woods – far away from stations and settlements. Mostly it trundles forth at an average speed of about 30mph (50km/h), crossing broad rivers, skirting little hamlets of scarlet cabins, puttering over wildflower-strewn meadows on its gentle journey northward.

Six hours on from Mora, the town of Östersund is the midway point on the railway. The main attraction here is Jamtli – a living history museum similar to Stockholm's Skansen, chronicling life through the centuries with the help of actors in period dress. A highlight is the recreation of 1970s Swedish life, replete with retro bungalows, old-school VW campervans and anti-Vietnam War protesters.

© GARY LATHAM | LONELY PLANET

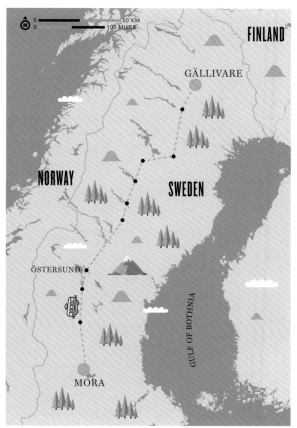

Setting out from Östersund on day two, it's a 13-hour journey to reach the northern terminus of the line in industrial Gällivare. Before long the train crosses the border into Lapland – followed by a modest sign declaring you have entered the Arctic Circle. Lots of passengers dismount in such towns as Sorsele, before following little roads west to the mountains that rise along the Norwegian border. Making use of this environment are anglers hoping to reel trout from fast-flowing mountain streams, and hikers looking to conquer Sweden's most famous long-distance trail, the Kungsleden, which runs parallel to the northern reaches of the Inlandsbanan. This region is also the home of the Sami, Europe's last indigenous people – stays in traditional teepees are easily arranged.

Although it's possible to get from one end of the line to the other in two days, to do so is to miss the point of the Inlandsbanan – a railway with a glacial speed that echoes the slowness of life at these northerly latitudes. In the age of 300mph (483km/h) trains and massive, crowded railway stations, Inlandsbanan preserves the miraculous calm of rail travel.

LAND OF THE MIDNIGHT SUN

Midsummer passengers will be able to witness the strange spectacle of the midnight sun. The southernmost point where it can be observed (weather permitting) is Arvidsjaur (20–21 June), though you'll have better odds at Gällivare (5 June–6 July) where Dundret hill is the traditional spot to watch the sun linger on the horizon.

❷ LIFE ON BOARD

By any measure, the Inlandsbanan trains are miniscule, consisting only of one or two carriage services, with standard class only. Snacks, teas and coffees are served on board, while substantial lunches and dinners can be bought during stops at lineside restaurants (make sure you don't miss the train). Inlandsbanan isn't a sleeper service, so all passengers will need to overnight in Östersund.

❸ MAKE IT HAPPEN

Inlandsbanan services typically run from early June to mid-August, with daily northbound/southbound departures running on the northern and southern sections of track (Mora-Östersund and Östersund-Gällivare). Some purists insist the original route

© JUSTIN FOULKES | LONELY PLANET

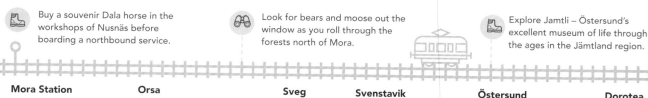

Buy a souvenir Dala horse in the workshops of Nusnäs before boarding a northbound service.

Look for bears and moose out the window as you roll through the forests north of Mora.

Explore Jamtli – Östersund's excellent museum of life through the ages in the Jämtland region.

Mora Station   Orsa   **Sveg**   Svenstavik   **Östersund**   Dorotea

CLOCKWISE FROM LEFT: The Inlandsbanan traverses Sweden's interior; passengers disembark en route for remote outposts and rural sites; preparing to board a northbound train. **PREVIOUS PAGE:** Reindeer navigate the snowy north.

begins in the town of Kristinehamn, south of Mora, though this stretch isn't operated by Inlandsbanan-branded trains. Tickets can be booked in advance online (inlandsbanan.se). The operator also offers holiday packages that include accommodation, additional excursions and detours over the border into Norway. The best way to travel is with the Inlandsbanan Card – which offers unlimited travel up and down the line for up to two weeks. Allow at least six days to fully explore.

Mosquitoes can be a pest during the Swedish summer – pack plenty of insect repellent. **OS**

Disembark the train for dinner in a lineside restaurant such as Martin Bergman – a fixture of early rail travel that survives on Inlandsbanan.

Watch the midnight sun from the hills above Gällivare, then take a detour into Swedish Lapland to experience Sami culture.

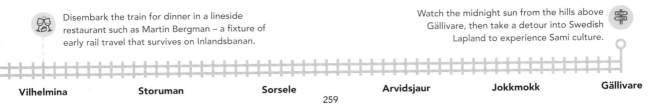

| Vilhelmina | Storuman | Sorsele | Arvidsjaur | Jokkmokk | Gällivare |

Ffestiniog & Welsh Highland Railways

WALES ●

START **CAERNARFON**

END **BLAENAU FFESTINIOG**

DEPARTS **DAILY (IN SEASON)**

DISTANCE **39 MILES (63KM)**

DURATION **4 HRS**

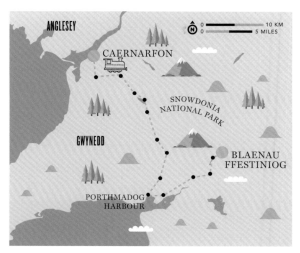

Proof that bigger doesn't always mean better, the Ffestiniog and Welsh Highland Railways are the spiritual home of narrow gauge – lines on which tiny steam locomotives putter through tiny stations and wind among the mighty mountains of North Wales. A trip combining the world's oldest operating railway company, Ffestiniog, and the UK's longest heritage line, Welsh Highland, can be completed in a day. Passing slate quarries and abandoned mines, passengers can witness how the industrial revolution altered the Welsh landscape forever, while at the same time seeing British nature at its most majestic, thanks to the dark forests, river valleys and windswept summits of Snowdonia.

❶ RIDING THE RAILS

Despite being beloved for its fleet of illustrious steam engines, Ffestiniog Railway actually began life without any locomotives – or indeed any passengers. Constructed in 1833 to transport slate from the quarries of Blaenau Ffestiniog to waiting ships on the Irish Sea, downhill trains were powered by gravity, with horses deployed to heave empty trucks back uphill. The horses were doubtless relieved when steam locomotives took over duties in the mid-19th century,

capable of carrying greater loads of slate to be shipped to rooftops across the British Empire.

Ffestiniog's northerly neighbour, the Welsh Highland Railway, opened for business in the 1920s, also hoping to plunder the mineral riches of the region – though both swiftly fell victim to declining demand for slate and the growing popularity of the motorcar. They had both closed completely to freight and passengers by the mid-1940s. It was 1982 before volunteers restored the Ffestiniog Railway to its original extent, and 2011 before Snowdonian hills echoed once again to the toot of the Welsh Highland Railway trains after years of legal wrangling and rebuilding. Though they are separate railways, they are operated by the same company and it's easy to buy a single ticket covering both lines.

Many visitors start their narrow-gauge odyssey on the Welsh Highland, catching a southbound service from the handsome seaside town of Caernarfon. Trains depart close to the battlements of its 13th-century castle – one of the largest and best preserved in the UK. Its mighty towers were built by Edward I to assert English control over North Wales, and are said to replicate the walls of Istanbul in their design. Look out for a slick new railway station opening in Caernarfon in 2018.

The line soon heads south and mountains begin to rise up on all sides – to the west are the gentle slopes of Mynydd Mawr – 'Elephant Mountain' – while to the east the serrated peaks of the Snowdon massif gradually inch into view. A few hikers get off at Rhyd Ddu and Snowdon Ranger, small stations that are the starting points for relatively quiet trails up the western flanks of Wales' highest mountain. Beddgelert follows soon after – it's perhaps the prettiest village in North Wales, with tearooms and pubs set in the shadow of Mt Snowdon.

Departing Beddgelert, the Welsh Highland continues along what is probably its most beautiful stretch where the steam engine races a fast-flowing river along the Aberglaslyn Pass, ducking in and out of tunnels among rhododendron-swathed slopes. Services finally reach Porthmadog two hours after leaving Caernarfon (the tracks rather alarmingly running down the middle of a main road).

At Porthmadog, stretch your legs for an hour or so before changing platforms for the Ffestiniog Railway, which is slightly shorter than its twin, though by no means less extraordinary. Trains initially chuff along the Cob – an embankment spanning the Glaslyn estuary, with a panoramic view over snow-dusted Snowdonian peaks for those sitting on the left. The railway then climbs steadily, passing fields full of grazing sheep, oak forests, cold lakes and little waterfalls. A highlight is the Dduallt spiral, where the railway loops around to gain elevation on its final push into the mountains.

The blustery precipices of the Moelwynion range loom ahead as the railway reaches its terminus at Blaenau Ffestiniog, where the little town is flanked by enormous slate heaps. Here, passengers can get to grips with the area's slate-quarrying heritage

© CROWN COPYRIGHT (2016) VISIT WAL

© GETTY IMAGES

A DETOUR TO PORTMEIRION

Just outside Porthmadog is the strange, sublime model village of Portmeirion. Inspired by Italian seaside towns, it was built between 1925 and 1975 by visionary architect Clough Williams-Ellis. It found fame as the location for the 1960s spy drama *The Prisoner* and more recently has become the venue for Festival Number 6 – a summer music festival.

Wander the battlements of Caernarfon Castle, before boarding a southbound Welsh Highland service.

Chuff beneath the foot of Mt Snowdon as the line skirts the shores of Llyn Cwellyn.

Stop for an ice cream in the picturesque village of Beddgelert, before the train descends into the Aberglaslyn Pass.

Caernarfon   **Waunfawr**   **Snowdon Ranger**   **Beddgelert**

© CROWN COPYRIGHT (2016) VISIT WAL

CLOCKWISE FROM LEFT: Caernarfon Castle; the slate mines and quarries of Blaenau Ffestiniog; powering along the route to Porthmadog. **PREVIOUS PAGE:** The Welsh Highland Railway passing through Beddgelert. **OVERLEAF:** Steaming over the Porthmadog Cob.

by descending into the Llechwedd Slate Caverns. In more recent years, Blaenau Ffestiniog has also gained a reputation for a crop of new adventure activities — from giant zip lines whooshing over former slate quarries, to the 'Bounce Below' network of trampolines, slides and walkways set in a vast subterranean cavern.

From Blaenau Ffestiniog, you'll have the option of returning to Porthmadog on the Ffestiniog Railway, or else change for normal service trains to the coast via the Conwy Valley. This is a beautiful journey in its own right and (with some clever planning) is also a means of completing a circular route back to Caernarfon. For many travellers, however, riding on these magnificent railways provides enough inspiration to strike out among the mountains, lakes and valleys of Snowdonia on foot, to see the wonderful landscapes under their own steam.

Gaze up at the peak of Cnicht – 'the Welsh Matterhorn' – on a Ffestiniog Railway service departing Porthmadog.

Admire the Dduallt spiral as the railway climbs higher into the mountains.

Porthmadog Harbour **Minffordd** **Dduallt**

❷ LIFE ON BOARD

Most passengers travel aboard standard 3rd-class carriages. You can also pay a supplementary fee to sit in 1st-class 'Pullman' style coaches, which feature plush fabrics, comfortable chairs and – best of all – tall windows giving superb mountain views. There's an on-board buffet serving hot and cold food on both lines, including toasted sandwiches and soups. Afternoon teas are also available on select services. Look out for special trains throughout the year, from Victorian-themed weekends to Christmas events.

Even if you're not a railway enthusiast, it's worth learning a little about the engines, a few of which have been pressed into service as far afield as South Africa and Australia. Look out for examples of the Double Fairlie engine: the curious double-ended locomotives that are the icon of the Ffestiniog Railway. The powerful Garratt design is commonly used on the Welsh Highland Railway, having been employed widely across the British Empire.

❸ MAKE IT HAPPEN

Trains on both lines have seasonal timetables: the Ffestiniog has up to eight daily departures in high summer (July and August), while the Welsh Highland has three daily departures during peak times. Both are closed for extended periods in the winter (November–February). The route is most beautiful in high summer, when the Welsh weather is at its most forgiving.

It's easy to book the railway services online at www.festrail.co.uk. Tickets are also available at principal stations. Timetable permitting, you can fully explore both lines in one day following a circular route, also incorporating mainline services. Catch the Welsh Highland from Caernarfon to Porthmadog, the Ffestiniog on to Blaenau Ffestiniog and then mainline trains on to Bangor via the Conwy Valley Line. Regular buses connect Bangor to Caernarfon, taking about 30 minutes. **OS**

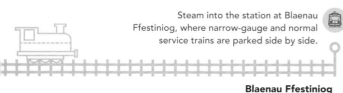

Steam into the station at Blaenau Ffestiniog, where narrow-gauge and normal service trains are parked side by side.

Blaenau Ffestiniog

© GAIL JOHNSON | SHUTTERSTOCK

Centovalli Express

SWITZERLAND & ITALY ●

```
START LOCARNO

END DOMODOSSOLA

DEPARTS DAILY          DURATION 2 HRS

DISTANCE 32 MILES (52KM)
```

Often eclipsed by Switzerland's more famous rail rides, this two-hour trundle from Locarno on the palm-rimmed shores of Lake Maggiore to Domodossola over the Italian border in Piedmont is something of an unsung beauty. Brush up your Italiano to swoon in sync with fellow passengers as the dinky train clatters across 83 bridges and burrows its way through 34 tunnels. The views make for spirit-lifting stuff: waterfalls shooting over cliff faces, hillside vineyards, gracefully arched viaducts, slate-roofed hamlets, glacier-carved ravines and mile after mile of chestnut and beech forests, all set against the puckered backdrop of mountains that are snow-capped in winter.

❶ RIDING THE RAILS

Switzerland has some truly epic rail journeys but, let's face it, many are far from secret. For a lesser-known, uncrowded alternative to the big hitters, the Centovalli Express comes up trumps. Launched in 1923, the railway combines a pinch of mountain grandeur with a welcome splash of Italian sunshine. And in an age where everything is high speed, there's something beautiful about travelling slowly through the Alps from one country to another, watching the architecture and landscapes change little by little.

The pint-sized train departs from Locarno, a mellow Swiss town that reclines on the shores of Lake Maggiore. It's worth lingering in for a sampling

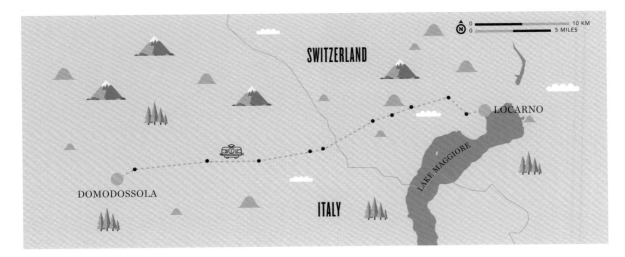

RIGHT & BELOW: The view from Intragna on the river Melezza; the market square in Domodossola at journey's end.
PREVIOUS PAGE: The town of Locarno nestles on the shores of Lake Maggiore.

of its cafe-rimmed piazzas, botanical gardens and Renaissance houses in ice-cream pastels.

You can ride these rails year-round, but little beats a cloudless autumn day when the beech, oak and chestnut woods light up in an ever-changing palette of golds and russets. One of the first stops is Ponte Brolla – much loved for its world-class cliff diving and rock climbing – where the train affords tantalising glimpses of the jade-green, boulder-speckled Maggia River. The little town marks the head of the valley that scythes is way into the Lepontine Alps north of Locarno, and from here the route dives west into the Centovalli ('Hundred Valleys'), which takes its name from the innumerable narrow side valleys that splinter away from it.

Climbing steadily, the train wends its way slowly up and over bridges and viaducts that balance precariously above ravines. Grey-stone, tiled-roofed hamlets perch like eyries on the hilltops, which in turn rise to steeply forested slopes. Below, the glassy green Melezza River carves out a path through the valley. Before reaching Intragna, the train rumbles over an iron viaduct 260ft (80m) high, which makes a sensational leap over the Isorno torrent. It was the site of Switzerland's first-ever bungee jump in 1993.

Topped by Ticino's highest church spire (213ft/ 65m), the village of Intragna crouches below the folds of craggy mountains. It's a great base for a couple of days of off-the-radar hiking, with old mule trails leading up into its wild heights. A little further on is Verdasio, where a cable car floats up to Rasa, a pipsqueak of a village, clasped between meadows and woods, which has the kind of peace you only find in places that are this cut off.

After Verdasio, the train rolls on into the Valle Vigezzo, where the Lepontine Alps – many of the

© AGF | GETTY IMAGES

THE ROUND TRIP

From Domodossola, it's a 30-minute train ride to Stresa, one of the loveliest towns on Lake Maggiore, with its views of sunrise across the lake, flowery promenade and intact *centro storico*. You could overnight here and catch the ferry back to Locarno in the morning. For timetables and fares, visit www.trenitalia.com and www.navigazionelaghi.it.

Linger in Locarno for strolls in subtropical gardens and the backstreets of the Renaissance Old Town.

Have your camera handy to capture the Isorno viaduct, site of Switzerland's first bungee jump.

Hike the old mule trails weaving up into the heights around Intragna.

Locarno

Ponte Brolla

Intragna

mountains reach the 9850ft (3000m) mark – soar above thick chestnut woods that are a riot of colour in the autumn. Waterfalls spill over the cliff faces in wispy threads. Beyond the border town of Camedo you reach Italy, ticking off pretty villages like rosary beads as you clank on to the highest point of the line at Santa Maria Maggiore (2723ft/830m), with its frescoed facades and art gallery devoted to the Vigezzo school of painting. The journey ends at the valley-floor town of Domodossola, Italian through and through with its medieval *centro storico* (historic centre), Renaissance *palazzo* and Unesco World Heritage–listed *Calvario* (calvary).

❷ LIFE ON BOARD

The train is tiny compared with most in Switzerland – it's comfortable but not ultra-plush, with large windows playing up the fabulous views. Sit on the left for the best vantage point. There's a trolley service from which you can buy snacks and hot drinks, or you can, of course, bring along your own picnic.

❸ MAKE IT HAPPEN

Several Centovalli Express trains run from Locarno to Domodossola every day. To view the full timetable, visit the Swiss Federal Railways site at www.centovalli. ch. Tickets can be purchased from machines at the station or in advance online at www.sbb.ch. Probably the only benefit of upgrading to 1st class, for which you'll fork out almost double the price of 2nd-class fares, is extra space and fewer crowds. All discount travel cards (Swiss Travel Pass, Half Fare Card, etc) are valid and yield significant discounts.

It's worth allowing time to stop in the Centovalli. You could combine the trip with a couple of days hiking to mountain villages, for instance. Trains operate year-round but autumn (September–November) is the best time to see the woods in all their golden glory. **KC**

Stop at Verdasio and take the cable car up to the impossibly pretty mountain village of Rasa.

Roll through dense beech forests to reach the route's high point: Santa Maria Maggiore at 2723 ft (830m).

Factor in time to explore the medieval town of Domodossola, and its Unesco-listed *Calvario*.

Verdasio **Camedo** **Domodossola**

OCEANIA

AMAZING TRAIN JOURNEYS

The Ghan

AUSTRALIA

START **ADELAIDE**	
END **DARWIN**	
DEPARTS **ONCE A WEEK**	DURATION **54 HRS**
DISTANCE **1851 MILES (2979KM)**	

 Cutting vertically across the Outback heart of Australia, straight through the desolate deserts of the Red Centre, the Ghan is one of the southern hemisphere's most unforgettable train journeys. Inaugurated in 1929, this cross-country train service has provided a vital link between Australia's north and south coasts, travelling just under 2000 miles (3000km) across the country from well-to-do, orderly Adelaide to the tropical, croc-filled creeks of Darwin. Luxurious and legendary, it's Australia's elegant riposte to the Orient Express.

❶ RIDING THE RAILS

Australia is vast, so it's fitting that at nearly two-thirds of a kilometre long, the Ghan is one of the world's longest passenger trains – a supersized railway for a continent that often seems to defy sensible dimensions. On average, this mighty train hauls thirty carriages along its 2000-mile (3000km) journey: power vans, crew quarters and supply wagons, as well as several sleeper carriages and a swish dinner lounge. There's no roughing it on the Ghan: this is a train that goes out of its way to spoil, from the afternoon teas and slap-up dinners served up by uniformed waiters to the turn-down chocolates on your pillow every night.

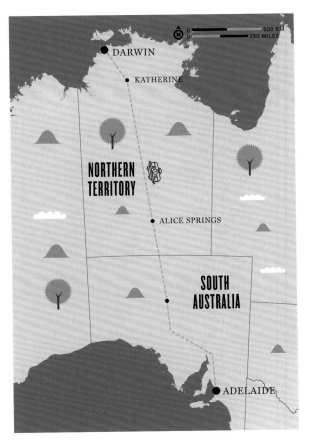

But then again, that's the curious thing about the Ghan. While its well-heeled guests sit back in the dining car, sipping glasses of chilled Aussie wine and tucking into crocodile sausage, grilled barramundi and kangaroo steak, just outside the window the savage Australian landscape whizzes constantly by. Beyond the confines of the train carriages, the prospects for anyone unfortunate enough to be

stranded here are grim indeed – but most travellers on the Ghan never give the matter a second thought, lapping up the luxury while a few yards on either side of the track, bones bleach and the desert sizzles.

The journey from Adelaide in the south to Darwin in the north usually covers three days and two nights. Day one begins with a leisurely route through the relatively gentle landscape of South Australia, chugging through Adelaide's suburbs into a patchwork of sheep farms, rolling pastureland and vineyards. The peaks of the Flinders Ranges zoom past. Gradually, farmland bleeds into scrub, and by nightfall, desert has filled the train windows, and passengers head off to their cabins, falling asleep under the Southern Cross.

When they wake, they discover that the Ghan has entered the Australia of the imagination: the Outback. Parched flatlands and red desert as far as the eye can see, dotted with spindly eucalyptus and gum trees. Cattle fences and telegraph poles spool past. Magical-sounding places are sprinkled over the map: Bookaloo, Pimba, Coondambo, Illoquara, Oodnadatta. Then the Ghan rattles over the border of South Australia and enters the wild Northern Territory.

For thousands of years, Aboriginal people had these barren lands to themselves, weaving a pantheon of mystical tales around their rocks, canyons and riverbeds. And few locations are as rich in legend as the area around Alice Springs, which the Ghan passes through just after lunchtime of the second day. This remote frontier town sits slap in the middle of the continent, and many passengers disembark for chopper rides over the MacDonnell Ranges, or to explore the trekking trails around Simpsons Gap and the otherworldly landscape of Uluru. The more daring hop onto camel-back for a safari-style camp in the Outback – a surreal experience after the fluffy pillows and warm duvets on offer in the Ghan's sleeper cabins.

© MATT MUNRO | LONELY PLANET

 Admire a wraparound view of the Outback from the viewing lounge.

 Stop off to search for gems at Coober Pedy, an underground opal-mining town.

Adelaide

Coober Pedy

© MATT MUNRO | LONELY PLANET

LEFT & BELOW: Crossing the country; a memorial to the line's builders. **PREVIOUS PAGE:** The Ghan locomotive.

THE 'GHANS

In the early 19th century, camel-herders were brought to Australia by the British, who thought their desert expertise would be ideal for surviving the arid Outback. Colloquially known as 'Ghans, from 'Afghans', in fact they probably came from what is now Pakistan – which means the Ghan should really be the Stan.

Beyond Alice Springs, the Outback rolls on – and on, and on. Emptiness unfolds, flat, orange and vast. Minutes rattle by, then hours, with nothing to mark the passage of time save for the occasional abandoned shack or skeletal tree. It's an extraterrestrial view – blue sky above, orange earth below – a bit like taking a train across the surface of Mars.

But as the sun begins to set, something remarkable happens: the flat earth is gloriously transformed as the low sun reveals cracks and contours in the parched earth, like crazy paving scaled to epic proportions, and uniform orange turns into a spectrum of ochres, scarlets, golds and tangerines. The Outback at twilight is a vision that stays with you once you've seen it: strange and otherworldly, like a Dalí dreamscape come to life.

And then, as a breakfast of eggs Benedict and French toast is served on the morning of day three, the Ghan rolls into yet another landscape. Yesterday it was rattling through the desert; today it's in the subtropics. Red desert gives way to greenery, flat earth to sandstone cliffs. The Katherine River appears, and beyond it, the creeks and gorges of Nitmiluk and Kakadu National Parks. Some conclude their journey here, disembarking the train to hike the forest trails or take riverboats along the crocodile-stocked creeks. Others remain on board all the way to Australia's northernmost city of Darwin, where the Ghan's journey comes to an end near the Timor Sea.

In 1862, bushman and explorer John McDouall Stuart took nearly fourteen months to complete the journey that the Ghan covers in three days. By the end, he was half-blind, wracked with scurvy and barely capable of walking; the Ghan's passengers, by contrast, emerge at Darwin Station rested, refreshed and supremely well-fed.

It might not be the world's longest train ride – but the Ghan certainly has to be one of the strangest.

Cross over the border between South Australia and the Northern Territory.

Take a guided tour around Alice Springs Desert Park.

Disembark at Katherine and cruise through Nitmiluk Gorge in search of Aboriginal cave art.

Alice Springs

Katherine

❷ LIFE ON BOARD

There are three service levels on the Ghan: Red, Gold and Platinum. Red Service buys you a recliner passenger seat, while Gold Service gets you your own private cabin, with seats that fold down into a day-bed, and shared corridor bathrooms. Platinum Service pulls out all the luxury stops: cabins twice as large as standard, with ottoman sofas that convert into a proper-sized bed, and your own private en suite bathroom with shower. You can even have breakfast served in your cabin. Gold and Platinum passengers get all-inclusive meals in the smart Queen Adelaide Restaurant, with complimentary booze and off-train excursions. Red passengers have to buy their own food from the licensed train cafe, although an upgrade to Red Premium includes meals. The Outback Explorer Lounge has the best view, and is perfect for mingling with your fellow passengers over a cold beer.

❸ MAKE IT HAPPEN

The Ghan runs once a week in each direction, leaving Adelaide on Sunday and Darwin on Wednesday. Buy tickets from Great Southern Rail (www.great southernrail.com.au); you can also buy tickets through third-party travel agents and train booking sites. You can travel in both directions between Darwin and Adelaide; the north-south route (the Ghan Expedition) takes four days rather than three. Alternatively, you can just book a return fare as far as Alice Springs. The cheapest time to travel is during low season from December to February; fares increase in shoulder months of October to November and March. May to September is the most expensive period. The train doesn't run from mid-December to mid-January. **OB**

RIGHT: The Outback, as seen from the comfortable carriages of the Ghan.

Explore the northern city of Darwin and nearby Kakadu National Park.

Darwin

© MATT MUNRO | LONELY PLANET

South Coast Line

AUSTRALIA

START **SYDNEY**

END **BOMADERRY**

DEPARTS **SEVERAL PER DAY**

DISTANCE **190 MILES (307KM)**

DURATION **3 HRS**

Escape Sydney's urban sprawl with this relaxing day-ride on the prettiest of commuter lines. Pass remnants of Gondwanaland rainforest and verdant bush resplendent with fascinating birdlife, delve through tunnels and deep ravines fringing one of the world's oldest national parks and be dazzled by stunning ocean vistas of rocky headlands, beckoning golden beaches and migrating whales. All within sipping distance of a decent latte, the cliff-hugging South Coast Line winds down through the coal-stained Illawarra to the rolling dairy hills of the Shoalhaven. Whether it's a swim, a walk, a picnic or just a lazy afternoon spent cafe-hopping, there's something for everyone.

❶ RIDING THE RAILS

After dodging early-morning commuters at bustling Central Station, you're soon slipping easily through Sydney's southern suburbs before your first glimpse of water crossing the Georges River at Como. The 'burbs end at Waterfall, gateway to Royal National Park, gazetted in 1879, making it the second-oldest national park in the world, though the station's namesake cascade isn't visible. The line now enters deep sandstone cuttings fringed by lush sub-tropical

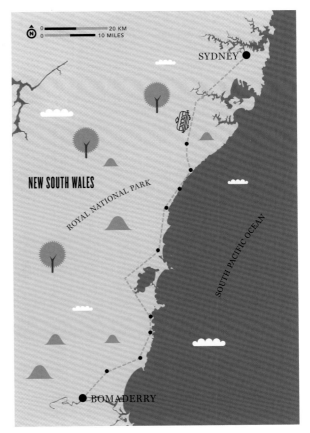

0 — 20 KM
0 — 10 MILES

SYDNEY

NEW SOUTH WALES

ROYAL NATIONAL PARK

SOUTH PACIFIC OCEAN

BOMADERRY

rainforest, tree ferns, flitting crimson rosellas and king parrots and the giant gymea lily (*Doryanthes excelsa*), whose triffidesque, red-topped flower spike can tower several metres. Pretty Otford Station, on a deep fern-filled bend, is a favourite with bushwalkers.

The train continues to snake along the national park boundary, through several tunnels until suddenly emerging above the Pacific Ocean at Stanwell Park, where's there's a lovely beach, plus paragliding

"The line winds in and out of ravines between the towering Illawarra Escarment and the sea"

and several cafes. The next section to Thirroul is particularly scenic, as the line winds in and out of ravines on a thin shelf between the towering sandstone Illawarra Escarpment and the restless seas below. Keep a keen eye out for humpback whales, migrating along the coast from April to October. A string of glorious beaches – Coledale, Wombarra, Austinmer – tempt the traveller with sublime ocean views, not to mention the clifftop pub at Scarborough. Some sightseers alight at aptly-named Coalcliff and walk over the amazing Sea Cliff Bridge, suspended mesmerisingly above the waves, before catching another train at Scarborough. Or continue on for a beer and pub counter lunch followed by a lazy swim at Wombarra, next along the line.

After Thirroul, the coast and escarpment recede as the train enters the flat, low-rise suburbs of Wollongong (aka 'The 'Gong'), the state's third-largest city and home to surfers, a respected university and some seriously heavy industry. You might have noticed the number of ships offshore, all queued waiting their turn for nearby Port Kembla, one of Australia's busiest, serviced by a branch line from Coniston. Most people are surprised that PK (or 'Port') is also home to several beautiful surf beaches.

You might catch a glimpse of Lake Illawarra, a large tidal lagoon, as the line detours inland to avoid it. The scenery softens again around alliterative Minnamurra with its pleasant river, while, next-up, tiny Bombo has a sensational location, almost on the dunes behind the beach. Pretty-as-a-postcard Kiama follows, and with its Norfolk Island pines, famous Blowhole, lighthouse and choice of funky cafes, makes a perfect destination

ABANDONED TUNNELS

The current line between Waterfall and Stanwell Park deviates from the original 19th-century route, where gradients proved too steep for fully laden steam locomotives. The abandoned Helensburgh Tunnels can be explored with a good torch, and the longest stretches over a mile. Expect graffiti, glow worms and an internal reservoir.

in itself, or a great place to break up the trip and whip out that picnic rug. As the electrified track ends here, there's usually enough time for a short stroll before a diesel railmotor makes the final 30-minute run over rolling green pastures to Bomaderry, on the north bank of the Shoalhaven River. Across on the southern side, the townsfolk of Nowra were offered a choice between road or rail bridges; they opted for cars and the trains have terminated at Bomaderry ever since. Rail buffs can spot an old turntable at the end of the tracks – follow the bike path outside the station.

A more energetic option, especially in whale season, is the easy, signposted 9-mile (14.5km) coastal path joining Kiama and subsequent stop, Gerringong. Never straying far from the railway, it offers uninterrupted ocean views as it tracks across beaches and headlands. Check the timetable carefully as the railmotor runs sporadically. Heading south, the quaint (somewhat touristy) village of Berry promises

Spot the giant red-tipped gymea lily flower-stalks in the national park between Waterfall and Otford.

Stare mesmerised at the dazzling Pacific Ocean between Stanwell Park and Thirroul.

Enjoy the beer garden of the Scarborough Hotel after walking across incredible Sea Cliff Bridge.

Sydney (Central)   **Waterfall**   **Stanwell Park**   **Coalcliff**   **Thirroul**

LEFT & BELOW: Sydney Central Railway Station; Kiama's cathedral rocks. **PREVIOUS PAGE:** Coastal vistas south of Sydney.

© MATT MUNRO | LONELY PLANET

a relaxed afternoon of soy lattes, scented candles and window shopping.

Wherever you get to, put your feet up for the return journey, as the incredible views rewind in reverse. Don't forget to change sides and flip your seat!

❷ LIFE ON BOARD

Trains are double-decked, single-class and without refreshments. The upstairs oceanside seats have the best view and can be 'flipped' to face the direction of travel. Some platforms are shorter than the train, so travel in the rear carriages if alighting midway. Mute your phone if travelling in a designated 'quiet' carriage. Weekends can be crazy packed.

❸ MAKE IT HAPPEN

Trains between Sydney and Kiama run hourly on weekends, more often in the week. Check the timetable carefully, not all stations receive the same service, particularly Waterfall to Thirroul. The Bomaderry railmotor runs two-hourly. Buy tickets on the day. A prepaid Opal card is cheaper. Start early for maximum sightseeing on this return day-trip, which is fantastic in all seasons. Find more info at www.sydneytrains.info.

Late spring to autumn (November–April) is perfect for lazy swimming and picnics, while the cooler months bring whales and milder conditions for exploration. Try to avoid public holidays. Avoid scheduled trackwork weekends, when delays are common and buses routinely replace trains for part of the journey. Bring a water bottle, a hat and sunscreen. **SW**

© TARAS VYSHNYA | TARASVYSHNYA | 500PX

Surf at Bombo then wander along the beach to Kiama's lighthouse and blowhole.

In late autumn, watch whales migrate from the coastal path between Kiama and Gerringong.

Stroll the cafes and boutiques of Berry.

Wollongong   **Bombo**   **Kiama**   **Gerringong**   **Berry**   **Bomaberry**

The TranzAlpine

NEW ZEALAND

START **CHRISTCHURCH**

END **GREYMOUTH**

DEPARTS **DAILY**

DISTANCE **139 MILES (223KM)**

DURATION **4 HRS 30 MINS**

In less than five hours, the journey renowned as one the world's finest and most scenic one-day train rides spans very distinct microclimates in the South Island of New Zealand. Commence the TranzAlpine experience in Christchurch, before speeding along the Canterbury Plains and then climbing quickly through the snow-capped mountains of the Southern Alps. After traversing some of the country's more remote alpine scenery, descend through a thrilling tunnel to emerge among the lakes, streams and rainforests of the South Island's West Coast. From there, more superb coastal and alpine scenery is on tap for independent travellers.

❶ RIDING THE RAILS

Be prepared to hear a tangle of languages and accents as you board the TranzAlpine at Christchurch. Most mornings the carriages are packed with visiting Australians, North Americans, and groups of Asian travellers, and a few New Zealanders eager for an up-close and personal experience of their country's Southern Alps. The Kiwis are usually a friendly bunch, so look forward to company and conversation as the train heads west through the rugged alpine spine of New Zealand's South Island.

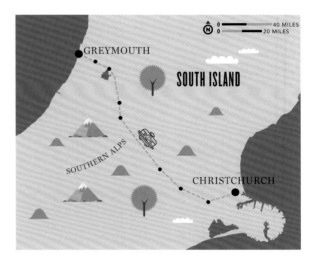

The initial stops across the Canterbury Plains are relatively unremarkable, and the rural towns of Darfield and Springfield roll by, anchored by heritage pubs and the well-tended pitches of local rugby clubs. Soon, however, the plains' agricultural patchwork is left behind, and the TranzAlpine begins a steady climb framed by the foothills of the Alps. For the journey from Christchurch to Springfield, the train largely follows the main highway, but the track's off-road diversion through 16 tunnels and five viaducts soon propels the train into more remote and inaccessible country.

Through the meandering gorge of the Waimakariri River, a procession of steel girder bridges and squat tunnels transports the train across a barren and stony riverbed, and the savviest travellers have already secured vista-friendly spots in the open-air viewing carriage. Visit outside of spring and summer, and nearby foothills are dusted in snow: scarves, fleece jackets and warming headgear are all as essential

a reason the West Coast is one of the country's most verdant regions – usually incorporate luminous lakeside rainbows, and from Moana, the TranzAlpine only needs another hour to complete the journey to Greymouth. From there, travellers can venture south by car or bus to the Fox and Franz Josef glaciers, and then continue from this spectacular ice show to action-packed Queenstown, or wait an hour and embark on an equally thrilling return journey east through the mountains back to Christchurch.

❷ LIFE ON BOARD

The TranzAlpine has one class with comfortable seating, panoramic windows and complimentary headphones to listen to an onboard commentary. Travellers can also stand in a spacious open-air viewing carriage that allows more immersion in the spectacular alpine scenery. This location also offers the best scope for photography, but dressing warmly is vital, especially outside of New Zealand's summer

as fully charged GoPro cameras and smartphones. Megabytes of memory are soon gobbled up as rugged mountain scenery quickly takes hold just an hour from Christchurch. Alpine settlements roll past in a cinematic scroll, and tiny Cass is announced by its compact but photogenic railway station. Approaching the village of Arthur's Pass, the mountains close in, and the broad expanses of the Canterbury Plains quickly fade into recent memory.

At an altitude of 2418ft (737m), Arthur's Pass is the country's highest railway station, and around 30 permanent residents share the spot with a few hundred keas, New Zealand's native alpine parrots. At Arthur's Pass, two additional locomotives are tacked to the rear of the train, and the TranzAlpine begins a steady ascent to the Otira Viaduct before descending through the 5.43-mile (8.6km) Otira Tunnel. This downhill journey in the dark soon emerges to a very different landscape of rainforest and lakes, and the TranzAlpine has entered another distinct New Zealand microclimate. Even the local place names have a rugged individuality, and Deception River and Crooked River both roll past as the train approaches the village of Moana on Lake Brunner.

Tea, coffee, or something more substantial are all on offer at Moana's heritage Edwardian railway station, and the trees around the often-misty lake are sometimes enlivened with the kotuku, New Zealand's native white heron. Frequent rain showers – there's

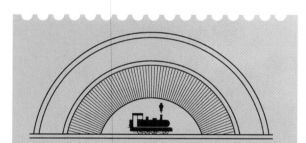

FAMOUS LITTLE TOWN

Immortalised in a 1936 New Zealand painting by the late Rita Angus, the tiny cherry-red railway station at the hamlet of Cass (population: one, a solitary railway worker lives on site) is a stark and poignant contrast to the massive alpine landscapes of the surrounding region.

Speed across the Canterbury Plains as the Southern Alps emerge on the horizon.

Traverse leviathan viaducts across the icy waters and braided channels of the Waimakariri river.

Christchurch   **Rolleston**   **Darfield**   **Springfield**

CLOCKWISE FROM LEFT: Crossing the Waimakariri Bridge; in the viewing carriage; between Cass and and Mt White Bridge; Arthur's Pass. **PREVIOUS PAGE:** The Alps that give the train its name.

months (December–February). Snacks, light meals and drinks are available from the train's dining car, and bringing your own food and beverage is allowed.

❸ MAKE IT HAPPEN

The service departs Christchurch daily at 8.15am, stops for an hour in Greymouth, then returns east to Christchurch. A day return is a popular option, but many visitors to New Zealand also use Greymouth as a jumping-off point to explore the South Island's rugged West Coast by bus or hire car, available at the Greymouth Railway Station. Book the TranzAlpine on www.greatjourneysofnz.co.nz, ideally a few months ahead for the popular December-to-April summer period. Winter in New Zealand (July to September) is also an excellent time for the journey, as the mountain landscapes are shrouded in snow. **BA**

ALL IMAGES COURTESY OF KIWIRAIL

 Stop at Arthur's Pass village and meet cheeky keas, New Zealand's native alpine parrots.

 Cross the Otira Viaduct and exit the Otira Tunnel to meet the rugged and isolated West Coast.

Enjoy a lakeside lunch at often misty Moana on the shores of Lake Brunner.

Arthur's Pass   **Otira**   **Moana (Lake Brunner)**   **Kokiri Greymouth**

West Coast Wilderness Railway

AUSTRALIA

START **STRAHAN**

END **STRAHAN**

DEPARTS **TWICE A WEEK**

DISTANCE **43 MILES (70KM)**

DURATION **8 HRS**

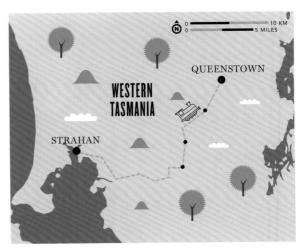

At the bottom of the world, in the dense rainforest of Tasmania's west, is a railway journey carved by epic resilience. In the 1890s, line workers pulled on soggy boots to complete a 22-mile (35km) stretch between the mining town of Queenstown and Strahan's port. It was the only link, built to transport copper to market. Rain, bushfires and a loco toppling into the harbour didn't halt these early pioneers. Today, the rail operates as a tourism route, recreating the journey and sharing century-old stories. Steep gorges, Huon pines and ambitious feats of engineering are yours to absorb from a comfy caboose while enjoying fluffy scones.

❶ RIDING THE RAILS

Tangled rainforest and horizontal scrub once described by journalist Randolph Bedford as 'a devilish vegetable that crawls over the land, and hasn't the courage to grow up like a real tree': this seemingly impenetrable terrain is what the West Coast Wilderness Railway's legacy is built upon.

The full-day journey departs from Strahan's harbourside Regatta Point Station where puffs of steam billow skyward. This is how the 30-ton (27-tonne) loco, with fire in her belly, warms up for the steepest steam haul in the southern hemisphere. It's an original Dubs & Co Abt locomotive from Glasgow, and engages a rare rack-and-pinion system to make the climb. No sooner do the carriages roll into action, than do the affable team, swiftly delivering Tasmanian sparkling wine to the passengers. Few mind that it's only 8.45am.

As with most Tasmanian journeys, wilderness is never far away. Within minutes, built dwellings are replaced with moss-blanketed trunks. Carriages dim in a naturally romantic manner, the rainforest canopy swallowing morning light. In these parts, gnarly Huon pines are plentiful, representing some of the oldest living organisms on the planet.

The petite back terrace, with its waist-height balustrade and protective side walls and roof, invites a wander into the forest air. Here, the constant 'thud-thud' of a slow moving loco is hypnotic, as wafts of steam disappear into the arms of ancient branches. The scent of Tasmania's wild is palpable.

© NICK OSBORNE

RACK AND PINION

The revolutionary rack-and-pinion system was devised by Swiss engineer and watchmaker Dr Roman Abt. In 2016, the railway was recognised as an engineering feat of global significance when awarded the Engineering Heritage International Marker. For a railway largely built with pick and shovel, its reputation is testament to those early pioneers.

First stop on the journey is Lower Landing, where a thick-trunked King Billy and deep green Huon pine stand among giant man ferns. Here, a variety of leatherwood honey samples are served up with stories of those who first brought hives to the region. Each stop along today's route delivers insight into the railway's past; the mining quests, young children who considered the train their 'school bus' and the untamed rainforest they called home. The workers came from everywhere, lured to Queenstown by Australia's largest copper mine of its day. At one point, more than 2000 axeworkers were charged with clearing the way.

The train makes an about-turn at Queenstown, where lunch is served at Tracks Café. Hop on the guided walk or wander at your own pace through a town whose underground resource drew prospectors from across the globe. At one point the town was

10,000 strong and home to 14 pubs, including one that doubled as a mortuary. Today, it's maintained its remote quirk.

Back on board, the steam locomotive comes into its own. climbing up the steep grades using a rack-and-pinion rail system. The return journey invites a spot of gold panning at Lynchford, a brief window into the illustrious hunt that captivated so many.

While you fuel up on Tasmanian soft cheese and afternoon drinks, the journey's gentle pace is a reminder to slow one's own. There's plenty of time to reflect on the hardy souls who forged the triumphant route. And although the rail has almost run out of steam on a number of occasions across its century-plus lifetime, it's their descendants who have ensured its survival. Those 'railway kids' who considered the train their school bus raised millions and, indeed, the loco rumbles on today.

Keep a look out for the formidable Iron Bridge just before Lower Landing Station.

Take a rainforest walk through vibrant green at Dubbil Barril, and wander beneath the mighty timber-built bridge.

Strahan (Regatta Point)

Lower Landing

Dubbil Barril

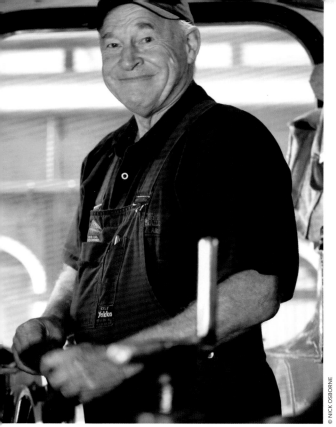

CLOCKWISE FROM LEFT: Driver AJ prepares the engine; the timber trestle bridge at Dubbil Barrill; edging up a section of 1:20-grade rack-and-pinion track. **PREVIOUS PAGE:** Steaming through the Tasmanian rainforest.

© NICK OSBORNE

❷ LIFE ON BOARD

The railway carriages have been fully restored yet remain true to original styling. Leather booth seating is generous, blending with native timber detailing throughout. Blankets are a cosy touch for wintry days.

There are two classes aboard: the Wilderness and Heritage carriages. The Wilderness Carriage provides a balcony, a glass of Tasmanian sparkling wine on arrival, morning tea, lunch, a Tasmanian tasting plate and unlimited hot drinks. Refreshments are available for purchase in the Heritage Carriage.

❸ ALTERNATIVE ROUTES

The route described is the Queenstown Explorer, but there are two other half-day steam journeys on the railway: the Rack & Gorge (from Queenstown) and the River & Rainforest (from Strahan); all return journeys. You can also join the pricey Footplate Experience on the Rack & Gorge route, where you can travel up front and work along with the driver and stoker.

❹ MAKE IT HAPPEN

The West Coast Wilderness Railway departs daily. To book tickets for Wilderness or Heritage class visit www.wcwr.com.au. Bookings can be made within 24 hours of departure, but seats fill quickly. The timetable is seasonal so do check the current departure times and dates. The best time of year to enjoy the rainforest walks is summer, but the experience does lend itself to rainy, brooding days. Pack a rain jacket! **AH**

© NICK OSBORNE

Pan for a prized gold nugget at Lynchford.

Don't miss a peek at the Paragon Theatre in Queenstown, a gorgeous 1930s art deco theatre.

Rinadeena   **Lynchford**   **Queenstown**

The Northern Explorer

NEW ZEALAND

© PENG SHI I 500PX

START **AUCKLAND**

END **WELLINGTON**

DEPARTS **WEEKLY**

DISTANCE **423 MILES (691KM)**

DURATION **10 HRS 40 MINS**

Traversing the rugged centre of New Zealand's North Island, the Northern Explorer is a superb alternative to flying, offering a slower, scenic journey linking two of the country's most important cities. Have breakfast beside the harbour in Auckland, lunch near snow-capped volcanic peaks in Tongariro National Park, and a late dinner among the energetic laneways of Wellington. Along the way, enjoy inland scenery combining isolated forested peaks and valleys, soaring viaducts and a tussock-trimmed alpine plateau. It's an extended combination that is far more compelling and inspiring than just another redeye flight fuelled by a rushed airport coffee.

❶ RIDING THE RAILS

Linking two very different cities – cosmopolitan and sprawling Auckland is New Zealand's economic capital while the political capital of Wellington is a more compact collection of neighbourhoods – the Northern Explorer is an adventure through the volcanic heart of the North Island. Between Auckland's West Coast surf beaches and boating on the Hauraki Gulf, and Wellingtonians' love of good food, coffee and fine craft beer, New Zealand's longest train journey incorporates

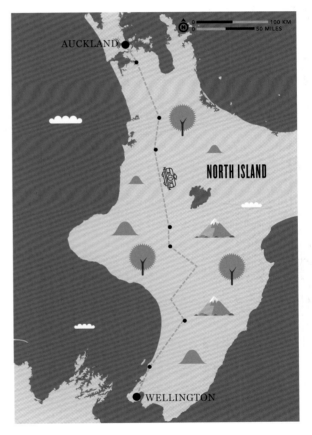

remote rural scenery, an expansive alpine plateau, and thrilling viaducts traversing river gorges. Flying between Auckland and Wellington is both cheaper and much faster, so don't expect to meet many New Zealanders on the Northern Explorer. Those Kiwis you do chat to will have signed up for a leisurely and reflective journey through spectacular landscapes often overlooked in the busyness of everyday life.

From Auckland's Strand Station, the Northern

Explorer begins its morning release from the country's biggest city by crossing Hobson's Bay causeway. Views of Rangitoto Island emerge from the left-hand side of the train, and this final harbour vista should be retained for as long as possible. In an island nation washed over by maritime influences, this is a journey where the scenic highlights are defiantly isolated from both the Tasman Sea and the South Pacific Ocean.

After a stop in the rural town of Pukekohe, the train continues through lush Waikato dairy farming country to Hamilton, in some parts skirting the sluggish, green-grey flow of the Waikato River. Travellers shouldn't get too comfortable with these bucolic farming scenes, as far more surprising scenery is impending. On through Te Awamutu, birthplace of Tim and Neil Finn from the Australasian band Crowded House, the Northern Explorer's next stop is at Otorohanga. A few overseas travellers usually join or leave the service here, as Otorohanga is a short 15-minute drive from the Waitomo Caves. And because it's adventurous, action-packed New Zealand, of course tourists can go abseiling or ziplining deep within the riverine caverns. Make the most of the Otorohanga stop with an organic coffee at the platform-side Origin Espresso, before taking in the Sir Edmund Hillary walkway, named after New Zealand's 1953 conqueror of Mt Everest, and an interesting display of retro Kiwiana memorabilia.

Beyond Otorohanga, the Northern Explorer enters the rugged King Country, a name inspired by the rebel Kingitanga Movement. This former bastion of independent Māoridom – Māori are New Zealand's indigenous people – was still off limits to colonial settlers until near the end of the 19th century. The area's rugged landscape consists of idiosyncratic rocky outcrops, either dotted with flocks of sheep or veiled in dense temperate rainforest. After a stop at Taumarunui – namechecked in a classic Kiwi folk

© TROY WEGMAN | SHUTTERSTOCK

Negotiate a labyrinthine path through the rugged and remote landscapes of the King Country.

IMAGE COURTESY OF KIWIRAIL

LEFT & BELOW: Tongariro National Park; Auckland. **PREVIOUS PAGE:** The park's Emerald Lakes.

MOVIE-STAR MOUNTAIN

Travelling through the alpine expanses of Tongariro National Park, don't be surprised if the volcanic cone of Mt Ngauruhoe looks familiar. The peak found fame as Mt Doom in the *Lord of the Rings* trilogy. Cinephiles can also alight at Hamilton and drive 45 minutes to *The Hobbit* movie set.

song, 'Taumarunui' (On the Main Truck Line) – the Northern Explorer negotiates one of New Zealand's most impressive engineering features.

In less than 16 miles (25km), the Raurimu Spiral ascends 1640ft (500m), a circuitous combination of horseshoe bends and tunnels very necessary to reach the elevated Central Plateau. A stop amid the tussocky alpine plains of Tongariro National Park provides the opportunity to spy on the park's triumvirate of often snow-clad volcanic peaks – Mts Ruapehu, Ngauruhoe and Tongariro, and the heritage National Park Station is quite probably New Zealand's cosiest location for an early-afternoon snack, especially if there's an open fire fending off the exterior chill.

Descending from the cooler elevations of the Central Plateau and Tongariro National Park, the Northern Explorer traverses the massive Hapuawhenua Viaduct before stopping at Ohakune, a hotspot for skiing and snowboarding in winter, and hiking, river-rafting and

mountain-biking in spring and summer. Look out the train's right-hand windows to possibly see bikers crossing the older, wooden Hapuawhenua Viaduct, now a highlight of the popular Ohakune Old Coach Road mountain bike trail.

Following more viaducts traversing the towering river gorges of the Rangitikei region, the Northern Explorer finally exhales after a few exciting hours of the central North Island's finest scenery, and cruises to a stop in the provincial city of Palmerston North. Students from Massey University provide rural 'Palmy' with much-needed energy, but the bars and cafes of Wellington are a better final destination.

South from Palmerston North, the journey's final stop before the buzz of the country's capital is Paraparaumu, and finally the ocean comes back into view. On the near horizon, Kapiti Island is a wildlife sanctuary best explored with Kapiti Island Nature Tours, run by a local Māori family. For train buffs,

Traverse the tunnels, curves and 360-degree circle of the Raurimu Spiral.

Travel through tussocky alpine plains past the imposing volcanic profiles of Mts Ruapehu and Ngauruhoe.

Be surrounded by the massive cliffs and bluffs of the Rangitikei river gorge.

National Park　　　　　**Ohakune**　　　　　**Palmerston North**

Steam Incorporated at nearby Paekakariki operates rail adventures on vintage locomotives. For everyone else, there's the chance to enjoy the Northern Explorer's final run around Wellington harbour, and the impending opportunity to toast the end of the journey amid the city's excellent nightlife.

❷ LIFE ON BOARD

The Northern Explorer offers one class incorporating comfortable seating, skylights and panoramic windows. An optional commentary can be accessed via complimentary headphones. To be more immersed in the spectacular scenic diversity, travellers can stand in a spacious open-air viewing carriage. This is the best location for photography, but you are advised to dress warmly, especially when the train is traversing the alpine landscapes around Tongariro National Park and the country's higher-altitude Central Plateau. Snacks, light meals and drinks are available on board.

❸ MAKE IT HAPPEN

Trains run southbound from Auckland on Monday, Thursday and Saturday, and northbound from Wellington on Tuesday, Friday and Sunday. Some travellers alight at Otorohanga, from where it's a short drive to the Waitomo Caves. Another option is to exit at National Park for winter sports, or to hike the one-day Tongariro Alpine Crossing during spring and summer. Booking a few months ahead on www.greatjourneysofnz.co.nz is recommended, especially for the December-to-April summer period. The journey is also spectacular during winter in New Zealand (July to September), when the three volcanic peaks of Tongariro National Park are often covered in snow. **BA**

RIGHT: Crossing the Hapuawhenua Viaduct.

Dissolve into a sunset with oceanside views of Kapiti Island.

Zip around Wellington harbour before alighting for excellent bars and restaurants.

© SOREN LOW

Paraparamu   **Wellington**

Kuranda Scenic Railway

AUSTRALIA

START	**CAIRNS**	
END	**KURANDA**	
DEPARTS	**DAILY**	**DURATION** **2 HRS**
DISTANCE **43 MILES (37KM)**		

Reach out and touch tropical World Heritage–listed rainforest millions of years old, as this heritage locomotive winds its rickety way through rugged mountains and steep ravines, from Cairns through Barron Gorge National Park to the picturesque village of Kuranda in Australia's Far North Queensland. In operation since 1891, this unique route of 15 handmade tunnels and more than 37 bridges is an architectural wonder: it was constructed by 1500 men using just picks and shovels, with the occasional bit of dynamite to blast through the terrain. Have your camera ready for the waterfalls and sheer enormity of Barron Gorge.

❶ RIDING THE RAILS

The palm-tree lined entrance to Cairns Station is the first clue that you're about to journey into a tropical paradise, though given this starting point is located within a shopping centre, you may find Freshwater Station (the next stop) to be a more atmospheric point to begin your adventure. Here, while you wait for the train, you can breakfast in an antique railway carriage, tour the museum and view a miniature replica of your route to heighten the anticipation. Wait, is that an engine approaching?

IMAGE COURTESY OF QUEENSLAND RAIL TRAVEL

Find your allocated seat (hopefully near a window) next to other tourists clad in shorts, T-shirts and flip-flops, and settle in. 'Welcome aboard the Kuranda Scenic Railway...' Yes, there's a handy audio commentary to guide you on the history and the highlights, but it'll soon compete with the soundtrack of the world's largest (and loudest) cicadas who start to hum in unison as the sun heats up the Queensland rainforest. Their tune somehow befits this slow, languid journey of vertiginous splendour, rising steadily from sea level to 1076ft (328m), especially when the cicada buzz seamlessly melds with the gush of Stoney Creek waterfall.

'There are magnificent views on this part of the line.' As the track curves across the Barron River, join everyone else in gleefully sticking your head out the open windows to enjoy views of the length of the entire train. The close-up of the rough terrain of Barron Gorge makes it clear what an astounding feat it was for this track to have been laid in the first place;

© FILIPE FRAZAO | SHUTTERSTOCK

SNAKY CARRIAGE COLOURS

The vibrant colour scheme of the front carriages is no accident; it represents the Legend of Buda-Dji, an Aboriginal Dreaming tale of a carpet snake that carved out the Barron River. And while the story varies, the Indigenous people from the Tablelands, Mareeba, Kuranda, Mossman, Cairns and Yarrabah all respect the legend.

little wonder that 32 men lost their lives in tragic accidents during the construction. Robb's Monument, a natural rock formation on the approach to Barron Gorge Hydro-Electric Power Station, is named in honour of John Robb: the builder of the railway. The rock also has Aboriginal Dreaming significance: a couple in an illegal relationship were said to have been punished by being turned into this stone.

If you're itching to stretch your legs and/or take a selfie or two, Barron Gorge Station is your cue. Depending on rainfall conditions, the waterfall at Barron Gorge can potentially be on a par with Niagara Falls, though it's wise not to set your expectations that high. Nevertheless, the 10-minute stop also allows time to enjoy the tropical sounds and sights of Barron Gorge National Park (keep your eyes peeled for rainbow lorikeets and, if you're really lucky, a cassowary).

As Kuranda Station signs loom into view, don't despair that the sightseeing is over. This heritage-listed, Federation-style station (completed in 1915) surrounded in lush plant life is one of the most photographed railway stations in the world. And there are few better ways to pass the time before your return trip than a jungle walk through the rainforest, or a visit to the butterfly sanctuary and koala gardens.

❷ LIFE ON BOARD

If you're after a smooth, luxurious ride, remember this is a vintage locomotive; the refurbished timber carriages, gentle rocking and occasional wheel screech are part of the charm. It's guaranteed to be a humid trip but there's filtered water in each carriage and a chilled refresher towel offered in summer. Splash out on Gold Class (available only on the 9.55am train from Freshwater Station/3.30pm from Kuranda) for

Admire the natural beauty of the Wet Tropics, Queensland's World Heritage–listed tropical rainforest.

Snap a pic of Stoney Creek Falls, cascading in front of the train's open-air windows.

Cairns Station

Freshwater Station

CLOCKWISE FROM LEFT: An actor in Kuranda's Tjapukai Culture Park; Stoney Creek Falls; Australian rainbow lorikeets. **PREVIOUS PAGE:** The enchanting Kuranda Station from 1915.

© EVAN TRAVELS | SHUTTERSTOCK

individual lounge-style seating, a gift pack, welcome drinks (local Sirromet wine, Great Northern Brewing Company lager or tropical mocktails), and morning/afternoon tea featuring sweet, buttery Wondaree macadamia nuts, freshly baked muffins and frozen mango treats.

❸ BUDGET ALTERNATIVE

The Savannahlander (www.savannahlander.com.au) offers a slightly cheaper one-way fare along the same route but only departs on Wednesdays at 6.30am from Cairns Station (note: the return from Kuranda on this service is not until Saturday, as this train carries on to a further destination). Food isn't offered on board but, like the Kuranda Scenic Railway, it also stops at Barron Falls Lookout to enjoy the views. This train is also not air-conditioned.

❹ MAKE IT HAPPEN

IMAGE COURTESY OF QUEENSLAND RAIL TRAVEL

The Kuranda Scenic Railway departs from Cairns Station at 8.30am and 9.30am daily all year round, except for Christmas Day. Make a booking enquiry on the website (www.ksr.com.au) or by phone. Book well in advance during school holidays. A popular choice is to take the train one-way then the SkyRail Rainforest Cableway back (select the Kuranda Classic Experience option). Trains are not air-conditioned and Far North Queensland summers are mercilessly hot and humid, so journeys are more comfortable in the cooler months (April to October). Wear a hat, sunglasses, plenty of sunscreen and insect repellent. **KN**

Learn about both the Indigenous and European significance of the Robb's Monument rock formation.

Alight at Barron Falls Station for unforgettable photos from the viewing platform over Barron Gorge.

Enjoy colourful, historic Kuranda Station, looking like a florist's interpretation of a transport hub.

Barron Falls Station

Kuranda Station

Index

Amazing Train Journeys

October 2018

Published by Lonely Planet Global Limited

CRN 554153

www.lonelyplanet.com

10 9 8 7 6 5 4 3 2 1

Printed in China

ISBN 978 1 78701 430 5

© Lonely Planet 2018

© photographers as indicated 2018

Managing Director, Publishing Piers Pickard

Associate Publisher Robin Barton

Commissioning Editor Dora Ball

Art Director & Design Daniel Di Paolo

Editors Bridget Blair, Nick Mee, Karyn Noble

Picture Research Tania Cagnoni

Cartography Corey Hutchison

Print Production Lisa Ford, Nigel Longuet

Thanks Neill Coen, Tina García, Simon Hoskins, Sandie Kestell, Flora Macqueen, Wayne Murphy, Isabella Noble, Yolanda Zappaterra

STAY IN TOUCH lonelyplanet.com/contact

Australia

The Malt Store, Level 3,

551 Swanston St, Carlton, Victoria 3053

T: 03 8379 8000

USA

124 Linden St, Oakland,

CA 94607

T: 510 250 6400

Ireland

Digital Depot, Roe Lane (off Thomas St),

Digital Hub, Dublin 8 D08 TCV4

Europe

240 Blackfriars Rd,

London SE1 8NW

T: 020 3771 5100

Writers Isabel Albiston (**IA**), Brett Atkinson (**BA**), James Bainbridge (**JB**), Sarah Baxter (SB), Oliver Berry (**OB**), Joe Bindloss (**JB**), Claire Boobbyer (**CB**), Kerry Christiani (**KC**), Gregor Clark (**GC**), Alex Crevar (**AC**), Megan Eaves (**ME**), Janine Eberle (**JE**), Ethan Gelber (**EG**), Bridget Gleeson (**BG**), Tom Hall (**TH**), Alice Hansen (**AH**), Carolyn Heller (**CH**), Jo Keeling (**JK**), Patrick Kinsella (**PK**), John Lee (**JL**), Emily Matchar (**EM**), Rebecca Milner (**RM**), Karyn Noble (**KN**), Zora O'Neill (**ZO'N**), Tim Richards (**TR**), Simon Richmond (**SR**), Oliver Smith (**OS**), Regis St Louis (**RSL**), Steve Waters (**SW**), Luke Waterson (**LW**), Yolanda Zappaterra (**YZ**).

Picture credits. **Front cover** Rocky Mountaineer (Pete Seaward | Lonely Planet). **Page 2-3** Northern Explorer (image courtesy of KiwiRail). **Pages 10-11** Elephants in Zimbabwe (Paula French | Shutterstock). **Page 36-37** Sunset Limted (Kris Davidson | Lonely Planet). **Page 110-11** Eastern & Oriental (image courtesy of Belmond). **Page 174-175** Inlandsbanan (Håkan Wike). **Page 270-71** The Ghan (Matt Munro | Lonely Planet). **Back cover** Clockwise from top left: Bernina Express (Justin Foulkes | Lonely Planet); Stafford Estate tea plantation (Matt Munro | Lonely Planet); Sunset Limited (Kris Davidson | Lonely Planet); African elephant (Jonathan Gregson | Lonely Planet); Jacobite crossing the Glenfinnan Viaduct (miroslav_1 | Getty Images); the Ghan (Matt Munro | Lonely Planet); travelling through Europe (Justin Foulkes | Lonely Planet); Reunification Express (Matt Munro | Lonely Planet).